A-Level Year 1 & AS

Mathematics

Exam Board: Edexcel

The best way to prepare for the AS Maths exams is practice. *Everybody* knows that. But at CGP, we don't just dish out obvious advice — we make a book packed with so much exam-style practice that you'll need a cumulative frequency diagram to keep track of it.

Inside, there are hundreds of questions covering every topic from the latest Edexcel course, plus a full set of practice exam papers at the end of the book. We've included step-by-step solutions and full mark schemes for every question too.

So don't just talk about practice — fill a flask with motivational tea, grab this book and get it *done*. When it comes to the real exams, you'll be so glad you did...

A-Level revision? It has to be CGP!

Published by CGP

Editors:
Chris Corrall, Alison Palin, David Ryan, Caley Simpson, Ethan Starmer-Jones

Contributors:
Kevin Bennett, Kieran Wardell, Charlotte Young

ISBN: 978 1 78294 736 3

With thanks to Alastair Duncombe and Andy Park for the proofreading.
With thanks to Laura Jakubowski for the copyright research.

Clipart from Corel®
Printed by Elanders Ltd, Newcastle upon Tyne

Based on the classic CGP style created by Richard Parsons.

Contents

☑ Use the tick boxes to check off the topics you've completed.

Exam Advice

Good exam technique can make a big difference to your mark, so make sure you read this stuff carefully.

Get familiar with the **Exam Structure**

For **AS-level Mathematics**, you'll be sitting **two papers**:

Paper	Weighting	Content
Paper 1 — Pure Mathematics **2 hours** **100** marks	**62.5%** of your AS-level	Covers the topics tested in **Section One** of this book.
Paper 2 — Statistics and Mechanics **1 hour 15 mins** **60** marks	**37.5%** of your AS-level	Covers the topics tested in **Sections Two & Three** of this book.

Paper 2 is split into Section A: Statistics and Section B: Mechanics — worth 30 marks each.
There may be some problem-solving questions in Paper 2 that need some pure maths.

Some *formulas are given in the* ***Formula Booklet***

In the exam you'll be given a **formula booklet** that lists some of the formulas you might need. The ones relevant for AS-level are shown on page 102 of this book.

You don't need to learn these formulas but you do need to know **how to use** them. The formula booklet also includes **statistical tables** — the relevant ones for this course are given on pages 97-101.

Manage Your Time *sensibly*

1) The **number of marks** tells you roughly **how long** to spend on a question — you've got just over a minute per mark in the exam. If you get stuck on a question for too long, it may be best to **move on** so you don't run out of time for the others.
2) You don't have to work through the paper **in order** — you could leave questions on topics you find harder until last.

Get **Familiar** with the **Large Data Set**

Throughout your course you'll be working with the **large data set**. This is a group of **tables** containing information about **weather conditions** (such as rainfall) in a number of towns in the years 1987 and 2015. The large data set will only be used in Paper 2 for AS-level Maths.

Questions in this paper might:
- Assume that you're familiar with the **terminology** and **contexts** of the data.
- Use **summary statistics** based on the large data set — this might reduce the time needed for some calculations.
- Include **statistical diagrams** based on the large data set.
- Be based on a **sample** from the large data set.

You might be expected to know specific details about the large data set — such as where the towns are located.

Watch out for **Modelling** *and* **Problem-Solving** *questions*

The AS Maths course has a few **overarching themes** — **proof**, **problem solving** and **modelling**. The first few questions in this book cover proof (and there are other proof questions dotted throughout the book). Problem solving and modelling questions are covered throughout the book, but they can be trickier to spot.

- **Problem-solving** questions involve skills such as **combining** different areas of maths or **interpreting information** given to identify what's being asked for. They're often worth a **lot of marks**, as there's a lot of maths involved in them.
- **Modelling** questions involve using maths to represent **real-life situations**. You might be asked to think about the **validity** of the model (how realistic it is) or to interpret values **in context**.

Algebra and Functions 1

Algebra is a pretty important part of maths — so it's a good idea to get to grips with it now. Some of this will be stuff you came across at GCSE and some of it will be brand spanking new. Ooooh, exciting.

1 Prove that $x^5 \geq 5^x$ for the integers $2 \leq x \leq 5$.

$x=2$, $2^5 = 32$, $5^2 = 25$, $32 > 25$
$x=3$, $2^3 = 8$, $5^3 = 125$
$x=4$, $2^4 = 16$, $5^4 = 625$
$x=5$, $2^5 = 32$, $5^5 = 3125$

(2 marks)

2 Find a counter example to disprove the following statement:

The sum of any two prime numbers is even.

$2 + 3 = 5$ → odd number

(2 marks)

3 Prove that, when n is an odd integer, $3n^2 - 12$ is always odd, and when n is an even integer, $3n^2 - 12$ is always even.

n odd integer → $n=3$ → $3(3)^2 - 12$
$27 - 12 = 25$ – odd

n even integer → $n=2$ → $3(2)^2 - 12$
$12 - 12 = 0$ – even

(3 marks)

4 Find a counter example to disprove the following statement:

If $x > y$, then $\frac{x}{y} > \frac{y}{x}$.

$x = -1$
$y = -2$
$-1 > -2$

$\frac{-1}{-2} > \frac{-2}{-1}$
↓
$\frac{1}{2} > 2$ False

(2 marks)

5 Prove that $n^3 + 2n^2 + 12n$ always has a factor of 8 when n is even.

$n = 2K$ → even
$(2K)^3 + 2(2K)^2 + 12(2K) =$
$8K^3 + 8K^2 + 24K =$
$8(K^3 + K^2 + 3K)$

(3 marks)

Algebra and Functions 1

6 Prove that $x(x + 2y + 4) \geq 4x - y^2$ for any integers x and y.

$x^2 + 2xy + 4x \geq 4x - y^2$

$x^2 + 2xy + y^2 \geq 0$

$(x+y)^2 \geq 0$

(2 marks)

7 Prove that the difference between the cube and square of any integer is always even.

n^2, n^3

$n^3 - n^2 =$

$n^2(n-1)$

(4 marks)

8 Prove that the product of any two distinct prime numbers has exactly four factors.

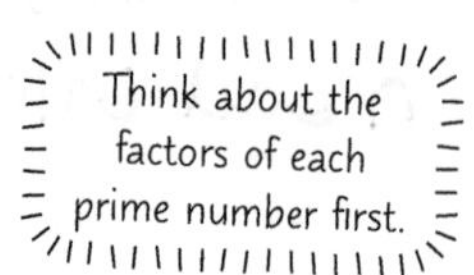

x, y

$xy =$ divisible by $xy, x, y, 1$

(3 marks)

9 Write down the exact value of $36^{-\frac{1}{2}}$.

$\frac{1}{\sqrt{36}} = \frac{1}{6}$

$\frac{1}{6}$

(1 mark)

10 Simplify $\frac{a^6 \times a^3}{\sqrt{a^4}} \div a^{\frac{1}{2}}$.

$\frac{a^9}{a^2} \div a^{\frac{1}{2}} = a^7 \times a^{-1/2} = a^{13/2}$

(2 marks)

Algebra and Functions 1

11 Find the value of x such that:

a) $27^x = 3$

$x = \frac{1}{3}$

(1 mark)

b) $27^x = 81$

$x = \frac{4}{3}$

(1 mark)

$(3ab^3)(3ab^3) = 9a^2b^6$

12 Fully simplify $\frac{(3ab^3)^2 \times 2a^6}{6a^4b}$.

$\frac{9a^2b^6 \times 2a^6}{6a^4b} = \frac{18a^8b^6}{6a^4b} = 3a^4b^5$

(2 marks)

13 Write $\frac{x + 5x^3}{\sqrt{x}}$ in the form $x^m + 5x^n$, where m and n are constants.

$\frac{x+5x^3}{x^{1/2}}$

$x^{-\frac{1}{2}}(x+5x^3) = x^{\frac{1}{2}} + 5x^{\frac{1}{2}}$

$x^{\frac{1}{2}} + 5x^{\frac{1}{2}}$

(2 marks)

14 Show that $\frac{(5 + 4\sqrt{x})^2}{2x}$ can be written as $\frac{25}{2}x^{-1} + Px^{-\frac{1}{2}} + Q$, where P and Q are integers.

$(5+4\sqrt{x})(5+4\sqrt{x}) = 25 + 40\sqrt{x} + 16x$

$\frac{25 + 40\sqrt{x} + 16x}{2x}$

$\frac{25}{2}x^{-1} + 20x^{-\frac{1}{2}} + 8$

(3 marks)

Algebra and Functions 1

15 Simplify $(\sqrt{3}+1)(\sqrt{3}-2)$.

$3-2\sqrt{3}+\sqrt{3}-2$

$1-\sqrt{3}$

$1-\sqrt{3}$ ✓

(2 marks)

16 Express $(5\sqrt{5}+2\sqrt{3})^2$ in the form $a+b\sqrt{c}$, where a, b and c are integers to be found.

$(5\sqrt{5}+2\sqrt{3})(5\sqrt{5}+2\sqrt{3}) =$

$125+20\sqrt{15}+12 =$

$137+20\sqrt{15}$

$a=137 \quad b=20 \quad c=15$

$137+20\sqrt{15}$ ✓

(4 marks)

17 Rationalise the denominator of $\frac{10}{\sqrt{5}+1}$.

$\frac{10(\sqrt{5}-1)}{(\sqrt{5}+1)(\sqrt{5}-1)} = \frac{10\sqrt{5}-10}{5-1} = \frac{10\sqrt{5}-10}{4}$

$\frac{5\sqrt{5}-5}{2}$

$\frac{5\sqrt{5}-5}{2}$ ✓

(3 marks)

18 Express $\frac{4+\sqrt{2}}{2+\sqrt{2}}$ in the form $a+b\sqrt{2}$, where a and b are integers to be found.

$\frac{(4+\sqrt{2})(2-\sqrt{2})}{(2+\sqrt{2})(2-\sqrt{2})} = \frac{8-2\sqrt{2}-2}{4-2} = \frac{6-2\sqrt{2}}{2} = 3-\sqrt{2}$

$3-\sqrt{2}$ ✓

(3 marks)

There's so much algebra to cover at AS Maths, I've decided to split it up into a few sections. This is the end of Part 1. Next, with crushing inevitability, comes Part 2...
Make sure you've got the different methods of proof clear before you move on. Exam questions usually won't tell you what method to use, and normally only one method will work.

Score

45

Algebra and Functions 2

7 Given that the equation $3jx - jx^2 + 1 = 0$, where j is a constant, has no real roots, find the range of possible values of j.

....

(4 marks)

8 $f(x) = \frac{1}{x^2 - 7x + 17}$

a) Express $x^2 - 7x + 17$ in the form $(x - m)^2 + n$, where m and n are constants.

....

(3 marks)

b) Hence find the maximum value of $f(x)$.

....

(2 marks)

9 Find the possible values of k if the equation $g(x) = 0$ is to have two real roots, where $g(x)$ is given by $g(x) = 3kx^2 + kx + 2$.

....

(3 marks)

10 Solve the simultaneous equations below.

$$y = -5x + 6 \text{ and } 7x + 2y - 6 = 0$$

$7x + 2(-5x + 6) - 6 = 0$

$7x - 10x + 12 - 6 = 0$

$-3x = -6$

$x = 2$

$y = -5(2) + 6$

$= -10 + 6$

$x =$ ....2.... $y =$ ....−4....

(4 marks)

Algebra and Functions 2

11 Consider the equations $x^2 + y^2 = 13$ and $x - 5y + 13 = 0$.

a) By eliminating x from the equations, show that $y^2 - 5y + 6 = 0$.

(2 marks)

b) Hence, or otherwise, solve the equations simultaneously.

$x =$ .... $y =$ .... or $x =$ .... $y =$ ....

(3 marks)

12 The curve C has equation $y = -x^2 + 3$ and the line l has equation $y = -2x + 4$.

a) Find the coordinates of the point (or points) of intersection of C and l.

....

(4 marks)

b) Sketch the graphs of C and l on the axes below, clearly showing where the graphs intersect the x- and y- axes.

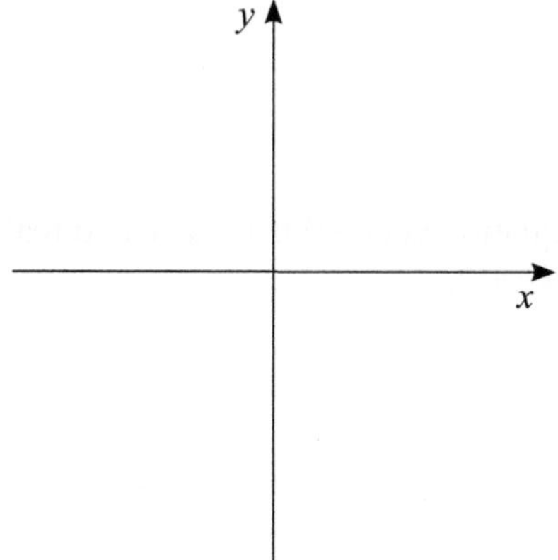

(5 marks)

13 Solve the simultaneous equations $y + x = 7$ and $y = x^2 + 3x - 5$.

$x =$ .... $y =$ .... or $x =$ .... $y =$ ....

(4 marks)

Algebra and Functions 2

14 Draw and label the region that satisfies the inequalities $y \geq x + 2$ and $4 - x^2 > y$.

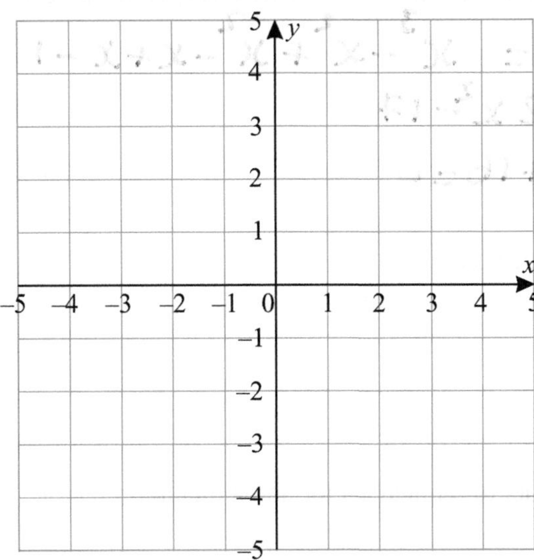

(3 marks)

15 Solve the inequality $x^2 - 8x + 15 > 0$. Give your answer in set notation.

$(x-5)(x-3) > 0$

$x = 5, 3$

$x < 3$, $x > 5$

(4 marks)

16 $f(x) = x^3 - 6x^2 - x + 30$

a) Using the factor theorem, show that $(x - 3)$ is a factor of $f(x)$.

$f(3) = 3^3 - 6(3)^2 - (3) + 30 = 0$

(2 marks)

b) Factorise $f(x)$ completely.

$x^2 - 3x - 10 \rightarrow (x-5)(x+2)$

$x - 3 \,\overline{)\, x^3 - 6x^2 - x + 30}$

$x^3 - 3x^2$

$-3x^2 - x$

$-3x^2 + 9x$

$-10x + 30$

$(x-5)(x+2)(x-3)$

(3 marks)

Algebra and Functions 2

17 $(x - 1)(x^2 + x + 1) = 2x^2 - 17$

a) Rewrite the equation above in the form $f(x) = 0$, where $f(x)$ is of the form $f(x) = ax^3 + bx^2 + cx + d$.

$(x^2+x+1)(x-1) = x^3 - x^2 + x^2 - x + x - 1$

$x^3 - 1 = 2x^2 - 17$

$x^3 - 2x^2 + 0x + 16 = 0$

....

(2 marks)

b) Show that $(x + 2)$ is a factor of $f(x)$.

(2 marks)

c) Hence write $f(x)$ as the product of a linear factor and a quadratic factor.

....

(2 marks)

d) By completing the square, or otherwise, show that $f(x) = 0$ has only one root.

(2 marks)

18 A function is defined by $f(x) = x^3 - 4x^2 - ax + 10$. $(x - 1)$ is a factor of $f(x)$.
Find the value of a and hence or otherwise solve the equation $x^3 - 4x^2 - ax + 10 = 0$.

Use the factor theorem to find the value of a.

$f(1) = (1)^3 - 4(1)^2 - a + 10$

$1 - 4 - a + 10 = 0$

$a = 7$

$x - 1 \overline{) x^3 - 4x^2 - 7x + 10}$

$a =$ ......7........ $x =$ ....

(6 marks)

Quadratics have a habit of popping up in exam questions where you least expect them (like in exponentials, trig equations or mechanics), not to mention in simultaneous equations, inequalities and cubics — so make sure you can handle them. It's worth practising your factorising skills, as it could save you a lot of time in the exam, and time is ~~money~~ marks.

Score

83

Algebra and Functions 3

This section should appeal to your artistic side — you get to draw some beautiful graphs. Although don't panic if you're not artistic — there's some equally beautiful algebra coming up later in the form of the binomial expansion.

1 Sketch each of the curves below on the axes provided.
Show clearly any points of intersection with the x- and y-axes and state the equations of any asymptotes.

a) 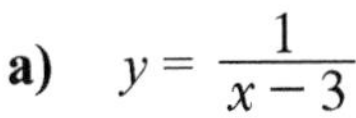 $y = \frac{1}{x-3}$

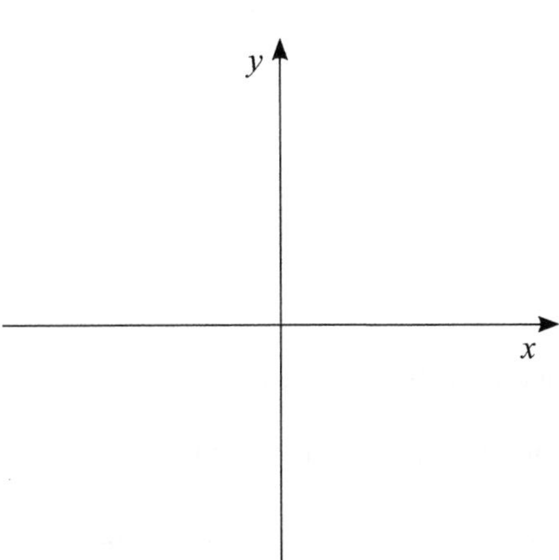

(3 marks)

b) $y = (x-1)(x+2)(3-x)$

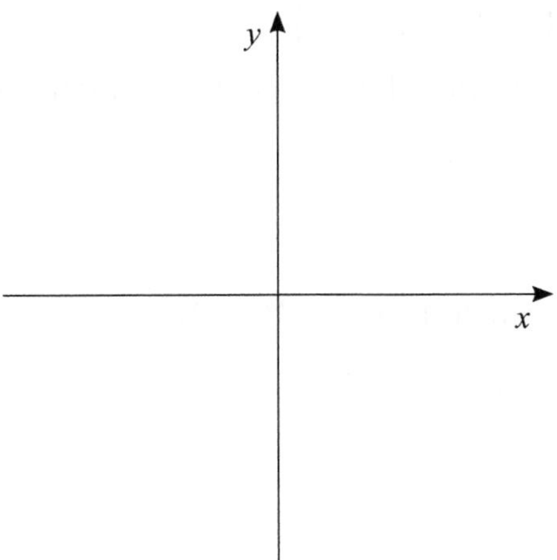

(3 marks)

c) $y = (x-2)^2(x+3)^2$

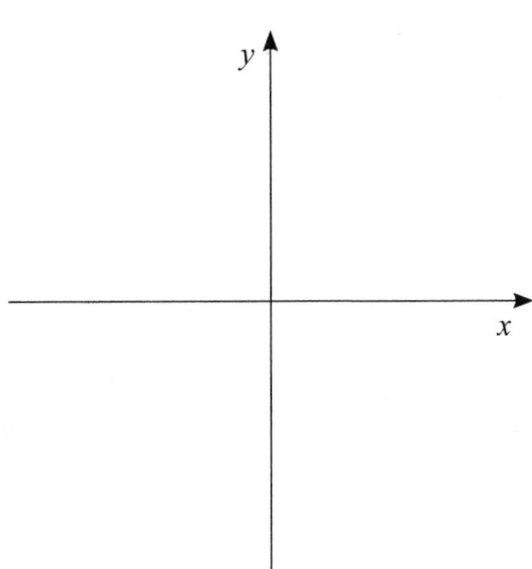

(3 marks)

Algebra and Functions 3

2 A travel agency offers a foreign currency exchange service. The number of dollars, d, is directly proportional to the number of pounds, p. On one day in July, £250 is exchanged for $320.

Sketch a graph showing this relationship and state the gradient of the line.

(2 marks)

3 The curve $y = \mathrm{f}(x)$ is to be transformed in different ways.

a) Describe fully the transformation that transforms the curve $y = \mathrm{f}(x)$ to the curve $y = -2\mathrm{f}(x)$.

....

....

(2 marks)

b) The curve $y = \mathrm{f}(x)$ is translated by the vector $\begin{pmatrix} 0 \\ 2 \end{pmatrix}$.
State the equation of the curve in terms of $\mathrm{f}(x)$ after the transformation.

....

(1 mark)

4 A curve has the equation $y = \mathrm{f}(x)$, where $\mathrm{f}(x) = (x - 1)^2 (x + 2)$.

On the axes below, sketch the graphs of:

a) $y = \mathrm{f}(x)$

(3 marks)

b) $y = \mathrm{f}(x - 3)$

(2 marks)

c) $y = 2\mathrm{f}(x)$

(2 marks)

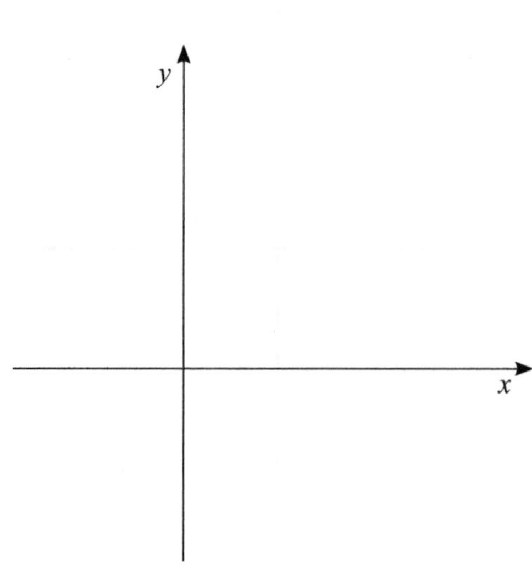

Algebra and Functions 3

5 Figure 1 shows a sketch of the function $y = f(x)$. The function crosses the x-axis at $(-1, 0)$, $(1, 0)$ and $(2, 0)$, and crosses the y-axis at $(0, 2)$.

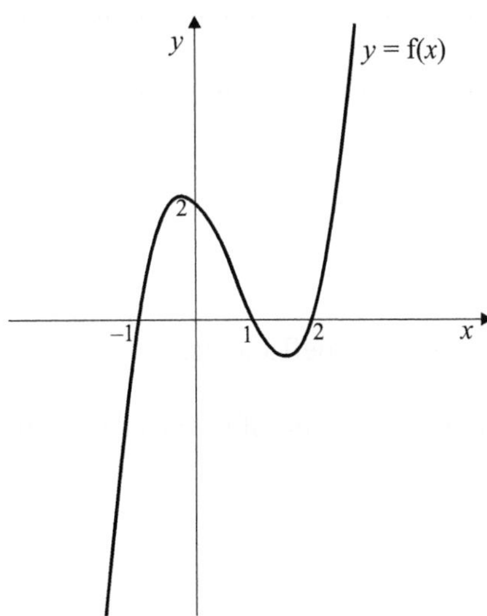

Figure 1

Sketch each transformation on the axes given below.
On each diagram, label any known points of intersection with the x- or y-axes.

a) $y = f\left(\frac{1}{2}x\right)$

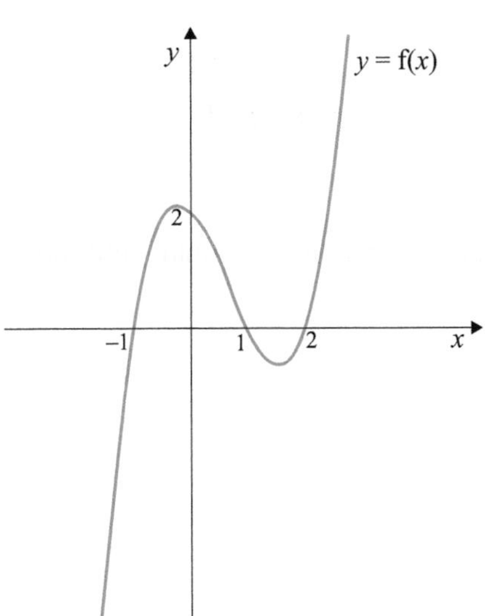

(3 marks)

b) $y = f(x - 4)$

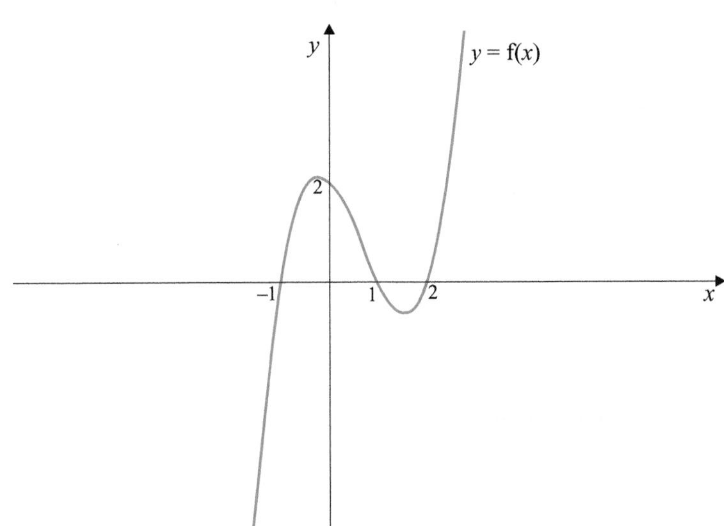

(2 marks)

Algebra and Functions 3

6 Describe what happens to the curve $y = x^3$ to transform it into the curve $y = (x - 4)^3$.

....

....

(2 marks)

7 Use the binomial expansion formula to find the coefficients.

a) Write down the first four terms in the expansion of $(1 + ax)^{10}$, $a > 0$, in ascending powers of x.

....

(4 marks)

b) Find the coefficient of x^2 in the expansion of $(2 + 3x)^5$.

$2^5 + {}^5C_1\, 2^4(3x) + {}^5C_2\, 2^3(3x)^2$

${}^5C_2 \times 2^3 \times 3^2 = 10 \times 8 \times 9$

$= 720$

720

(2 marks)

c) If the coefficients of x^2 in both expansions are equal, find the value of a.

$a =$ ....

(2 marks)

8 Find the coefficients of x, x^2 and x^3 in the binomial expansion of $(4 + 3x)^9$.

$4^9 + {}^9C_1\, 4^8(3x)$

$+ {}^9C_2\, 4^7(3x)^2$

$+ {}^9C_3\, 4^6(3x)^3$

$+ {}^9C_4\, 4^5(3x)^4$

...., ..., ...

(4 marks)

Algebra and Functions 3

9 Binomial expansions can be used to estimate values of powers.

a) Find the first 3 terms of the expansion of $\left(1+\frac{x}{3}\right)^8$ in ascending powers of x. Give each term in its simplest form.

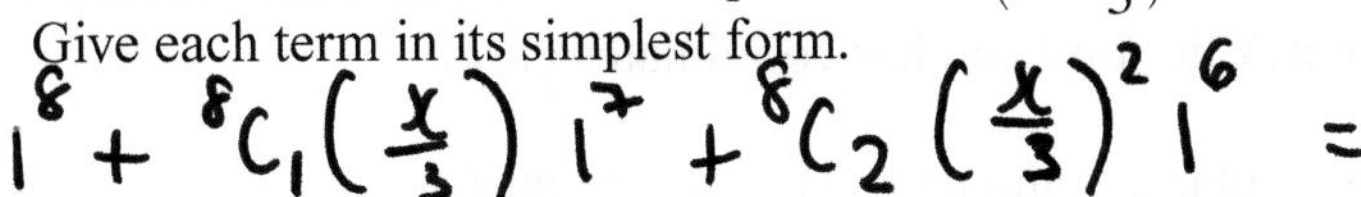

....

(3 marks)

b) Hence estimate the value of $(1.002)^8$ to 4 decimal places.

....

(3 marks)

10 This question is about the expansion of $(1+3x)^6$.

a) Find, in ascending powers of x, the first three terms of the expansion of $(1+3x)^6$, giving each term in its simplest form.

....

(3 marks)

b) Assuming x is small so that x^3 and higher powers can be ignored, show that

$$(1-2x)(1+3x)^6 \approx 1+16x+99x^2$$

(2 marks)

It doesn't matter what your preferred format for writing out the coefficients in the binomial expansion is — using the formula or using Pascal's triangle. As long as the examiner can understand what you've put down, and you've got each one correct, you should get full marks. That's not a license to scribble down any old nonsense though, it still has to be right...

Score

51

Coordinate Geometry

This topic is about lines and circles. Unfortunately, lines and circles can get quite complicated when it comes to exam questions. But remember the important gradient rules and circle properties and you'll be fine.

1 The line l has equation $y + 2x - 5 = 0$. Point A lies on l and has coordinates $(1, k)$.

Find the equation of the line that is perpendicular to l and passes through point A, giving your answer in the form $ax + by + c = 0$, where a, b and c are integers.

$$y = -2x + 5$$
$$m = -2$$

(4 marks)

2 The point A lies at the intersection of the lines l_1 and l_2, where the equation of l_1 is $x - y + 1 = 0$ and the equation of l_2 is $2x + y - 8 = 0$.

a) Find the coordinates of point A.

(3 marks)

b) The points B and C have coordinates $(6, -4)$ and $\left(-\frac{4}{3}, -\frac{1}{3}\right)$ respectively, and D is the midpoint of AC. Find the equation of the line through B and D in the form $ax + by + c = 0$, where a, b and c are integers.

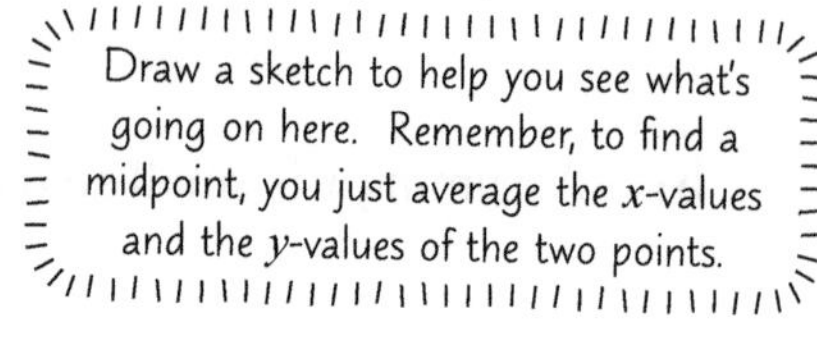

(5 marks)

c) Show that the triangle ABD is a right-angled triangle.

(3 marks)

Coordinate Geometry

3 The diagram shows a square ABCD, where point B has coordinates $(3, k)$. The line through points B and C has equation $-3x + 5y = 16$.

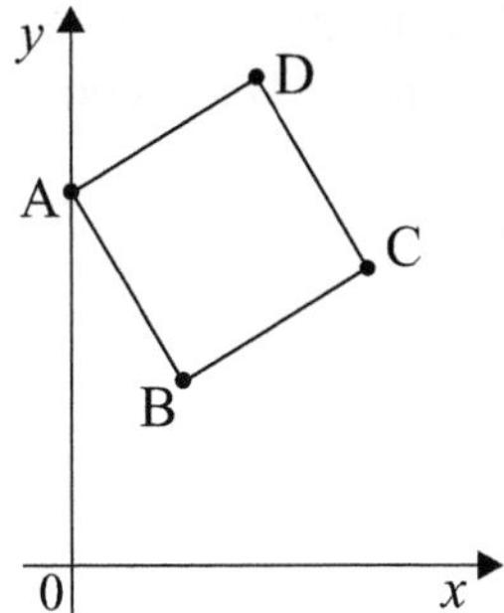

a) Show that the line through points A and B has equation $3y + 5x = 30$.

(4 marks)

b) Find the area of square ABCD.

....

(3 marks)

c) Show that the line with equation $5x + 3y - 6 = 0$ is parallel to the line through points A and B.

(2 marks)

4 The points A(2, 1) and B(0, –5) lie on a circle, where the line AB is a diameter of the circle.

a) Find the centre and radius of the circle.

centre = ..., radius = ...

(3 marks)

b) Show that the point (4, –1) also lies on the circle.

(2 marks)

c) Show that the equation of the circle can be written in the form $x^2 + y^2 - 2x + 4y - 5 = 0$.

(2 marks)

d) Find the equation of the tangent to the circle at point A, giving your answer in the form $y = mx + c$.

....

(3 marks)

Coordinate Geometry

5 The diagram shows a circle with centre P. The line AB is a chord with midpoint M.

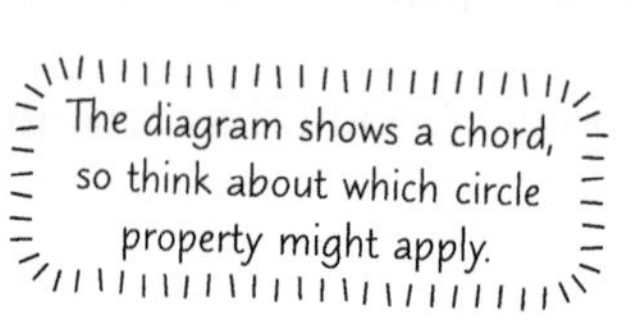

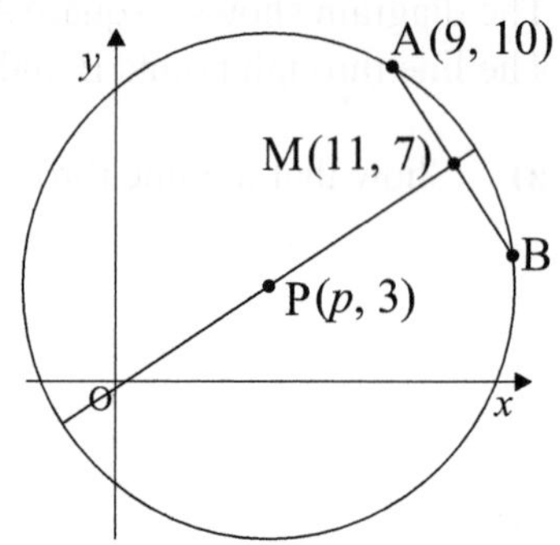

a) Show that $p = 5$.

(5 marks)

b) Find the equation of the circle.

....

(3 marks)

6 The circle with equation $x^2 - 6x + y^2 - 4y = 0$ crosses the y-axis at the origin and the point A.

a) Find the coordinates of point A.

....

(2 marks)

b) Write the equation of the circle in the form $(x - a)^2 + (y - b)^2 = c$.

....

(3 marks)

c) Write down the radius and the coordinates of the centre of the circle.

radius = ..., centre = ...

(2 marks)

d) The tangent to the circle at point A meets the x-axis at point B. Find the exact distance AB.

....

(6 marks)

If you're not given a diagram in the question, it's wise to sketch one — if you can picture where points are, it's much easier to see which rules for line gradients or properties of circles you can use. Make sure you give equations in the form you're asked for in the question — you wouldn't want to throw away marks by leaving them in the wrong form.

Score

55

Trigonometry

Aaah, you might have thought you'd left the triangular wonders of trigonometry behind when you finished GCSE Maths. But no, they're back to bring you unbridled joy and unlimited thrills once again.

1 Given that $\cos\theta = \frac{5}{6}$ and $0° < \theta < 90°$, find the exact values of $\sin\theta$ and $\tan\theta$.

$\sin\theta =$ ...., $\tan\theta =$ ....

(4 marks)

2 Sketch the graphs of $y = \sin x$ and $y = \sin\frac{x}{2}$ in the range $0° \leq x \leq 720°$ on the same set of axes, showing the points at which the graphs cross the x-axis.

(3 marks)

3 Find the missing length a and angle θ in the triangle shown in Figure 1.

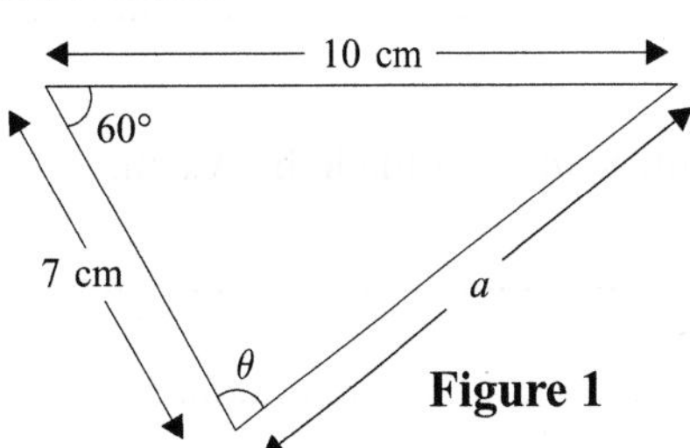

Figure 1

$a =$ .... cm

$\theta =$ ....°

(4 marks)

Trigonometry

4 A sheep pen is modelled as a triangle with side lengths of 50 m, 70 m and 90 m.

a) Find the area of the sheep pen to the nearest square metre.

.... m^2

(5 marks)

b) Comment on the accuracy of the model.

....

....

(1 mark)

5 Adam and Bethan have each attempted to solve the equation $\sin 2t = \sqrt{2}\cos 2t$ for the range $-90° < t < 90°$. Their working is shown below.

<u>Adam</u>

$\sin 2t = \sqrt{2}\cos 2t$

$\tan 2t = \sqrt{2}$

$\tan t = \frac{\sqrt{2}}{2}$

$t = 35.26...°$

<u>Bethan</u>

$\sin 2t = \sqrt{2}\cos 2t$

$\sin^2 2t = 2\cos^2 2t$

$1 - \cos^2 2t = 2\cos^2 2t$

$\cos^2 2t = \frac{1}{3}$

$\cos 2t = \pm\frac{1}{\sqrt{3}}$

$t = \pm 27.36...°$

a) Show that Adam's solution is incorrect.

....

....

(1 mark)

b) Identify an error made by Adam.

....

....

(1 mark)

c) Bethan's teacher explains that one of her solutions is incorrect.
Identify and explain the error Bethan has made.

....

....

(2 marks)

Trigonometry

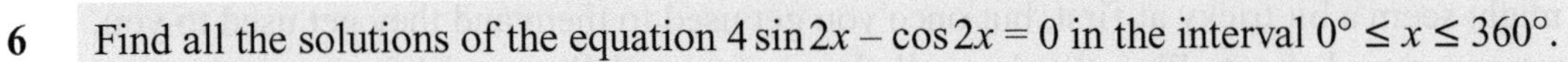

6 Find all the solutions of the equation $4\sin 2x - \cos 2x = 0$ in the interval $0° \leq x \leq 360°$.

....

(4 marks)

7 The function $f(\theta) = \tan^2\theta + \frac{\tan\theta}{\cos\theta}$ is defined for $0° \leq \theta \leq 360°$, $\theta \neq 90°, 270°$.

a) Show that the equation $\tan^2\theta + \frac{\tan\theta}{\cos\theta} = 1$ can be written in the form $2\sin^2\theta + \sin\theta - 1 = 0$.

(4 marks)

b) Hence find all solutions to the equation $f(\theta) = 1$ in the interval $0° \leq \theta \leq 360°$.

....

(3 marks)

8 Solutions to this question based entirely on graphical or numerical methods are not acceptable.

Find all the values of x, in the interval $0° \leq x \leq 180°$, for which

$$7 - 3\cos x = 9\sin^2 x$$

....

(5 marks)

When solving trig equations, make sure you check the question for the range it's asking for solutions in. It's no good giving all the solutions from 0° to 180° if the question asks for solutions between 360° and 540°. You'd just be throwing away easy marks right at the end of the answer, after doing all the hard work. Don't say I didn't warn you.

Score

37

Exponentials and Logarithms

Exponentials and logs might seem a bit tricky at first, but once you get used to them and they get used to you, you'll wonder what you ever worried about. Plus, they're really handy for modelling real-life situations.

1 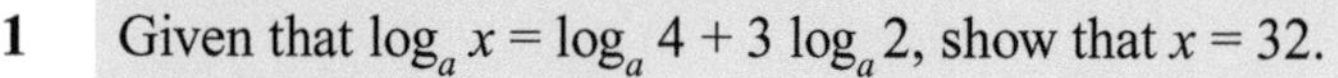
Given that $\log_a x = \log_a 4 + 3\log_a 2$, show that $x = 32$.

(2 marks)

2 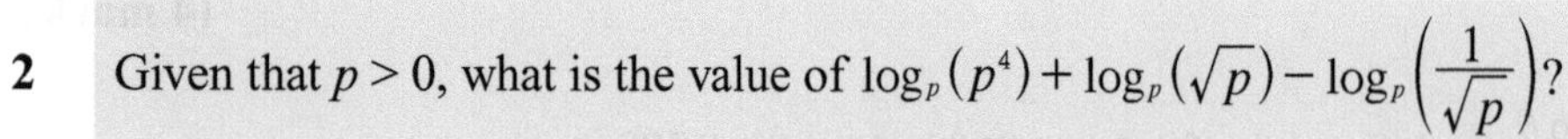
Given that $p > 0$, what is the value of $\log_p(p^4) + \log_p(\sqrt{p}) - \log_p\left(\frac{1}{\sqrt{p}}\right)$?

....

(3 marks)

3 It is given that $2^x = 9$.

a) Find the value of x, giving your answer to 2 decimal places.

$x =$ ....

(2 marks)

b) Hence, or otherwise, solve the equation $2^{2x} - 13(2^x) + 36 = 0$, giving each solution to an appropriate degree of accuracy.

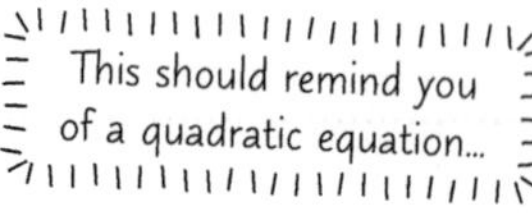

....

(5 marks)

4 Solve the equation $3^{(y^2 - 4)} = 7^{(y + 2)}$, giving your answers to 3 significant figures where appropriate.

Start by taking logs of both sides.

....

(5 marks)

Exponentials and Logarithms

5 For the positive integers p and q, $\log_4 p - \log_4 q = \frac{1}{2}$.

a) Show that $p = 2q$.

(3 marks)

b) The values of p and q are such that $\log_2 p + \log_2 q = 7$.
Use this information to find the values of p and q.

$p =$ .... $q =$ ....

(5 marks)

6 For the function $f(x) = 3 \ln x - \ln 3x$, $x > 0$, find the exact value of x when $f(x) = 0$.

$x =$ ....

(2 marks)

7 The curve below has equation $y = e^{kx}$.

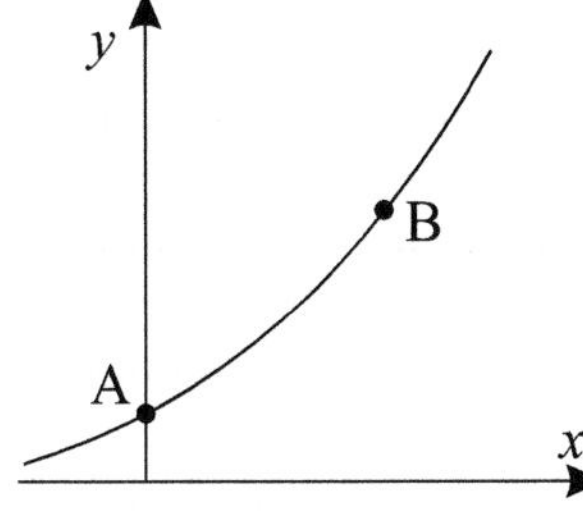

a) Write down the coordinates of A.

....

(1 mark)

b) The gradient of the curve at A is 4.
Write down the value of k.

$k =$ ....

(1 mark)

c) Find the exact gradient of the curve at the point where $x = -1$.

....

(1 mark)

d) The gradient of the curve at B is $4e^8$. Find the coordinates of B.

....

(2 marks)

Exponentials and Logarithms

8 In 2010, a bird of prey species was introduced into a country.
The bird of prey hunts an endangered species of bird, as well as other animals.

- The population, P, of the endangered species is modelled by the equation: $P = 5700e^{-0.15t}$.
- The population, Q, of the bird of prey is modelled by the equation: $Q = 2100 - 1500e^{-0.15t}$.

Where $t \geq 0$ is time in years, and $t = 0$ represents the beginning of the year 2010.

a) Find the year in which the population of the bird of prey is first predicted to exceed the population of the endangered species according to these models.

....

(4 marks)

b) The graph showing the predicted population of the bird of prey is shown on the right. Add a curve to the graph to show the predicted population of the endangered species of bird over the same time period.

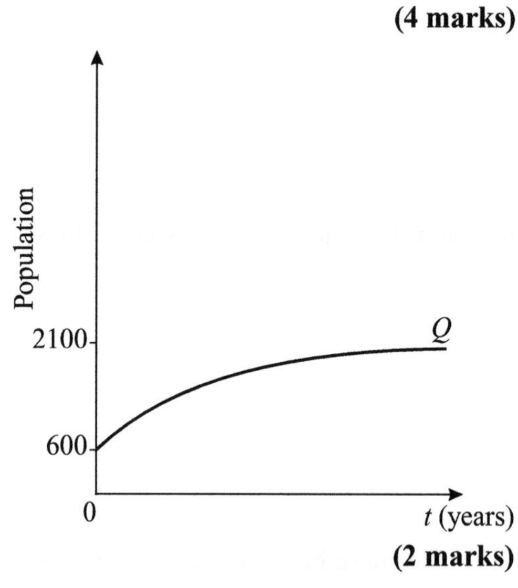

(2 marks)

c) Comment on the validity of each population model.

....

....

....

....

(2 marks)

d) Predict the year that the population of the endangered species will drop to below 1000.

....

(2 marks)

e) When this population drops below 1000, conservationists start enacting a plan to save the species. Suggest one refinement that could be made to the model to take this into account.

....

....

(1 mark)

Exponentials and Logarithms

9 The number of supporters of a local football club has increased since it was founded in 2010. The following table shows the average home game attendance for the club from 2011 to 2015.

Year	2011	2012	2013	2014	2015
Attendance (in hundreds, to the nearest hundred)	1	2	4	8	14

The attendance can be modelled by an equation of the form $y = ab^t$, where y is the average home game attendance in hundreds, t is the number of years from 2010, and a and b are constants to be found.

a) Show that $y = ab^t$ can be written in the form $\log_{10}y = t\log_{10}b + \log_{10}a$.

(2 marks)

b) Complete the following table, giving values correct to 3 d.p.:

t	1	2	3	4	5
$\log_{10}y$	0	0.301			

(1 mark)

c) Plot the graph of $\log_{10}y$ against t. Draw by eye a line of best fit for your data and calculate the values of a and b.

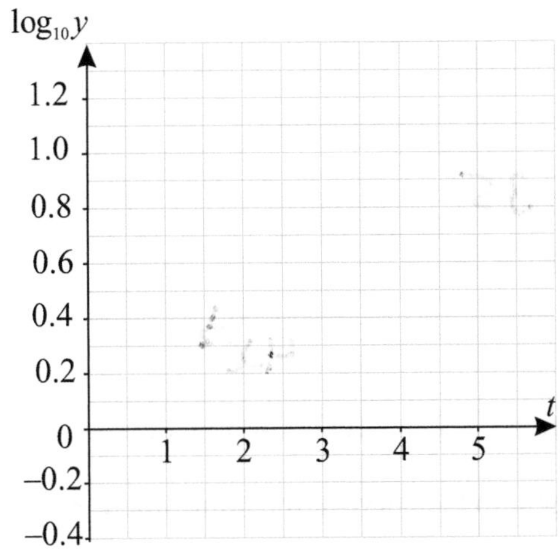

a = ... b = ...

(4 marks)

d) The chairman has promised a new stadium for the club when the average home game attendance reaches 5000. Find the value of t when this happens, according to the model.

....

(2 marks)

EXAM TIP

If you're asked to comment on the validity of models, or asked for limitations or refinements, think about anything that stops the model being realistic. For example, it might predict that a quantity will continue to rise until it becomes infinitely big, which might not be likely in a real-life situation — so you could refine the model by introducing an upper limit.

Score

52

Differentiation

Whenever you see a question about gradients, tangents or normals, you should immediately think, “Oho, that’ll be differentiation.” It’s also handy for curve sketching and for finding maximum and minimum values of functions.

1 Given that $y = x^7 + \frac{2}{x^3}$, find:

$x^7 + 2x^{-3}$

a) $\frac{\mathrm{d}y}{\mathrm{d}x}$

$\frac{dy}{dx} = 7x^6 - 6x^{-4}$

$7x^6 - 6x^{-4}$

(2 marks)

b) $\frac{\mathrm{d}^2y}{\mathrm{d}x^2}$

$\frac{d^2y}{dx^2} = 42x^5 + 24x^{-5}$

$42x^5 + 24x^{-5}$

(2 marks)

2 A curve has equation $y = 3x + 4 + x^4$.

The point A (2, 26) lies on the curve. Find the gradient of the curve at point A.

$y' = 4x^3 + 3$

$x = 2, \quad 4(2)^3 + 3$

$32 + 3 = 35$

(4 marks)

$4x^{\frac{1}{2}}$

3 The curve C is given by the equation $y = 2x^3 - 10x^2 - 4\sqrt{x} + 12$.

a) Find the gradient of the tangent to the curve at the point where $x = 4$.

$y = 6x^2 - 20x +$

(4 marks)

b) Hence find an equation for the normal to the curve at this point.
Give your answer in the form $ax + by + c = 0$.

(4 marks)

Differentiation

4 $f(x) = x^3 - 7x^2 + 8x + 9$

a) Sketch the graph of $y = f'(x)$, showing clearly the points of intersection with the axes.

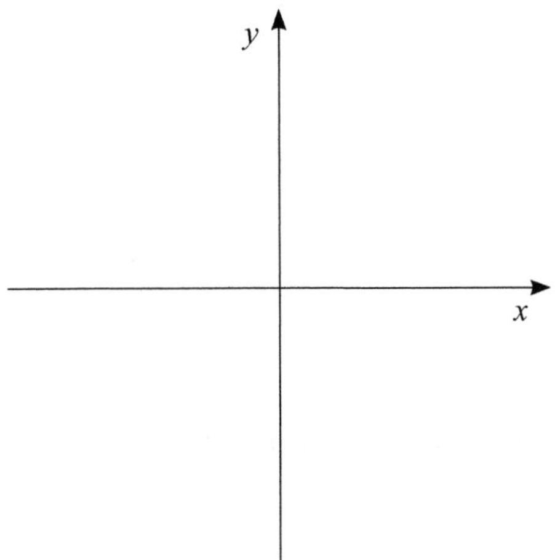

(4 marks)

b) Explain the significance of the x-intercepts on your sketch with regards to the graph of $y = f(x)$.

....

....

(1 mark)

5 A curve has equation $y = kx^2 - 8x - 5$, for a constant k. The point R lies on the curve and has an x-coordinate of 2. The normal to the curve at point R is parallel to the line with equation $4y + x = 24$.

a) Find the value of k.

k = ...

(5 marks)

b) The tangent to the curve at R meets the curve $y = 4x - \frac{1}{x^3} - 9$ at the point S. Find the coordinates of S.

....

(5 marks)

Differentiation

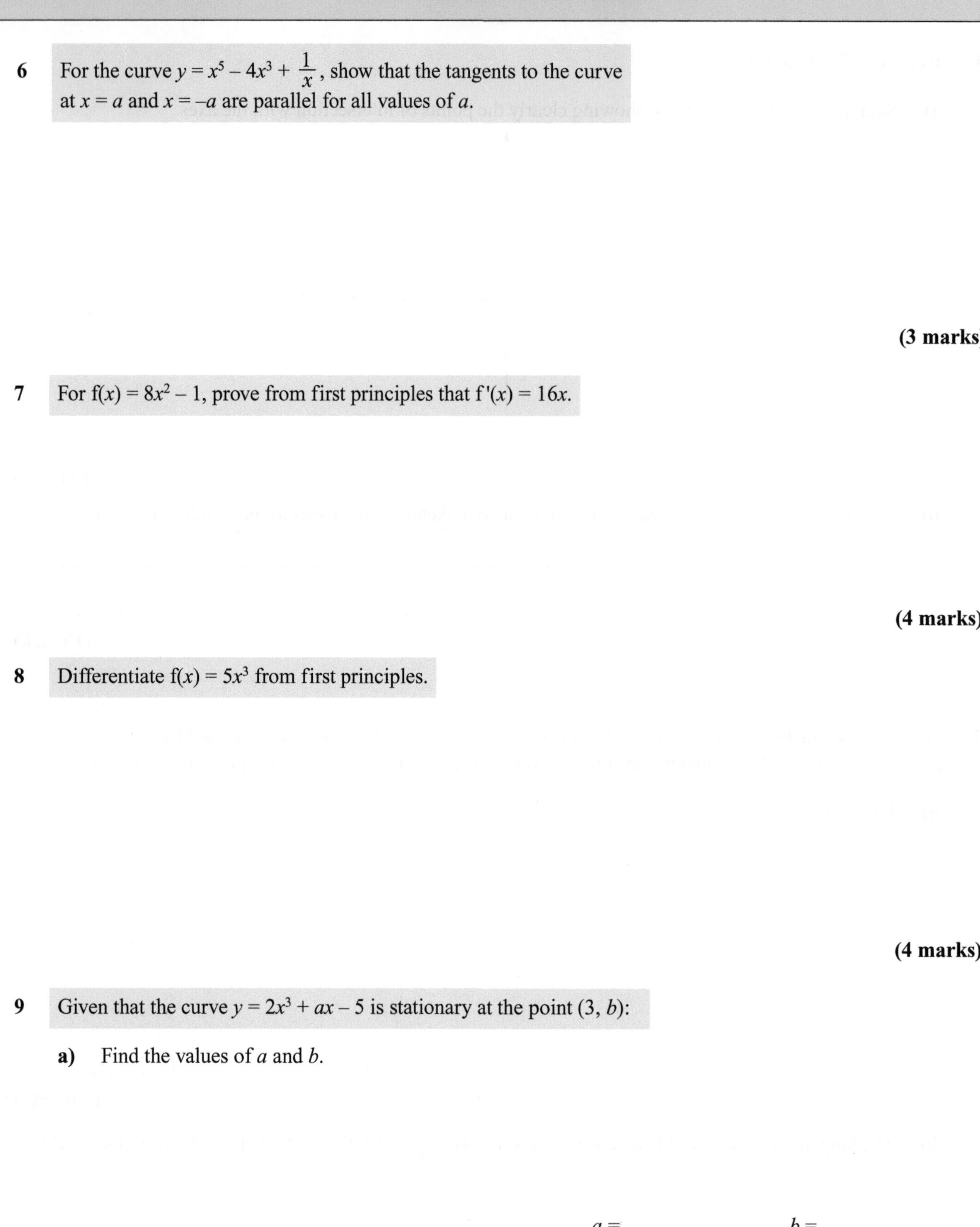

6 For the curve $y = x^5 - 4x^3 + \frac{1}{x}$, show that the tangents to the curve at $x = a$ and $x = -a$ are parallel for all values of a.

(3 marks)

7 For $f(x) = 8x^2 - 1$, prove from first principles that $f'(x) = 16x$.

(4 marks)

8 Differentiate $f(x) = 5x^3$ from first principles.

(4 marks)

9 Given that the curve $y = 2x^3 + ax - 5$ is stationary at the point $(3, b)$:

a) Find the values of a and b.

a = ... b = ...

(5 marks)

b) Determine whether $(3, b)$ is a maximum or minimum point.

....

(2 marks)

Differentiation

10 Joe claims that the function $f(x) = 3x^3 + 9x^2 + 25x$ is an increasing function for all values of x.

Show that Joe's claim is correct.

(4 marks)

11 The function $f(x) = 2x^4 + 27x$ has one stationary point.

a) Find the coordinates of the stationary point.

....

(3 marks)

b) Find the range of values of x for which the function is increasing and the range of values of x for which it is decreasing.

Increasing for: ...., decreasing for: ....

(2 marks)

c) Hence sketch the curve $y = f(x)$, showing where it crosses the axes.

To check what happens to the curve as x gets big, factorise f(x) by taking the highest power of x outside the brackets. Then if you imagine x getting very big, you can see what f(x) will tend towards.

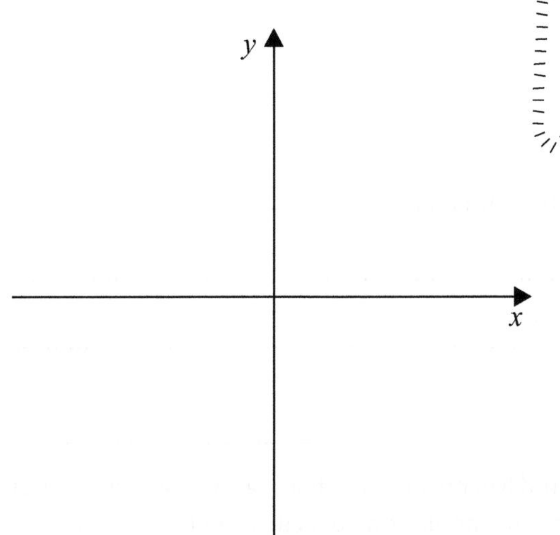

(3 marks)

Differentiation

12 An ice cream parlour needs an open-top stainless steel container with a capacity of 40 litres, modelled as a cuboid with sides of length x cm, x cm and y cm, as shown in Figure 1.

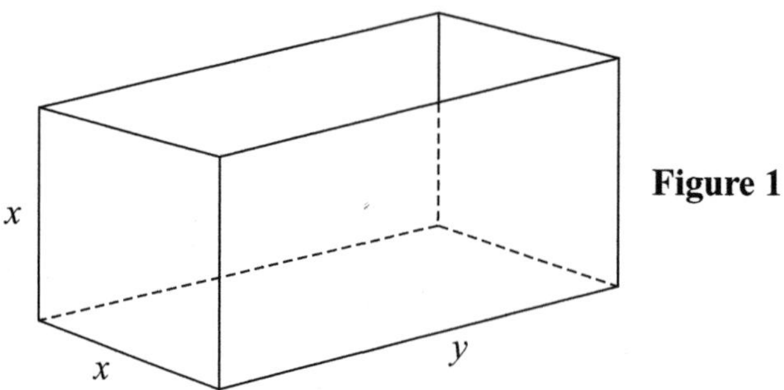

Figure 1

a) Show that the external surface area, A cm^2, of the container is given by $A = 2x^2 + \frac{120\,000}{x}$

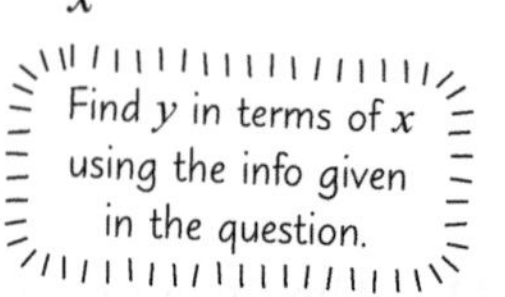

(4 marks)

b) Find the value of x to 3 s.f. at which A is stationary, and show that this is a minimum value of A.

(6 marks)

c) Calculate the minimum area of stainless steel needed to make the container. Give your answer to 3 s.f.

.... cm^2

(2 marks)

d) Comment on the validity of this model.

....

....

(1 mark)

Work carefully through differentiation questions, as it's easy to get a bit mixed up. Remember that tangents have the same gradient as the curve, and normals are perpendicular to the curve. To find stationary points, differentiate once, then differentiate again to determine the nature of the point — don't forget that negative means maximum and positive means minimum.

Score

74

Integration

Remember, integration is the reverse process of differentiation — so powers should increase when you integrate (I've been doing integration for years and I've only just thought of that way of remembering it).

1 Find $\int (4x^3 + 6x + 3)\,dx$.

$= \frac{4x^4}{4} + \frac{6x^2}{2} + 3x + C$

$= x^4 + 3x^2 + 3x + C$

$x^4 + 3x^2 + 3x + C$

(3 marks)

2 Find $\int \left(2\sqrt{x} + \frac{1}{x^3}\right) dx$.

$\int (2x^{\frac{1}{2}} + x^{-3})\,dx$

$= \frac{2x^{\frac{3}{2}}}{3/2} + \frac{x^{-2}}{-2} =$

$\frac{4}{3}x^{3/2} + \frac{x^{-2}}{-2}$

(3 marks)

3 Find $\int \left(\frac{x^2 + 3}{\sqrt{x}}\right) dx$.

$\int (x^{3/2} + 3x^{-1/2})\,dx$

$= \frac{x^{5/2}}{5/2} + \frac{3x^{1/2}}{1/2} + C$

$\frac{2}{5}x^{5/2} + 6x^{1/2} + C$

(3 marks)

4 A curve that passes through the point (0, 0) has derivative $\frac{dy}{dx} = 3x^2 + 6x - 4$. Find the equation of the curve.

You're given the derivative of the curve — so integrate to find its equation.

$= \frac{3x^3}{3} + \frac{6x^2}{2} - 4x$

$x^3 + 3x^2 - 4x$

(4 marks)

5 The curve C has the equation $y = f(x)$, $x > 0$. $f'(x)$is given as $2x + 5\sqrt{x} + \frac{6}{x^2}$.

A point P on curve C has the coordinates (3, 7). Find $f(x)$, giving your answer in its simplest form.

....

(6 marks)

Integration

6 Evaluate $\int_{p}^{4p}\left(\frac{1}{\sqrt{x}} - 4x^3\right)dx$, where $p > 0$, leaving your answer in terms of p.

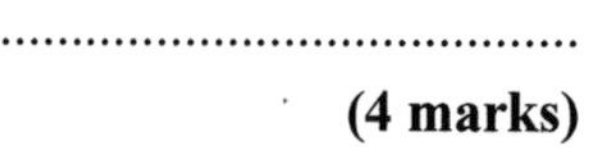

(4 marks)

7 Region A is bounded by the curve $y = \frac{2}{\sqrt{x^3}}$ $(x > 0)$, the x-axis and the lines $x = 2$ and $x = 4$.

Show that the area of A is $2\sqrt{2} - 2$.

(5 marks)

8 Find the possible values of k that satisfy $\int_{\sqrt{2}}^{2}(8x^3 - 2kx)\,dx = 2k^2$, where k is a constant.

....

(5 marks)

Integration

9 A curve has equation $y = f(x)$, where $\frac{dy}{dx} = 4(1 - x)$.
The curve passes through the point A, with coordinates (2, 6).

a) Find the equation of the curve.

....

(4 marks)

b) Hence find the area of the region under the curve that lies above the x-axis.

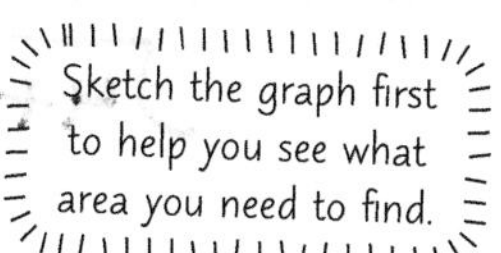

....

(6 marks)

10 The curve $y = 2x^3 - 3x^2 - 11x + 6$ is shown below. It crosses the x-axis at (–2, 0), (0.5, 0) and (3, 0).
Find the area of the shaded region bounded by the curve, the x-axis and the lines $x = -1$ and $x = 2$.

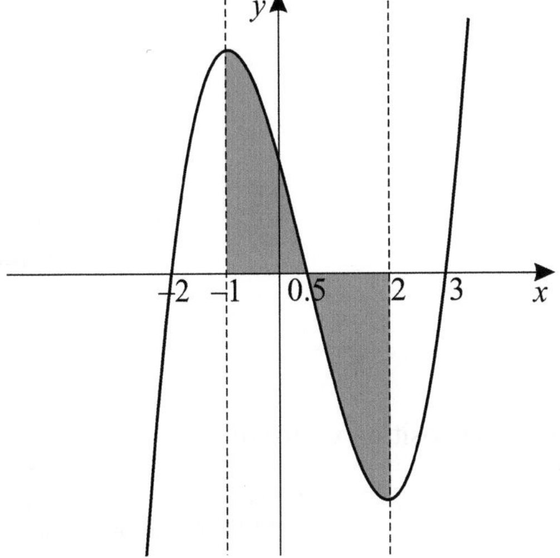

....

(6 marks)

Knowing your index laws inside out is a big help when it comes to integration — always write out fractions and roots as powers of x before integrating (it'll save a lot of heartache further down the line). The examiners might try to confuse you by sneaking some extra algebra in there or wording the question weirdly, but the basic integration process is the same each time.

Score

49

Vectors

Aaah, good old dependable vectors. They've got a certain magnitude about them, and they always have a clear direction. Much like an inspirational leader. It's kind of how I see myself after I've brought about the revolution.

1 Point A has position vector $4\mathbf{i} + 2\mathbf{j}$ and point B has position vector $6\mathbf{i} - 3\mathbf{j}$.

a) Find the vector $\overrightarrow{AB}$.

$\overrightarrow{AB} = B - A$

$= (6i - 3j) - (4i + 2j)$

$2i - 5j$

$2i - 5j$ ....

(2 marks)

b) Find the exact magnitude of vector $\overrightarrow{AB}$.

$\sqrt{4 + 25} = \sqrt{29}$

$\sqrt{29}$ ....

(2 marks)

2 Points A, B and C have position vectors $-\mathbf{i} + 7\mathbf{j}$, $5\mathbf{i} - 3\mathbf{j}$ and $8\mathbf{i} + 4\mathbf{j}$ respectively. M is the midpoint of AB.

a) Show that $|\overrightarrow{AM}| = \sqrt{34}$.

$\overrightarrow{AB} = B - A = (5i - 3j) - (-i + 7j)$

$= 6i - 10j$

$\overrightarrow{AM} = 3i - 5j$

$= \sqrt{9 + 25}$

$= \sqrt{34}$

(3 marks)

b) Find the position vector of the point D, such that $\overrightarrow{AC} = \overrightarrow{BD}$.

....

(3 marks)

3 Points A and B have position vectors $\begin{pmatrix} 1 \\ 4 \end{pmatrix}$ and $\begin{pmatrix} -3 \\ 5 \end{pmatrix}$ respectively.
Point C is the point on the line AB such that $AC : CB = 1 : 3$. Find the position vector of C.

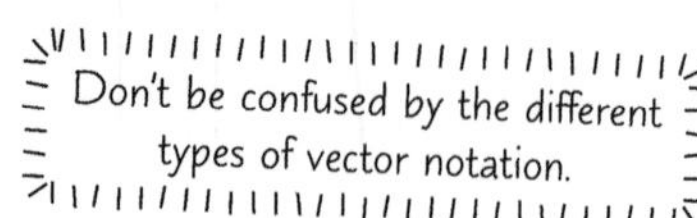

....

(4 marks)

Vectors

4 Find the magnitude and direction of the resultant vector **a** + **b** + **c**, where **a** = (4**i** + 6**j**), **b** = (**i** – 2**j**) and **c** = –3**j**.

$a+b+c$

$\begin{pmatrix}4\\6\end{pmatrix}+\begin{pmatrix}1\\-2\end{pmatrix}+\begin{pmatrix}0\\-3\end{pmatrix} = \begin{pmatrix}5\\1\end{pmatrix}$

$\text{mag} = \sqrt{25+1}$
$= \sqrt{26}$

$\text{mag} = \sqrt{26}$ ....

(5 marks)

5 A vector of magnitude 7 acts vertically upwards. Another vector, of magnitude $4\sqrt{2}$, acts at an angle of 45° below the positive horizontal direction. The resultant of the two vectors is **r**.

a) Find **r** in terms of **i** and **j**.

r = ...

(2 marks)

b) The vector **s** acts parallel to **r**, and has magnitude 35. Find **s** in terms of **i** and **j**.

s = ...

(3 marks)

6 The point P is 14 m from point O. The point Q is 11 m from O. The angle between the position vectors $\overrightarrow{OP}$ and $\overrightarrow{OQ}$ is 105°.

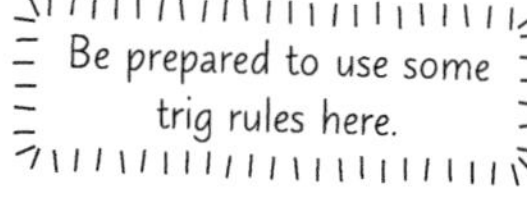

a) Find the distance between the points P and Q.

.... m

(2 marks)

b) Find the size of angle OPQ.

.... °

(2 marks)

Vectors

7 Four cones are placed in a field, forming a parallelogram *ABDC* as shown below. The position vectors of three of the cones relative to a fixed origin are $A = (5\mathbf{i} + 2\mathbf{j})$ m, $B = (\mathbf{i} - 4\mathbf{j})$ m and $C = (19\mathbf{i} + 2\mathbf{j})$ m. Find the exact perimeter of the parallelogram in m.

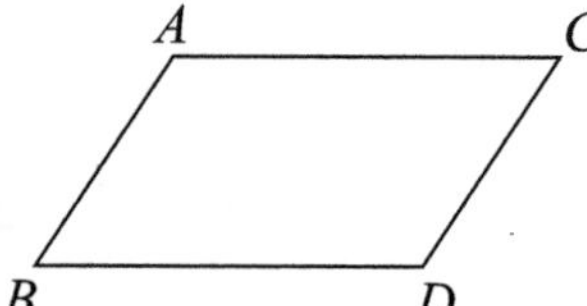

.... m

(6 marks)

8 Figure 1 shows a sketch of a triangle, *PQR*. Given that $\overrightarrow{PQ} = \begin{pmatrix} 2 \\ -9 \end{pmatrix}$ and $\overrightarrow{QR} = \begin{pmatrix} 14 \\ 6 \end{pmatrix}$, find the angle at *P*.

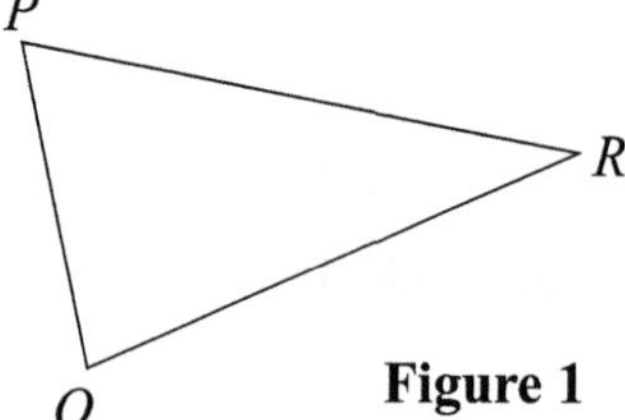

Figure 1

.... °

(5 marks)

Once you've grasped the magnitude of this topic, and got these questions cracked, you'll be heading in the right direction for exam success. Make sure you're comfortable with finding the length of vectors using Pythagoras, and using trig to find angles. There's not too much more to it to be honest. Don't forget to underline your **i** and **j** vectors, or use column notation.

Score

39

Data Presentation and Interpretation

Questions on presenting and interpreting data are the perfect chance for the examiners to test you on the large data set — so now would be a good time to have another look at those massive spreadsheets...

1 A group of 10 friends play a round of minigolf and record their scores, x. It is given that $\sum x = 500$ and $\sum x^2 = 25\ 622$.

a) Find the mean and the standard deviation for the data.

mean = ..., standard deviation = ...

(3 marks)

b) Another friend wants to incorporate his score of 50. Giving reasons, but without further calculation, explain the effect of adding this score on:

(i) the mean,

....

....

(2 marks)

(ii) the standard deviation.

....

....

(2 marks)

2 The daily mean air temperature (t °C) in Jacksonville, Florida, was recorded each day in May 2015. The results are summarised in the table below.

Daily mean air temperature (t °C)	$17.5 \leq t < 20.0$	$20.0 \leq t < 22.5$	$22.5 \leq t < 24.0$	$24.0 \leq t < 25.0$	$25.0 \leq t < 27.5$
Frequency	4	3	8	8	8

Morwenna draws a histogram to represent the data.
The bar for the $24.0 \leq t < 25.0$ class has a width of 0.5 cm and a height of 4 cm.

Find the width and height of the bar for the $25.0 \leq t < 27.5$ class.

Find the area of the bar you're given and use it to work out what 1 cm² represents.

width = ... cm, height = ... cm

(3 marks)

Data Presentation and Interpretation

3 All the Year 12 students in a school were asked how much their monthly phone bill is (in £). The incomplete table and histogram below show the results.

a) Complete the table and the histogram.

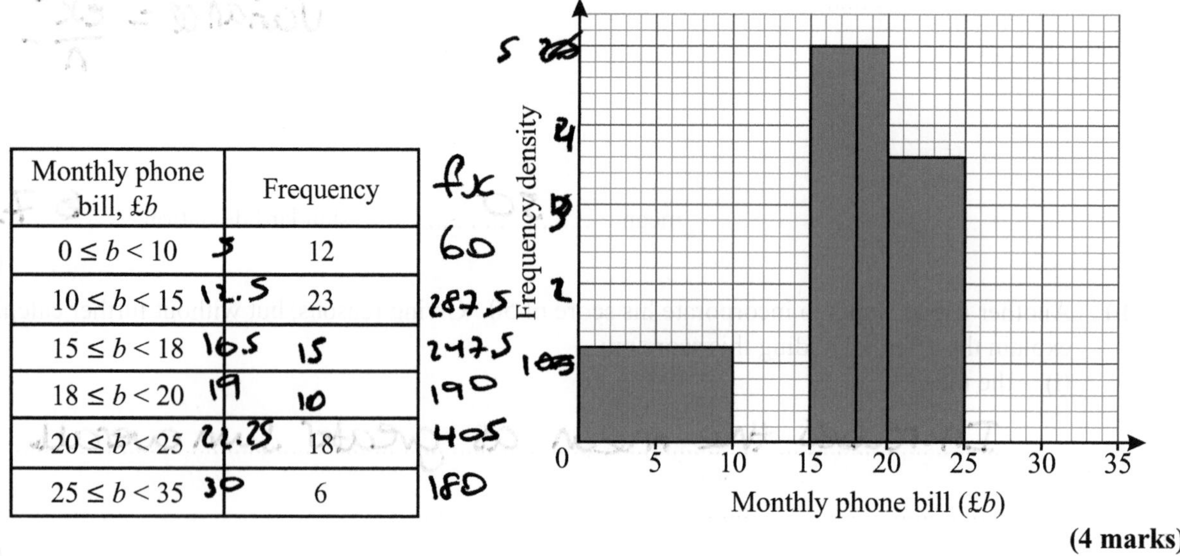

Monthly phone bill, £b	Frequency
$0 \le b < 10$	12
$10 \le b < 15$	23
$15 \le b < 18$	
$18 \le b < 20$	
$20 \le b < 25$	18
$25 \le b < 35$	6

(4 marks)

b) Estimate the number of students that have a monthly phone bill of between £12.50 and £17.50.

....

(2 marks)

c) Estimate the mean monthly phone bill for the Year 12 students.

You might find it helpful to add some columns to the table above for parts c) and d).

£ ....

(3 marks)

d) Estimate the standard deviation for the data.

£ ....

(3 marks)

e) Estimate the 20th percentile of the data.

£ ....

(3 marks)

Data Presentation and Interpretation

4 The heights of giraffes living in a zoo were measured.
The results are shown in the frequency table below.

Height, h (metres)	$0 < h \leq 2$	$2 < h \leq 3$	$3 < h \leq 4$	$4 < h \leq 5$	$5 < h \leq 6$
Frequency	0	5	12	10	3

a) Use the table to calculate an estimate of the median height of these giraffes.

.... m

(3 marks)

b) Draw a cumulative frequency graph for the heights of the giraffes in the zoo.

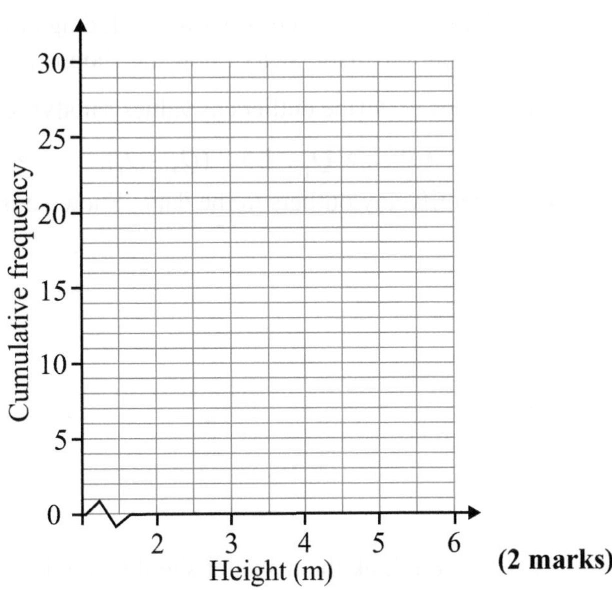

(2 marks)

c) Use your cumulative frequency graph to estimate the lower and upper quartiles of the data. Then calculate an estimate for the interquartile range.

lower quartile = ... m, upper quartile = ... m, interquartile range = ... m

(3 marks)

The tallest giraffe in the zoo measures 5.56 m and the shortest giraffe measures 2.7 m.

The heights of giraffes living in a game reserve were also measured.
This data is summarised in the box plot below.

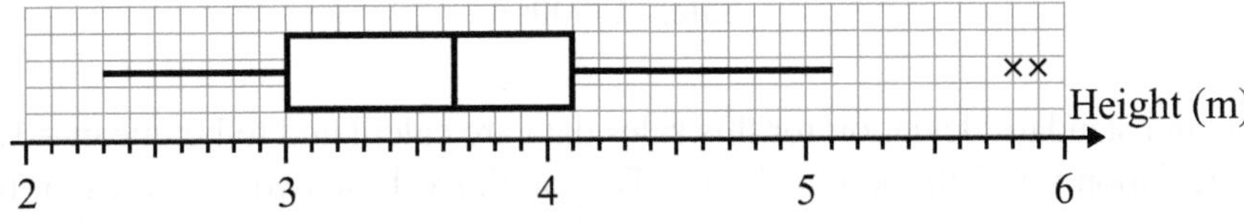

d) Compare the heights of the two groups of giraffes.

....

....

....

(3 marks)

Data Presentation and Interpretation

5 The sales figures, x, for a gift shop over a 12-week period are shown below.

Week	1	2	3	4	5	6	7	8	9	10	11	12
Sales, x (£'000s)	5.5	4.2	5.8	9.1	3.8	4.6	6.4	6.2	4.9	5.9	6.0	4.1

a) Find the median and quartiles of the sales data.

median = £ ...., lower quartile = £ ...., upper quartile = £ ....

(3 marks)

The shop's manager is considering excluding any outliers from his analysis of the data, to get a more realistic idea of how the shop is performing.

He decides to define outliers as values satisfying either of the following conditions:

- below $Q_1 - 1.5 \times (Q_3 - Q_1)$
- above $Q_3 + 1.5 \times (Q_3 - Q_1)$.

b) Identify any outliers in the data. Show your working.

....

(2 marks)

c) Do you think the manager should include any outliers in his analysis? Explain your answer.

....

....

(1 mark)

d) Draw a box plot to represent this data on the grid below.

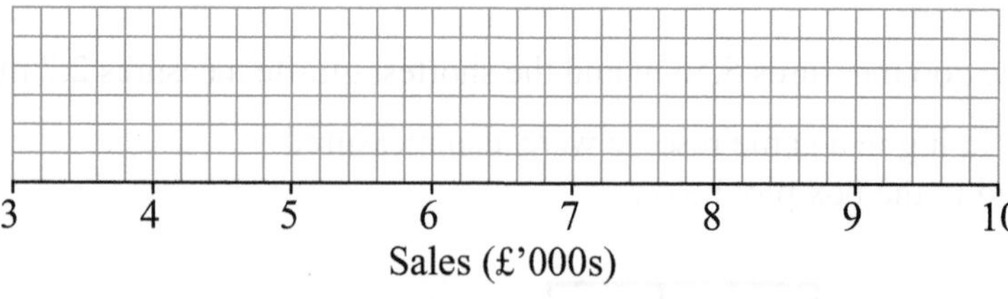

(2 marks)

e) The mean and standard deviation for this sales data are calculated to be: mean = £5540, standard deviation = £1370 (both to 3 s.f.). Do you think these two measures, or the median and interquartile range, are more useful measures of location and spread for this data? Explain your answer.

....

....

....

(2 marks)

Data Presentation and Interpretation

6 The total daily rainfall figures for Heathrow and Hurn over 15 days in October 1987 are shown on the line graph below.

The mean for Heathrow over this period was 8.31 mm and the standard deviation was 13.2 mm (both to 3 s.f.).
For Hurn, the mean was 7.73 mm and the standard deviation was 7.85 mm (both to 3 s.f.).

a) Match each of the towns Heathrow and Hurn to the corresponding line on the diagram. You must explain your reasoning for each town.

Town A = ...

Reason: ....

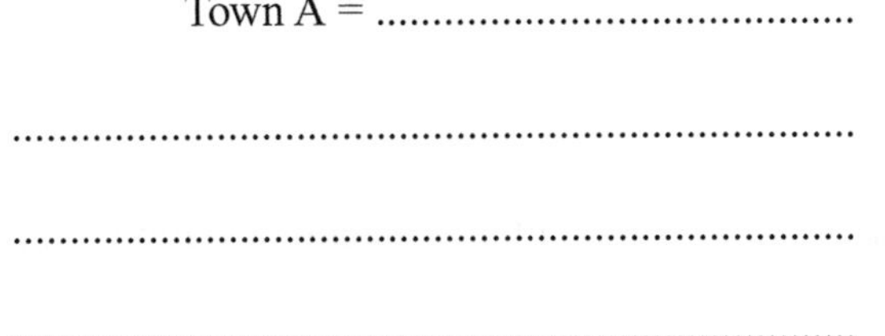

Town B = ...

Reason: ....

(2 marks)

b) An outlier is defined as a value that lies more than three standard deviations from the mean. Using the graph and the information given above, identify any outliers for each town and circle them on the graph. You must show your working.

(2 marks)

c) With reference to the data, suggest a reason for any outliers.

....

....

(1 mark)

Data Presentation and Interpretation

7 The daily mean pressure, p (measured in hPa), in Leeming was recorded for 10 days in June 2015. The data was coded using $q = \frac{p - 1000}{2}$ and the summary statistics for q were $\sum q = 104$ and $\sum q^2 = 1492$.

Find the mean and standard deviation of the original data.

mean = ... hPa, standard deviation = ... hPa

(4 marks)

8 Some ecologists carry out an investigation into the reindeer populations at different locations. They also recorded the human population density at the same locations. Their results are displayed in the scatter diagram below.

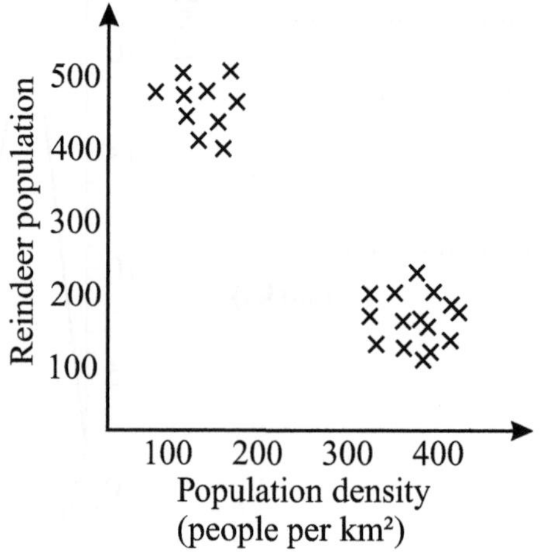

a) Jiao claims that there is negative correlation between human population density and reindeer population. Use the scatter diagram to comment on Jiao's claim.

....

....

....

(2 marks)

b) Killian claims that more people living in an area cause there to be fewer reindeer in that area. Do you agree with Killian's claim? Explain your answer.

....

....

....

(2 marks)

Data Presentation and Interpretation

9 A construction company measures the length, y metres, of a cable when put under different amounts of tension, T kN (kilonewtons). The results of its tests are shown below.

T (kN)	1	2	3	5	8	10	12	15	20
y (metres)	3.05	3.1	3.13	3.15	3.27	3.4	3.1	3.5	3.6

a) Draw a scatter diagram to show these results.

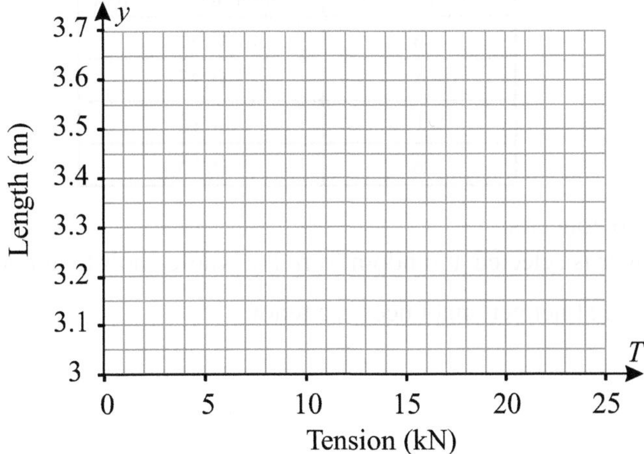

(2 marks)

b) One of the readings has been recorded inaccurately. Put a ring around this reading on your graph.

(1 mark)

c) Describe the correlation shown on your scatter diagram.

....

(1 mark)

An engineer believes a linear regression line of the form $y = a + bT$ could be used to accurately describe the results. She ignores the outlier, and calculates the equation of the regression line to be $y = 3 + 0.03T$.

d) Explain what these values of a and b represent in this context.

....

....

(2 marks)

e) Use the regression line to predict the length of the cable when put under a tension of 30 kilonewtons.

.... m

(1 mark)

f) Comment on the reliability of your estimate for part e).

....

....

(1 mark)

You'll be given the method to find outliers in the question (or be asked to spot them on a graph) — but you need to know what to do with them. You might have to decide whether to include them in your analysis or exclude them — think about what effect they have on different measures, and whether they're likely to be errors in recording or actual unusual results.

Score

67

Probability

In all probability, you'll love this topic. After all, it's been scientifically proven that Venn diagrams are the single most exciting thing you can do with circles. And who doesn't love a table or two...

1 In a choir, there are four different types of voice: soprano (S), alto (A), tenor (T) and bass (B). Each person in the choir fits into one of these categories.
The table below shows the proportion of each different type of voice in the choir.

Type of voice	Proportion in choir
S	0.36
A	0.27
T	0.22
B	0.15

The choir performs in two concerts.
At each concert, one singer is selected at random from the whole choir to announce the songs.

a) Find the probability that neither announcer is a tenor.

....

(2 marks)

b) Find the probability that both announcers have the same type of voice.

....

(3 marks)

2 Jessica has two packs of cards. One pack has some cards missing. The probability of selecting a heart, P(S), from this pack is 0.3. Jessica selects one card from this pack and one card from her complete pack of cards.

a) Find the probability that at least one of the two cards is a heart.

....

(2 marks)

b) Find the probability that exactly one of the two cards is a heart.

....

(3 marks)

Probability

3 Riyad carries out a survey on his classmates to find out what after-school clubs they attend. He uses a Venn diagram to show his findings. A represents the number of pupils who do archery, B represents the number of pupils who play badminton and C represents the number of pupils who play chess.

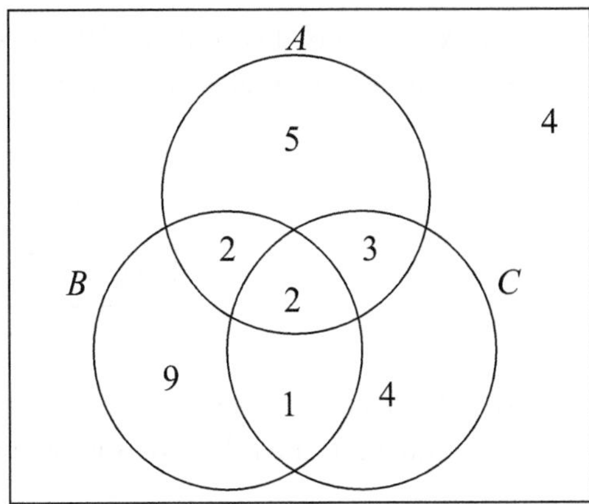

a) Riyad claims that a classmate chosen at random is more likely to not play badminton than to do either archery or chess. State whether or not Riyad is correct, giving reasons for your answer.

Make sure you read the question carefully — you're interested in pupils who don't play badminton.

....

(3 marks)

b) Calculate the probability that a classmate chosen at random is a member of the badminton club or the chess club, but not both.

....

(1 mark)

4 A film club with 20 members meets once a week. 14 of the members go every week and 13 plan to renew their membership for another year. Of those planning to renew their membership, 10 go every week. One member of the club is selected at random.

a) Find the probability that the person selected plans to renew their membership and goes to the club every week.

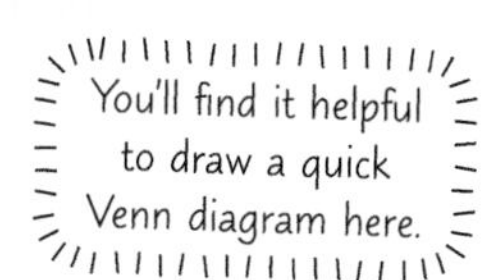

....

(2 marks)

b) Show whether or not the events 'selected member goes to the club every week' and 'selected member plans to renew their membership' are independent.

(2 marks)

Probability

5 A box of chocolates contains 20 chocolates, all of which are either hard or soft centred. Some of the chocolates contain nuts. The table below shows the number of each type of chocolate.

	Hard centre	Soft centre	Total
Nuts	6	4	10
No nuts	7	3	10
Total	13	7	20

a) A chocolate is selected at random. Find the probability that the chocolate either has a hard centre or contains nuts.

....

(2 marks)

b) If three chocolates are selected at random without replacement, find the probability that exactly one has a hard centre.

....

(3 marks)

6 This incomplete Venn diagram shows the probabilities of two independent events L and M. Calculate the probability that neither L nor M occur.

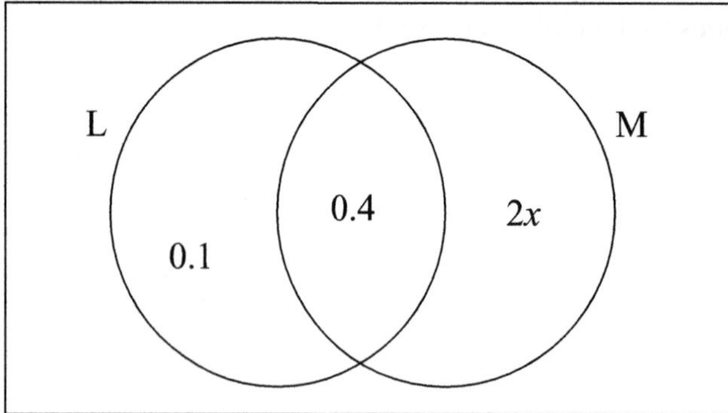

....

(4 marks)

Probability

7 The events A and B are mutually exclusive. P(A) = 0.1 and P(B) = 0.4.
Event C has probability P(C) = 0.3.
Events B and C are statistically independent, and the probability of both events A and C occurring is 0.06.

a) Draw a Venn diagram showing the probabilities of events A, B and C.

(5 marks)

b) Are events A and C independent? Explain your answer.

....

....

(2 marks)

c) Find the probability that either event B or C but not both occurs.

....

(1 mark)

d) Find the probability that neither event A nor event B occurs.

....

(1 mark)

EXAM TIP

You might not be asked to draw a diagram (of the Venn or tree variety), but you'd be a fool not to. They make it so much easier to keep track of all those pesky probabilities and help you to avoid mistakes. It doesn't have to be a work of art, just a quick sketch will do (as long as the probabilities are correct) — and watch out for independent and mutually exclusive events.

Score

36

Statistical Distributions

Another treat of a topic for probability fans (like me), and your first glimpse of the binomial distribution. If you don't warm to the binomial distribution here, you'll get another chance with hypothesis testing in the next topic.

1 The discrete random variable X has the probability function shown below.

$$P(X=x) = \begin{cases} \frac{kx}{6} & \text{for } x = 1, 2, 3 \\ \frac{k(7-x)}{6} & \text{for } x = 4, 5, 6 \\ 0 & \text{otherwise} \end{cases}$$

a) Find the value of k.

$\frac{K}{6} + \frac{2K}{6} + \frac{3K}{6} + \frac{3K}{6} + \frac{2K}{6} + \frac{K}{6} = \frac{12K}{6} = 2K$

$k =$ ....$\frac{1}{2}$....

(2 marks)

b) Find $P(1 < X \leq 4)$.

$P(X=2) + P(X=3) + P(X=4) =$

$\frac{1}{6} + \frac{1}{4} + \frac{1}{4} = \frac{2}{3}$

....$\frac{2}{3}$....

(2 marks)

A discrete random variable Y has the probability function $P(Y = y) = 0.2$ for $y = 1, 2, 3, 4, 5$.

c) State the name of the distribution of Y.

....discrete uniform distribution....

(1 mark)

2 The number of points awarded to each contestant in a talent competition is modelled by the discrete random variable X with the following probability distribution:

x	0	1	2	3
$P(X=x)$	0.4	0.3	a	b

A contestant is twice as likely to be awarded 2 points as they are to be awarded 3 points.

By finding the values of a and b, calculate the probability that for two randomly chosen contestants, one scores 2 points and the other scores 3 points.

$0.4 + 0.3 + a + b = 1$

$0.7 + a + b = 1$

$a + b = 0.3$

$a = 2b$

$2b + b = 0.3$

$3b = 0.3$

$b = 0.1$

$a = 0.2$

....

(4 marks)

Statistical Distributions

3 In a game, a player tosses three fair coins. If three heads occur then the player wins 20p. If two heads occur then the player wins 10p. For any other outcome, the player wins nothing.

a) If X is the random variable 'amount won in pence', draw a table to show the probability distribution of X.

3H = 1/2 × 1/2 × 1/2 = 1/8

2H = 1/8 × 3 = 3/8

(3 marks)

The player pays 10p to play each game.

b) Use the probability distribution to find the probability that the player makes a profit over two games.

....

(2 marks)

4 5% of chocolate bars made by a particular manufacturer contain a 'golden ticket'. A student buys 5 of the chocolate bars every week for 8 weeks.

The number of golden tickets he finds is represented by the random variable X.

a) State two necessary conditions for X to follow the binomial distribution B(40, 0.05).

....

....

(2 marks)

Assuming that $X \sim$ B(40, 0.05):

b) Find $P(X > 1)$.

You can use the binomial tables or your calculator here.

0.6009

(2 marks)

c) Find the probability that more than 35 of the chocolate bars bought by the student do not contain a golden ticket.

....

(2 marks)

Statistical Distributions

5 A particular model of car, the Dystopia, is prone to developing a rattle in the first year after being made. The probability of any particular Dystopia developing the rattle in its first year is 0.65.

A random sample of 20 one-year-old Dystopias is selected.

a) Find the probability that at least 12 but fewer than 15 of the cars rattle.

....

(3 marks)

b) Find the probability that more than half of the cars rattle.

....

(2 marks)

c) A further five random samples of Dystopias are tested. There are 20 cars in each sample. Find the probability that more than half of the cars in exactly three of these five samples rattle.

Define a new random variable that follows a binomial distribution with $n = 5$ and p = P(more than half of cars rattle).

....

(3 marks)

6 An ice cream shop owner finds that, on 1st July, 880 out of the 1100 customers chose a sugar cone.

a) A random sample of 20 customers from 2nd July is selected. Use a binomial distribution and the data from the previous day to estimate the probability that exactly 12 of them chose a sugar cone.

Use the info to find p.

....

(3 marks)

The owner claims that 42% of customers buy an ice cream with at least one scoop of chocolate ice cream.

b) Assuming that this claim is correct, and that the next 75 customers form a random sample of customers, find the probability that more than 30 of them choose at least one scoop of chocolate ice cream.

....

(3 marks)

c) Comment on the validity of the binomial model you used in part b).

....

....

(1 mark)

EXAM TIP

Remember, the binomial distribution is discrete, which means that $P(X < x)$ does not equal $P(X \leq x)$ — so you need to be extra careful with the inequality signs when you're finding probabilities. Make sure you're clued-up on how the binomial functions on your calculator work — you'll definitely need to use them if n or p aren't given in the binomial tables.

Score

35

Statistical Hypothesis Testing

This topic covers hypothesis tests for a proportion in a binomial distribution — you saw the binomial distribution in the previous topic, so it should feel like an old friend. You also get to criticise people's sampling methods...

1 Splash Electronics Ltd. sell waterproof cameras. Before the company sends a batch of cameras out, they test a sample of cameras to see how long they can stay underwater for before water leaks in.

a) Give a reason why the company would test a sample of their cameras rather than the whole population.

All cameras would be destroyed by the water

(1 mark)

The company decides to test a random sample of 15 cameras from a batch of 300 cameras.
Every camera in the batch has a unique product code on the inside cover.

b) Describe how the company could obtain a simple random sample of size 15 from the batch of cameras.

Generate 15 random numbers using lottery generating method.

(3 marks)

2 Josie wants to find out what the most popular type of music is amongst the pupils in her school. She decides to ask a sample of the pupils.

a) Identify the population that Josie is interested in.

Pupils in her school

(1 mark)

Mike says that it would be better to carry out a census, rather than take a sample.

b) Give one reason why he might have said this.

Data wouldn't be affected by sampling bias.

(1 mark)

Josie decides to select all the students in her GCSE music class as her sample.

c) Name the sampling method Josie is using.

Opportunity

(1 mark)

d) Explain whether or not Josie's sample is likely to be representative of the population.

unlikely as individuals in the sample are not representing the whole school as much.

(1 mark)

Statistical Hypothesis Testing

3 Jamila is investigating the pay rises given to working adults in her town last year. The table below shows the number of working adults in Jamila's town.

Age (in years)	18-27	28-37	38-47	48-57	Over 57
No. of working adults	1200	2100	3500	3200	1500

a) Jamila plans to use stratified sampling to select a sample of 50 working adults from her town. Calculate how many people from each age group should be in the sample.

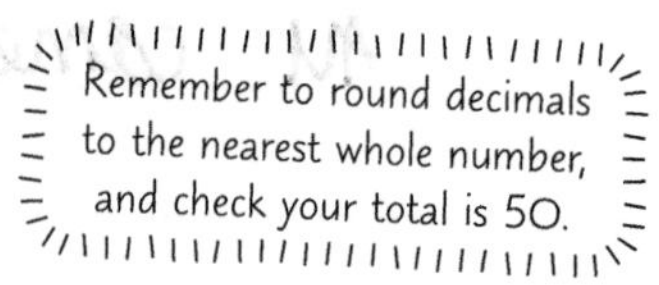

18-27 = ..., 28-37 = ..., 38-47 = ..., 48-57 = ..., Over 57 = ...

(4 marks)

b) Jamila wants to investigate the pay rises given to working adults across the UK last year. Can she use her sample data to draw conclusions about the whole population? Explain your answer.

....

....

(1 mark)

4 The residents of a town are being asked about a plan to build a wind farm in the area. Past records show that 10% of residents were against the plan. Campaigners claim that the proportion of residents who are against the plan has increased. A random sample of 50 residents is surveyed.

a) Write down suitable hypotheses to test the campaigners' claim.

$X \sim B(50, 0.1)$

$H_0: p = 0.1 \quad H_1: p > 0.1$

(1 mark)

b) Of the sampled residents, 6 are against the plan. Using a 1% significance level, test whether there is evidence to suggest that the proportion of residents opposed to the plan has increased.

$P(X \geq 6) = 1 - P(X \leq 5) = 1 - 0.6161 = 0.3839$

$0.3839 > 0.01$

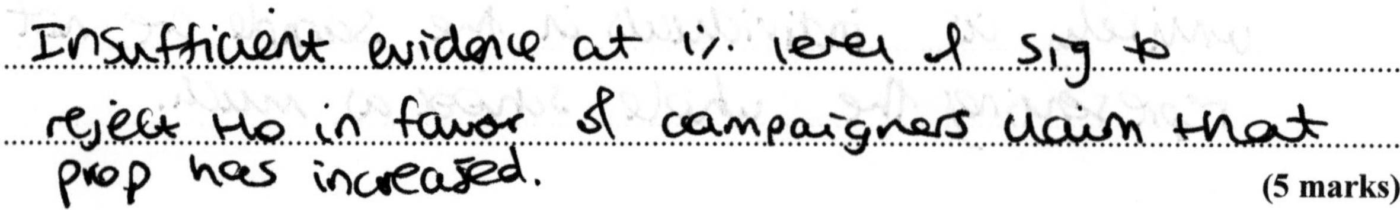

Insufficient evidence at 1% level of sig to reject Ho in favor of campaigners claim that prop has increased.

(5 marks)

Statistical Hypothesis Testing

5 Nate teaches judo classes at 'basic' and 'advanced' levels. Last year, the proportion, p, of his students who had done judo for at least two years was 0.2. Nate moves to a different judo club and claims that at this club, the proportion of his students who have done judo for at least two years has changed. To test this, he plans to survey a sample of 20 of his new students.

a) State suitable hypotheses that could be used to test Nate's claim.

$H_0: p = 0.2$

$H_1: p \neq 0.2$

(1 mark)

b) Find the critical region for a two-tailed test of Nate's claim at the 5% level of significance. The probability of rejection in each tail should be less than 0.025.

Use the binomial tables (see p97-101) or a calculator to find the values that give the correct probability in each tail.

$X \sim B(20, 0.2)$

lower: $P(X \leq 0) = 0.0115$

$P(X \leq 1) = 0.0692$

upper: $P(X \geq 9) = 1 - 0.990 = 0.01$

$P(X \geq 8) = 1 - 0.9679 = 0.0321$

CR $(X = 0)$ $(X \geq 9)$

(3 marks)

c) Find the actual significance level of a test based on your critical region from part b).

$0.0115 + 0.001 = 0.0125$

0.0215

(1 mark)

d) Given that 7 of the sampled students have done judo for at least two years, carry out the test of Nate's claim.

7 does not lie in the critical region so do not reject H0. Insufficient evidence at the 5% level that the prop who have done judo has changed.

(2 marks)

e) To select his sample, Nate chose 20 students from the same judo class. Comment on the validity of the model used to carry out the test of Nate's claim. Explain your answer.

Members not selected randomly so not likely to be independent.

(2 marks)

Statistical Hypothesis Testing

6 For Heathrow during the period May to October 1987, it is known that 50% of the days had a maximum temperature of less than 19 °C. Adil wants to carry out a hypothesis test to investigate whether the proportion of days with a maximum temperature of less than 19 °C was different for the same period in 2015.

a) Adil uses the large data set to randomly sample 30 days from the period May to October 2015. 14 of the days had a maximum temperature of less than 19 °C. Use this information to carry out Adil's test at the 10% level of significance.

You can either work out the p-value or find the critical region.

....

....

(6 marks)

b) Adil also plans to investigate the daily maximum temperature for Hurn during the period May to October 2015. He takes a sample from the large data set using systematic sampling. Suggest one reason why systematic sampling might give a more representative sample than simple random sampling.

....

....

(1 mark)

7 The records for 2016 suggest that 45% of the members of a gym use the swimming pool. The gym's manager thinks that the popularity of the swimming pool has decreased over recent months.

a) Out of a random sample of 16 gym members, 3 of them use the pool. Using a 5% level of significance, test whether there is evidence to suggest that the popularity of the pool has decreased.

$X \sim B(16, 0.45)$

$H_0: p = 0.45$

$H_1: p < 0.45$

$P(X \leq 3) = 0.0281 < 0.05$. There is evidence at 5% signficance level to suggest popularity of pool has ↓.

(6 marks)

b) The manager decides that the same test should be done again, but this time using a larger sample. He surveys a random sample of 50 members and carries out the test. He concludes that at the 5% level of significance there is evidence to suggest that the popularity of the pool has decreased.

Find the maximum possible number of gym members in the sample of 50 who use the pool.

$X \sim B(50, 0.45)$ $P(X \leq 17) = 0.0765$

$P(X \leq 16) = 0.0427$

16

(4 marks)

With hypothesis tests, think carefully about whether it's easier to find the p-value or the critical region — and whether it's easier to use the binomial tables or your calculator functions. And make sure you always write a proper conclusion. For example, don't just say 'reject H_0', you also need to explain what rejecting H_0 means in the context of the question.

Score

45

Kinematics

It's the section you've all been waiting for... Kinematics. Push the pedal to the metal and enjoy high-octane thrills and spills calculating velocity, acceleration and displacement. I've even thrown in a roller-coaster — what a treat.

1 A motorcyclist is travelling at 15 ms^{-1}. As she passes point A on a straight section of road, she accelerates uniformly for 4 s until she passes point B at 40 ms^{-1}. She then immediately decelerates at 2.8 ms^{-2} so that when she passes point C she is travelling at 26 ms^{-1}.

a) Find her acceleration between A and B.

....

(2 marks)

b) Find the time it takes her to travel from B to C.

....

(2 marks)

c) Find the distance from A to C.

....

(3 marks)

2 A van is travelling with velocity 21 ms^{-1}. As it nears its destination, the driver brakes and the van decelerates uniformly to rest in 6 seconds. The van is stationary for 10 seconds, then sets back off in the direction it came, accelerating uniformly to a velocity of $-U$ ms^{-1} in 4 seconds. It maintains this speed for 5 seconds.

a) Taking when the driver starts to brake as $t = 0$ s, draw a velocity-time graph showing the van's motion.

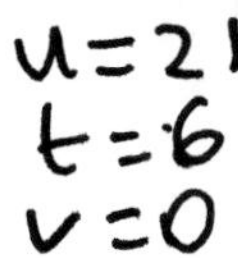

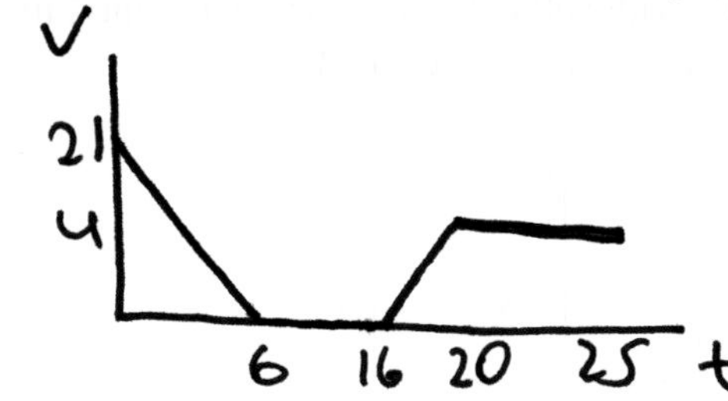

(3 marks)

b) Find the van's deceleration.

....

(2 marks)

c) In total, the van travels a distance of 161 m during the measured time. Find the value of U.

$U =$ ....

(3 marks)

d) Calculate the van's displacement at time $t = 25$ s from its position at time $t = 0$ s.

....

(2 marks)

Kinematics

3 The diagram below shows how the speed of a roller coaster varies along a straight section of its track.

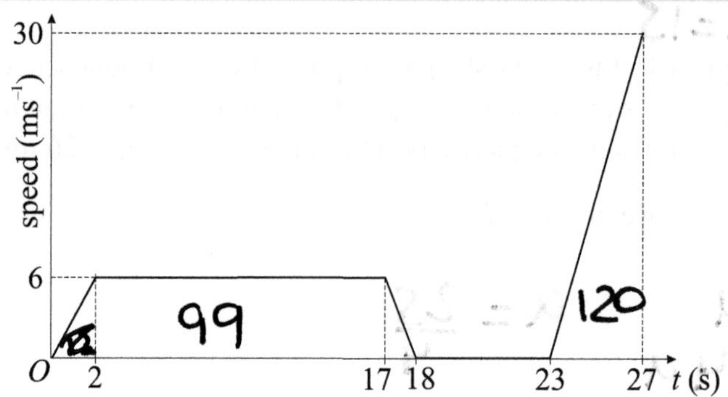

a) Find the greatest acceleration experienced by the roller coaster.

$7.5ms^{-2}$

(2 marks)

b) Calculate the total distance travelled by the roller coaster.

120+99 =

219m

(3 marks)

4 A ball is thrown vertically upwards with velocity 5 ms^{-1} from a point 2 m above the ground. The velocity-time graph below shows the motion of the ball.

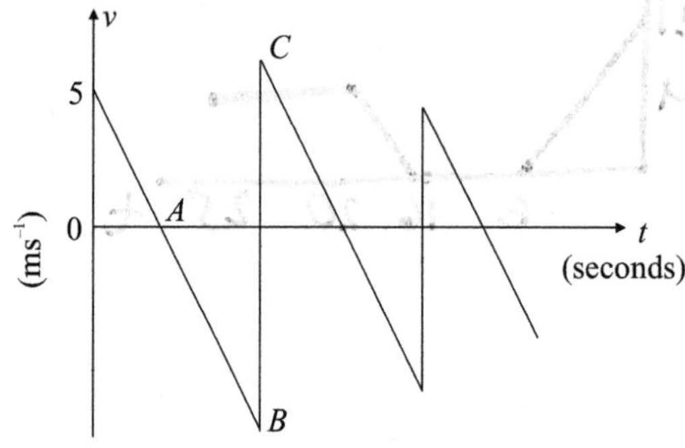

As these are straight lines, you know acceleration is constant. So you can use the suvat equations.

a) Find the time taken by the ball to reach point A.

....

(3 marks)

b) Find the velocity of the ball when it reaches point B.

....

(3 marks)

Kinematics

5 A toy car is travelling along a straight horizontal path with constant acceleration. It passes points A, B and C in that order, where AB = 1.5 m and BC = 5 m. It takes the car 3 seconds to get from A to B, and 4 seconds to get from B to C.

a) Find the acceleration of the toy car.

AB
s = 1.5
t = 3
a =

BC
s = 5
t = 4
a =

$a =$ ....

(6 marks)

b) Calculate the speed of the toy car at the instant it passes B.

....

(2 marks)

6 A particle P sets off from the origin at $t = 0$ and starts to move along the x-axis in the direction of increasing x. After t seconds, P has velocity v ms^{-1}, where v is given by:

$$v = \begin{cases} 11t - 2t^2 & 0 \le t \le 5 \\ 25 - 4t & t > 5 \end{cases}$$

a) Find the displacement of P from the origin at $t = 5$.

....

(4 marks)

b) Find the time taken for P to return to the origin.

....

(5 marks)

Kinematics

7 A student is attempting to model the flight of a toy rocket. He models the rocket as a light particle that sets off from rest at the origin and travels along the y-axis in the direction of y increasing. He models the acceleration, a ms^{-2}, of the rocket with the equation $a = 3t^2 - \frac{t^3}{3}$, where t is time in seconds.

a) According to the model, explain what happens to the rocket at $t = 9$ s.

....

....

(2 marks)

b) The student observes that it actually takes the toy rocket 5 s to reach a vertical height of 75 m. Comment on the accuracy of the student's model in light of this observation. Justify your claims.

....

....

(7 marks)

c) Suggest one way in which this model could be improved.

....

(1 mark)

8 The displacement, x m, of a particle from a fixed point O at time t s is $x = t^4 - 4t^3 - 8t^2 + 1$, where $t \geq 0$.

a) Determine the times at which the particle is stationary.

....

(5 marks)

b) Find the total distance travelled by the particle during the first 5 seconds of motion.

....

(4 marks)

c) Determine the time at which the particle's acceleration is zero.

....

(5 marks)

EXAM TIP

Look out for questions which mention 'constant' or 'uniform' acceleration — that's your cue to break out the suvat equations. If acceleration varies with time, you'll need to use calculus, so make sure you're completely happy with it. You also need to be really confident with when to differentiate and when to integrate — you don't want to get mixed up in the exam.

Score

69

Forces and Newton's Laws

This section contains more pulleys and ropes than a medieval siege weaponry convention. Jokes aside, the maths can get pretty messy when you're working on these questions, so take your time and don't skip steps.

1 A box of weight x N is being pulled along a horizontal table by a force of 12 N. The box is moving in the direction of the pulling force and is accelerating at 2 ms^{-2}. Shinji draws the following diagram to help him model the forces acting on the box:

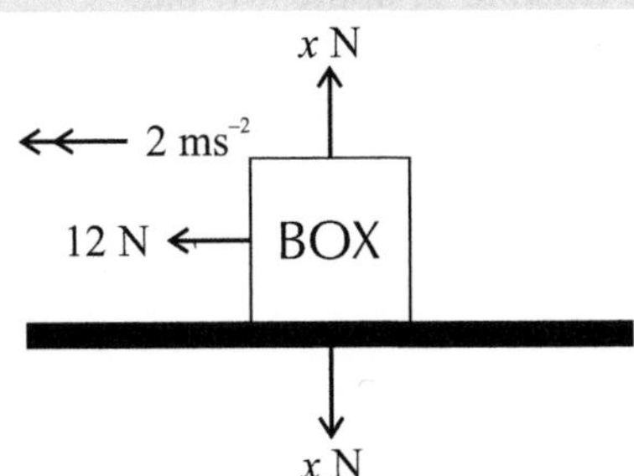

a) Look at Shinji's diagram. Identify **two** modelling assumptions that Shinji has made.

-weight = normal reaction force

- Table is smooth?

(2 mark)

b) Calculate x.

F=ma

12 - 2m = 0

12=2m

m=6

x = 6g =

x = 58.8

(3 marks)

2 A rocket with mass 1 400 000 kg is launched vertically upwards by engines providing a force of 34 000 000 N.

a) Scientists model the rocket's flight assuming no other forces act on the rocket. Find the rocket's expected acceleration using this model.

....

(2 marks)

b) Observers on the ground notice that the rocket's actual acceleration is 12 ms^{-2}. Find the magnitude of the total resistive force, R, acting on the rocket.

R = ...

(2 marks)

c) Besides assuming that acceleration is constant, state one other assumption made in part b).

....

....

(1 mark)

Forces and Newton's Laws

3 A car, of mass 1600 kg, is towing a horse box of mass 3000 kg along a straight, horizontal road. The car experiences a resistive force of magnitude 400 N and the horse box experiences a constant resistive force of magnitude R N. A driving force of magnitude 4300 N acts on the car. The vehicles accelerate at 0.8 ms^{-2}.

a) Assuming that the tow bar connecting the car to the horse box is horizontal, find the tension, T, in the tow bar.

T = ...

(3 marks)

b) Find the resistance force, R, acting on the horse box.

R = ...

(3 marks)

When the car and horse box are travelling at a speed of 7 ms^{-1}, the horse box becomes detached from the car. Assume that the only horizontal force now acting on the horse box is the resistive force R.

c) Find the deceleration of the horse box.

....

(2 marks)

d) Find the distance the horse box travels before it comes to rest.

You'll need to use a suvat equation to answer this question.

....

(3 marks)

4 A particle of mass 0.5 kg moves under the action of two forces, $\mathbf{F}_1$ and $\mathbf{F}_2$, where $\mathbf{F}_1 = (3\mathbf{i} + 2\mathbf{j})$ N and $\mathbf{F}_2 = (2\mathbf{i} - \mathbf{j})$ N. Find the acceleration of the particle, giving your answer in **i** and **j** vector form.

....

(3 marks)

Forces and Newton's Laws

5 A truck of mass 3000 kg and a rock of mass 500 kg are connected by a rope.
The rope passes over a pulley P as shown in the diagram.

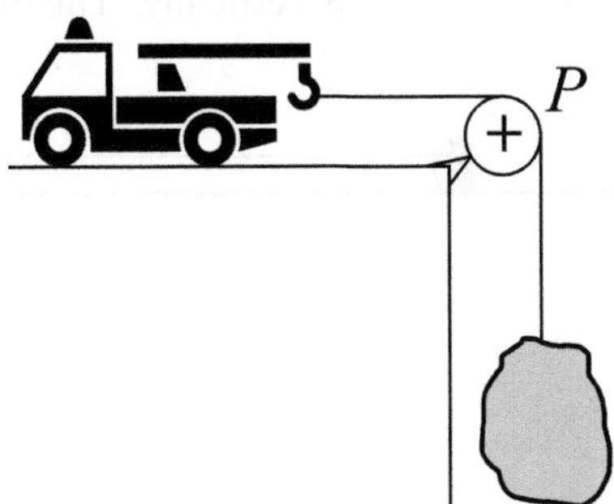

The system begins at rest and the rope is taut. The truck begins to move away from P.
Its engine produces a constant driving force of 10 000 N. A constant resistance force between the truck and the ground is modelled as having a magnitude of 800 N.

The rope is modelled as light and inelastic. The pulley is modelled as light and smooth.

a) Using this model, find the acceleration of the rock towards the pulley P.
Give your answer to three significant figures.

....

(5 marks)

It was found that the rock was actually accelerating at 0.8 ms^{-2}.

b) Using this information, suggest one improvement that could be made to the model.
Give a reason for your answer.

....

....

(2 marks)

6 A woman is travelling in a lift. The lift is rising vertically and is accelerating at a rate 0.75 ms^{-2}.
The lift is pulled upwards by a light, inextensible cable. The tension in the cable is T N and the lift has mass 500 kg. The floor of the lift exerts a force of 675 N on the woman. Find T.

T = ...

(4 marks)

Forces and Newton's Laws

7 A particle, A, is attached to a weight, W, by a light inextensible string which passes over a smooth pulley, P, as shown. When the system is released from rest, with the string taut, A and W experience an acceleration of 4 ms^{-2}. A moves across a rough horizontal plane and W falls vertically. The mass of W is 1.5 times the mass of A.

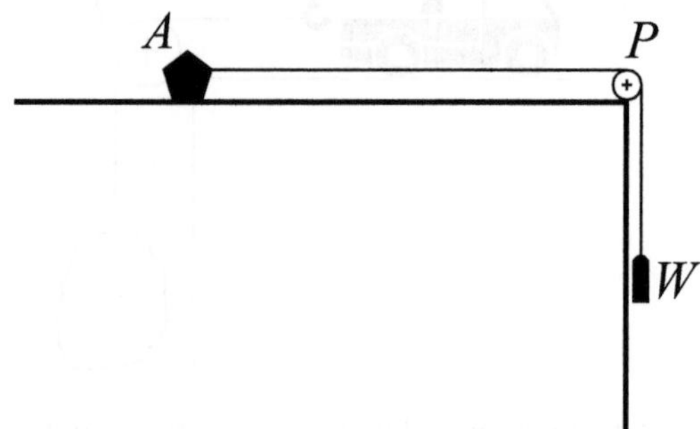

a) Given that the mass of A is 0.2 kg, find the resistance force acting on A in the horizontal plane.

....

(4 marks)

W falls for h m until it hits the ground and does not rebound. A continues to move until it reaches P with speed 3 ms^{-1}. The initial distance between A and P is $\frac{7}{4}h$ m.

b) Find the value of h.

....

(5 marks)

c) Find the time taken for W to hit the ground.

....

(2 marks)

d) How did you use the information that the string is inextensible?

....

....

(1 mark)

There's usually a few easy marks to be picked up on difficult mechanics questions by being able to talk about the modelling assumptions that have been made. Also, you could be asked to talk about how the model could be improved. So, make sure you know what all those fiddly mechanics terms like 'particle', 'inextensible', 'light', 'rough' and 'smooth' mean. Exciting stuff...

Score

47

General Certificate of Education
Advanced Subsidiary (AS) Level

AS Mathematics
Practice Exam Paper 1: Pure Mathematics

Time Allowed: 2 hours

There are 100 marks available for this paper.

Statistical tables and formulas are given on pages 97 to 102.

1 A graph shows the height, y cm, of a candle plotted against the time, x hours, that it has been burning. The candle is 10 cm tall 1 hour after it was lit. After 5 hours of burning, it is 7 cm high. The relationship between the height and the time is linear.

a) Find the equation of the graph.

(3 marks)

b) Explain, in this context, what the gradient of the graph shows and the significance of the y-intercept.

(2 marks)

2 Without evaluating the expression, write $\sqrt{2} \times 32^3 \div 2^{-6}$ in the form 2^k, where k is a number to be found. Show each step of your working.

(3 marks)

3 A right-angled triangle has an area of $(4 + \sqrt{2})$ cm². The length of one of the shorter sides is $(2 - \sqrt{2})$ cm. Show that the length of the other shorter side can be written as $2(a + b\sqrt{2})$ cm, where a and b are integers to be found.

(4 marks)

4 The point M has coordinates (3, 7). $\overrightarrow{NM} = -4\mathbf{i} + 3\mathbf{j}$.

a) Find the position vector of the point N.

(2 marks)

b) The line NM is the diameter of a circle. Find the length of the radius of the circle.

(2 marks)

5 Find the equation of the tangent to the curve $y = 8\sqrt{x} - x$ at the point on the curve where $x = 4$. Give your answer in the form $y = mx + c$.

(6 marks)

6 **a)** Find the first 3 terms of the binomial expansion $(2 + x)^6$, in ascending powers of x. Give your answer in its simplest form.

(4 marks)

b) Use your answer to part a) to find an approximation to 2.001^6. You must show your working.

(2 marks)

c) Explain why you would not be able to use your answer to part a) to find an approximation to 3.001^6.

(1 mark)

7 The line $y = 19$ intersects the curve $y = 2^{3x+2}$ at the point P. Find the x-coordinate of P, giving your answer to 3 significant figures.

(4 marks)

8 **a)** $f(x) = \sqrt{x} - 10 + \dfrac{21}{\sqrt{x}}, x \geq 0.$

Find the coordinates of the points at which the graph of $y = f(x)$ crosses the x-axis.

(5 marks)

b) $g(x) = \sqrt{2x} - 10 + \dfrac{21}{\sqrt{2x}}$

By considering a transformation of the graph of $f(x)$, find the coordinates of the points where $g(x)$ crosses the x-axis.

(2 marks)

9 A right-angled triangle has a perimeter of 40 m and a hypotenuse that is 18 m in length. Find the lengths of the two shorter sides, giving your answer in metres to 2 decimal places.

(6 marks)

10 **a)** The polynomial $x^3 - 8x^2 + 9x + 18$ has a factor $(x - a)$, where a is a positive integer and $a < 5$. Find the value of a, showing your working clearly.

(2 marks)

b) Sketch the graph of $y = x^3 - 8x^2 + 9x + 18$, clearly showing the coordinates of the points at which the graph intersects both the x- and the y-axes.

(4 marks)

c) A different polynomial can be factorised to give $(x + 2)(x^2 - kx + 9)$. Given that $x = -2$ is the only real root of the polynomial, find the possible values of k.

(3 marks)

11 Solve for $-90° < x < 90°$:

$$6\tan^2 x - \frac{19\tan x}{\cos x} + \frac{10}{\cos^2 x} = 0.$$

Give your answer(s) correct to 1 decimal place.

(5 marks)

12 Prove that $\sin x + x^2 - 4x + 6 > 0$ for all real values of x.

(4 marks)

13 a) Write $2\log_6 x + \log_6(x^2 - 25) - \log_6(x^2 + 5x)$ as a single logarithm.

(3 marks)

b) Hence solve the inequality $2\log_6 x + \log_6(x^2 - 25) \leq \log_6(x^2 + 5x) + 2$, where $x > 5$.

(5 marks)

14 The graph shows $f(x) = 2x^3 + x^2 - 7x - 6$.
It crosses the x-axis at $x = -1.5$, -1 and 2.

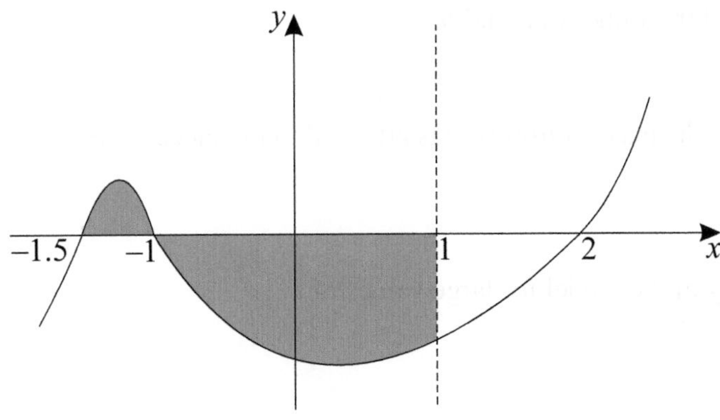

a) Find $\int f(x)\,dx$, giving your answer in its simplest form.

(3 marks)

b) Find the total shaded area. Give your answer to 3 significant figures.

(4 marks)

15 A zoo keeper needs to build a rectangular pen.

- The pen needs to have two partitions in it to keep the animals separate whilst she cleans the enclosure.
- The partitions must be parallel to the width of the pen as shown in the diagram on the right.
- She uses 200 m of fencing to build the sides and partitions of the pen.

w

partitions

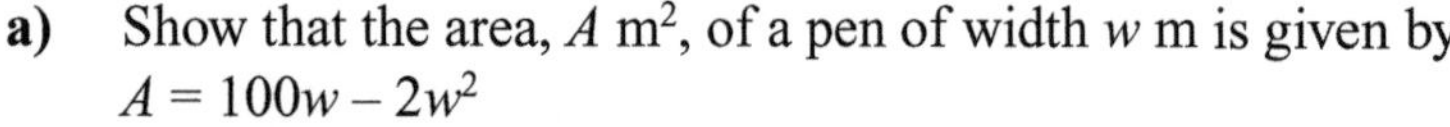

a) Show that the area, A m^2, of a pen of width w m is given by $A = 100w - 2w^2$

(3 marks)

b) Using differentiation, find the value of w which gives the greatest total area in the pen.

(2 marks)

c) Find the maximum area of the pen.

(2 marks)

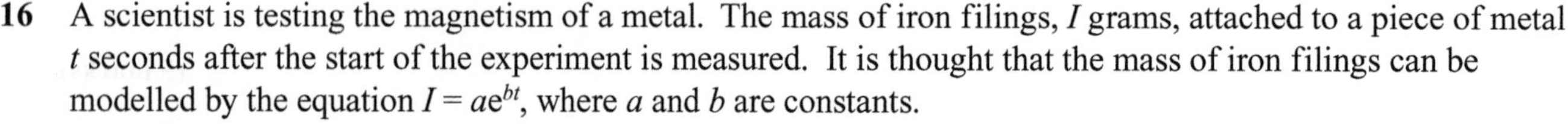

16 A scientist is testing the magnetism of a metal. The mass of iron filings, I grams, attached to a piece of metal t seconds after the start of the experiment is measured. It is thought that the mass of iron filings can be modelled by the equation $I = ae^{bt}$, where a and b are constants.

a) Show that this equation can be written in the form $\ln I = mt + c$, where m and c are given in terms of the constants a and b.

(2 marks)

b) The scientist records the result for the first 20 seconds of the experiment and plots a graph of $\ln I$ against t. The data points lie approximately on a straight line. The points (5, 4.012) and (8, 4.072) both lie on the line. Find the values of a and b.

(3 marks)

c) Use the model to predict the mass of iron filings attached to the piece of metal after 15 seconds.

(1 mark)

d) Comment on the validity of the model for large values of t.

(1 mark)

17 Find the equation of the circumcircle of the triangle ABC, where A = (3, 1), B = (0, 2) and C = (1, 5).

(7 marks)

END OF EXAM PAPER

TOTAL FOR PAPER: 100 MARKS

General Certificate of Education
Advanced Subsidiary (AS) Level

AS Mathematics
Practice Exam Paper 2: Statistics and Mechanics

Time Allowed: 1 hour 15 minutes

There are 60 marks available for this paper.

Statistical tables and formulas are given on pages 97 to 102.

Section A: Statistics

1 An investigation was done into the lengths of delays experienced by people using a main city train station. 100 people leaving one waiting room were asked how long their train had been delayed for.

a) Name the sampling method being used in this investigation and explain one possible problem with this method.

(2 marks)

The cumulative frequency graph below shows the results of the investigation.

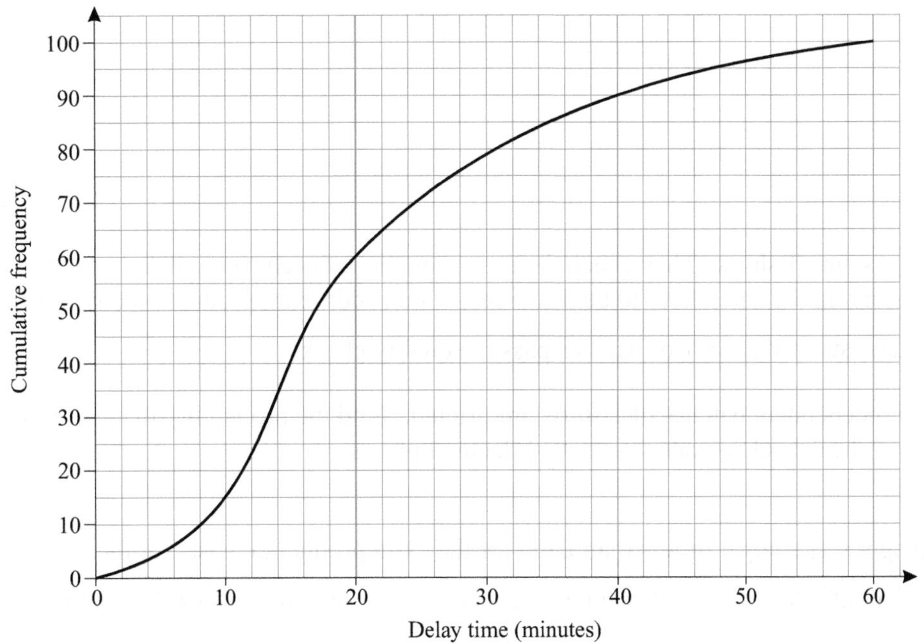

b) Complete the following table.

Delay time (t, minutes)	Frequency	Cumulative frequency
$0 \leq t < 10$		
$10 \leq t < 20$	45	
$20 \leq t < 40$		
$40 \leq t < 60$		100

(2 marks)

c) Use linear interpolation to estimate the median delay time.

(2 marks)

2 Jim, Kira and Harry often attend classic car shows at the weekend. Kira attends events independently of both Harry and Jim.

- The probability of Jim attending a show is 0.6.
- The probability of Harry attending a show is 0.4.
- The probability of Jim and Harry both attending a show is 0.2.
- The probability of Kira and Jim both attending a show is 0.12.
- The probability of Jim, Kira and Harry all attending a show is 0.04.
- The probability of none of them attending a show is 0.16.

a) Model the above information in a Venn diagram.

(4 marks)

b) Is the event 'Jim attending a show' statistically independent of the event 'Harry attending a show'? Explain your answer.

(1 mark)

c) If everyone's attendance at one weekend's show is independent of their attendance at any other weekend's show, what is the probability that the three of them will all attend a show on two particular consecutive weekends?

(1 mark)

3 A factory prints designs onto T-shirts. They check the design quality of each batch of T-shirts. If a batch fails the checks, all the T-shirts in the batch have to be discarded, which adds extra production costs of £120.

The production manager states that 85% of batches pass the quality checks.

a) In one week, 25 independent batches of T-shirts are printed. Find the probability that every batch passes the quality checks. Give your answer to 4 decimal places.

(2 marks)

The production manager sets a target of less than £500 for the extra production costs for the week.

b) What is the probability that this target will be exceeded? Give your answer to 4 decimal places.

(2 marks)

The production data shows that out of 50 batches of T-shirts, three batches failed the quality checks.

c) By assuming that the 50 batches are independent, carry out a hypothesis test at the 10% significance level to test whether there is evidence that the proportion of batches that pass the quality check is actually higher than the production manager states.

(6 marks)

4 Karen is investigating the daily maximum temperature, M °C, for Heathrow in the period May to October 2015. She selects a sample of size 30 from the large data set and calculates the following values:

$\sum M^2 = 9466.98$, standard deviation $= 2.36$

a) Calculate the mean temperature for Karen's data sample. Give your answer to 2 decimal places.

(2 marks)

An outlier is a value that is more than 3 standard deviations above or below the mean.

b) Show that a daily maximum temperature of 26 °C would be an outlier for Karen's data.

(2 marks)

5 Amit is doing a project that looks at the relationship between daily total rainfall, R mm, and daily total sunshine, S hours. He takes a sample of data from the large data set for Camborne in the period May to October 2015.

Amit draws the following scatter diagram for his sample data:

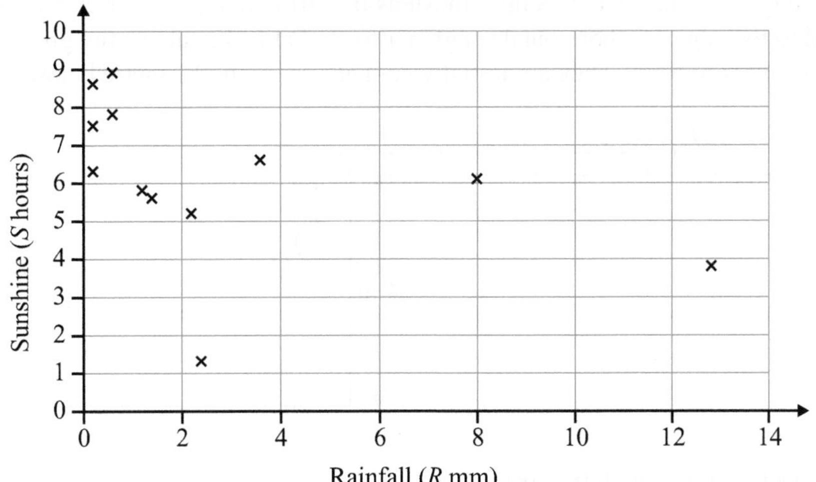

a) Describe the correlation between rainfall and hours of sunshine.

(1 mark)

The regression line of S on R for this data is calculated to be $S = 6.801 - 0.24291R$.

b) Give an interpretation of the gradient and the intercept of this regression line.

(2 marks)

c) Amit uses the regression line to predict that there will be 2.43 hours of sunshine when there is 18 mm of rainfall. Comment on the reliability of his prediction.

(1 mark)

TOTAL FOR SECTION A: 30 MARKS

Section B: Mechanics

6 A car initially starts at rest. It accelerates constantly for 20 seconds, reaching a speed of V ms^{-1}.
It then continues at this speed for T seconds, before decelerating at a rate of 0.25 ms^{-2} until it comes to a halt.

a) Sketch this situation on a speed-time graph.

(2 marks)

During the first 10 seconds, the car covers a distance of 100 m.

b) Calculate the value of V.

(1 mark)

The total distance travelled by the car is 6.4 km.

c) Calculate the value of T.

(4 marks)

7 Two particles, P and Q, are connected by a light inextensible string that passes over a smooth pulley.
The pulley is fixed to the edge of a horizontal rough platform that is 4 m above the ground.
Both P and Q have a mass of 5 kg. They are initially held at rest, with Q 1 metre below the horizontal platform.

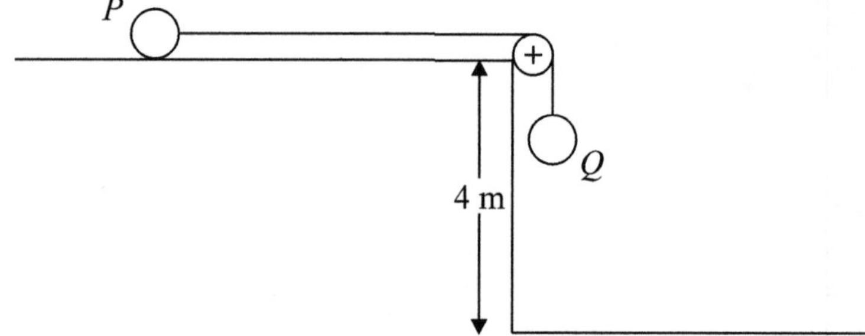

The system is released from rest with the string taut.
A resistance force with a magnitude of 30 N opposes the motion of P.

Using the equations of motion for each particle, find:

a) **(i)** the acceleration in the system,
(ii) the magnitude of T, the tension in the string.

(5 marks)

After Q has covered a distance of 0.95 m, the string snaps and Q falls freely.

b) What is the speed of Q as it hits the ground? Give your answer to 3 significant figures.

(4 marks)

8 A particle P of mass 3 kg moves along a straight horizontal line under the action of a force.
Its displacement, s metres, from the fixed point O can be modelled using:

$$s = 9t^2 - 2t^3 + 11, \quad \text{where } 0 \leq t \leq 5 \text{ seconds.}$$

a) Find the maximum displacement of P from O.

(5 marks)

b) Find, in terms of t, the force acting on P.

(2 marks)

9 A train is moving along a straight horizontal track with constant acceleration.
The train enters a tunnel which is 760 m long and exits 24 seconds later.
8 seconds before entering the tunnel, the train passes a sign. The sign is 110 m from the tunnel's entrance.

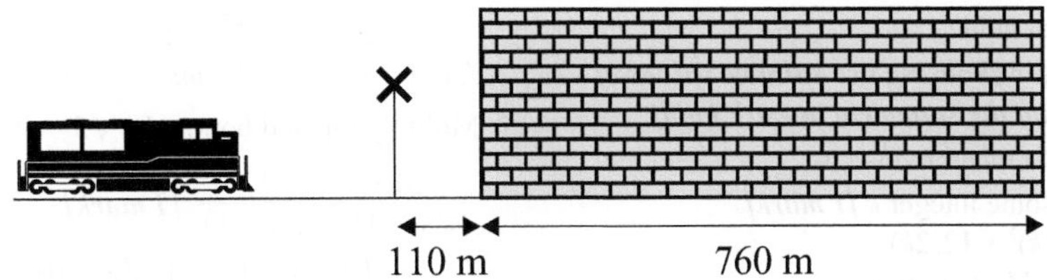

Find the train's acceleration and its speed when it passes the sign.

(7 marks)

END OF EXAM PAPER

TOTAL FOR SECTION B: 30 MARKS
TOTAL FOR PAPER: 60 MARKS

Section One — Pure Maths

Pages 3-6: Algebra and Functions 1

1 Find the values of x^5 and 5^x for $x = 2, 3, 4$ and 5:

x:	x^5:	5^x:	
2	32	25	so $x^5 > 5^x$
3	243	125	so $x^5 > 5^x$
4	1024	625	so $x^5 > 5^x$
5	3125	3125	so $x^5 = 5^x$

So $x^5 \geq 5^x$ for $x = 2, 3, 4$ and 5.
[2 marks available — 1 mark for working out values of x^5 and 5^x, 1 mark for comparing and stating conclusion]
This is a simple proof by exhaustion.

2 E.g. Take 2 and 3, which are both prime numbers. Then $2 + 3 = 5$, which is odd, so the statement is false.
[2 marks available — 1 mark for choosing two suitable prime numbers, 1 mark for showing that their sum is odd]
You could have used 2 and any other prime number here.

3 Factorising $3n^2 - 12$ gives:
$3n^2 - 12 = 3(n^2 - 4) = 3(n + 2)(n - 2)$ ***[1 mark]***
If n is odd, then $n + 2$ and $n - 2$ will also be odd, so:
$3n^2 - 12 = 3(n + 2)(n - 2) = (\text{odd}) \times (\text{odd}) \times (\text{odd}) = (\text{odd})$ ***[1 mark]***
Similarly, if n is even, then $n + 2$ and $n - 2$ will also be even, so:
$3n^2 - 12 = 3(n + 2)(n - 2) = (\text{odd}) \times (\text{even}) \times (\text{even}) = (\text{even})$
[1 mark]

4 E.g. Take $x = -1$ and $y = -2$.
Then $\frac{x}{y} = \frac{-1}{-2} = \frac{1}{2}$ and $\frac{y}{x} = \frac{-2}{-1} = 2$.
$2 > \frac{1}{2}$, so the statement does not hold.
[2 marks available — 1 mark for choosing two suitable values of x and y, 1 mark for showing that the statement doesn't hold]
Any two distinct negative numbers would work here.

5 As n is even, write n as $2k$ for some integer k ***[1 mark]***.
So $n^3 + 2n^2 + 12n = (2k)^3 + 2(2k)^2 + 12(2k)$
$= 8k^3 + 8k^2 + 24k$ ***[1 mark]***
This can be written as $8x$, where $x = k^3 + k^2 + 3k$, so is always a multiple of 8 when n is even ***[1 mark]***.

6 Start by multiplying out the brackets:
$x^2 + 2xy + 4x \geq 4x - y^2$
Rearrange to get all the terms on one side:
$x^2 + 2xy + 4x \geq 4x - y^2 \Leftrightarrow x^2 + 2xy + y^2 \geq 0$
$\Leftrightarrow x^2 + 2xy + y^2 = (x + y)^2 \geq 0$ ***[1 mark]***
The square of any number is greater than or equal to 0, so $(x + y)^2 \geq 0$, so the original statement is true ***[1 mark]***.

7 For any integer n, its square is n^2 and its cube is n^3.
The difference between these is $n^3 - n^2 = n^2(n - 1)$ ***[1 mark]***.
When n is odd, n^2 is odd and $n - 1$ is even, and odd × even = even, so the difference is even ***[1 mark]***.
When n is even, n^2 is even and $n - 1$ is odd, and even × odd = even, so the difference is even ***[1 mark]***.
Therefore, as any integer must either be odd or even, the difference between the cube and the square is always even for any integer n ***[1 mark]***.

8 Take two prime numbers, p and q ($p \neq q$ and $p, q > 1$). As p is prime, its only factors are 1 and p ***[1 mark]***, and as q is prime, its only factors are 1 and q ***[1 mark]***. So the product pq has factors 1, p, q, and pq ***[1 mark]*** (these factors are found by multiplying the factors of each number together in every possible combination). $pq \neq 1$ as $p, q > 1$. Hence the product of any two distinct prime numbers has exactly four factors.

9 $36^{-\frac{1}{2}} = \frac{1}{36^{\frac{1}{2}}} = \frac{1}{\sqrt{36}} = \frac{1}{6}$ ***[1 mark]***

10 $\sqrt[m]{a^n} = a^{\frac{n}{m}}$ so $\sqrt{a^4} = a^2$ and $a^6 \times a^3 = a^{6+3} = a^9$
So $\frac{a^6 \times a^3}{\sqrt{a^4}} \div a^{\frac{1}{2}} = \frac{a^9}{a^2} \div a^{\frac{1}{2}} = a^7 \times a^{-\frac{1}{2}}$ ***[1 mark]***
$= a^{7-\frac{1}{2}} = a^{\frac{13}{2}}$ ***[1 mark]***

11 a) $3 = \sqrt[3]{27} = 27^{\frac{1}{3}}$, so $x = \frac{1}{3}$ ***[1 mark]***
b) $81 = 3^4 = (\sqrt[3]{27})^4 = 27^{\frac{4}{3}}$, so $x = \frac{4}{3}$ ***[1 mark]***

12 $\frac{(3ab^3)^2 \times 2a^6}{6a^4b} = \frac{3^2 \times a^2 \times (b^3)^2 \times 2a^6}{6a^4b} = \frac{18a^8b^6}{6a^4b} = 3a^4b^5$
[2 marks available — 1 mark for simplifying the numerator to get $18a^8b^6$, 1 mark for the correct answer]

13 $\frac{x + 5x^3}{\sqrt{x}} = x^{-\frac{1}{2}}(x + 5x^3)$ ***[1 mark]***
$= x^{\frac{1}{2}} + 5x^{\frac{5}{2}}$ ***[1 mark]***

14 $\frac{(5 + 4\sqrt{x})^2}{2x} = \frac{25 + 40\sqrt{x} + 16x}{2x}$ ***[1 mark]***
$= \frac{1}{2}x^{-1}(25 + 40x^{\frac{1}{2}} + 16x)$ ***[1 mark]***
$= \frac{25}{2}x^{-1} + 20x^{-\frac{1}{2}} + 8$ ***[1 mark]***
So P = 20 and Q = 8.

15 $(\sqrt{3} + 1)(\sqrt{3} - 2) = 3 - 2\sqrt{3} + \sqrt{3} - 2$ ***[1 mark]***
$= 1 - \sqrt{3}$ ***[1 mark]***

16 $(5\sqrt{5} + 2\sqrt{3})^2 = (5\sqrt{5} + 2\sqrt{3})(5\sqrt{5} + 2\sqrt{3})$
$= (5\sqrt{5})^2 + 2(5\sqrt{5} \times 2\sqrt{3}) + (2\sqrt{3})^2$
First term: $(5\sqrt{5})^2 = 5\sqrt{5} \times 5\sqrt{5}$
$= 5 \times 5 \times \sqrt{5} \times \sqrt{5} = 5 \times 5 \times 5 = 125$ ***[1 mark]***
Second term: $2(5\sqrt{5} \times 2\sqrt{3}) = 2 \times 5 \times 2 \times \sqrt{5} \times \sqrt{3}$
$= 20\sqrt{15}$ ***[1 mark]***
Third term: $2\sqrt{3} \times 2\sqrt{3} = 2 \times 2 \times \sqrt{3} \times \sqrt{3}$
$= 2 \times 2 \times 3 = 12$ ***[1 mark]***
So $(5\sqrt{5})^2 + 2(5\sqrt{5} \times 2\sqrt{3}) + (2\sqrt{3})^2$
$= 125 + 20\sqrt{15} + 12 = 137 + 20\sqrt{15}$ ***[1 mark]***
(So a = 137, b = 20 and c = 15.)

17 Multiply top and bottom by $\sqrt{5} - 1$:
$\frac{10 \times (\sqrt{5} - 1)}{(\sqrt{5} + 1) \times (\sqrt{5} - 1)}$ ***[1 mark]***
$= \frac{10(\sqrt{5} - 1)}{5 - 1} = \frac{10\sqrt{5} - 10}{4} = \frac{5\sqrt{5} - 5}{2}$
[1 mark for simplifying top, 1 mark for simplifying bottom]

18 Rationalise the denominator by multiplying top and bottom by $(2 - \sqrt{2})$:
$\frac{4 + \sqrt{2}}{2 + \sqrt{2}} \times \frac{2 - \sqrt{2}}{2 - \sqrt{2}} = \frac{8 - 4\sqrt{2} + 2\sqrt{2} - 2}{4 - 2}$
$= \frac{6 - 2\sqrt{2}}{2} = 3 - \sqrt{2}$
[3 marks available — 1 mark for multiplying numerator and denominator by the correct expression, 1 mark for correct multiplication, 1 mark for the correct answer]

Pages 7-12: Algebra and Functions 2

1 $\frac{x^2 + 5x - 14}{2x^2 - 4x} = \frac{(x + 7)(x - 2)}{2x(x - 2)} = \frac{x + 7}{2x}$
[2 marks available — 1 mark for factorising either the numerator or the denominator, 1 mark for the correct answer]

2 $\frac{(x^2 - 9)(3x^2 - 10x - 8)}{(6x + 4)(x^2 - 7x + 12)} = \frac{(x + 3)(x - 3)(3x + 2)(x - 4)}{2(3x + 2)(x - 3)(x - 4)}$
$= \frac{x + 3}{2}$
[3 marks available — 1 mark for factorising the numerator, 1 mark for factorising the denominator and 1 mark the correct answer]

3 Expanding the brackets on the RHS gives the quadratic $mx^2 + 4mx + 4m + p$.
Equating the coefficients of x^2 gives $m = 5$.
Equating the coefficients of x gives $n = 4m$, so $n = 20$.
Equating the constant terms gives $14 = 4m + p \Rightarrow p = -6$.
[2 marks available — 2 marks for all three values correct, otherwise 1 mark for two values correct]

4 If the quadratic $ax^2 + bx + c = 0$ has no real roots, this means the discriminant gives a negative value: $b^2 - 4ac < 0$ ***[1 mark]***.
So: $(-4)^2 - [4 \times 1 \times (k - 1)] < 0$ ***[1 mark]***
$\Rightarrow 16 - (4k - 4) < 0$
$\Rightarrow 20 - 4k < 0$ ***[1 mark]***
$\Rightarrow 20 < 4k$
$\Rightarrow k > 5$ ***[1 mark]***

5 a) (i) First, rewrite the quadratic as: $-h^2 + 10h - 27$ and complete the square ($a = -1$):
$-(h - 5)^2 + 25 - 27 = -(h - 5)^2 - 2$
Rewrite the square in the form given in the question:
$T = -(-(5 - h))^2 - 2 \Rightarrow T = -(5 - h)^2 - 2$
[3 marks available — 1 mark for $(5 - h)^2$ or $(h - 5)^2$, 1 mark for 25 – 27, 1 mark for the correct final answer]
The last couple of steps are using the fact that $(-a)^2 = a^2$ to show that $(m - n)^2 = (n - m)^2$...

(ii) $(5 - h)^2 \geq 0$ for all values of h, so $-(5 - h)^2 \leq 0$.
Therefore $-(5 - h)^2 - 2 < 0$ for all h, so T is always negative ***[1 mark]***.

b) (i) The maximum temperature is the maximum value of T, which is –2 (from part a) ***[1 mark]***, and this occurs when the expression in the brackets = 0. The h-value that makes the expression in the brackets 0 is 5 ***[1 mark]***, so maximum temperature occurs 5 hours after sunrise.

(ii) At sunrise, $h = 0$, so $T = 10(0) - 0^2 - 27 = -27$°C, so the graph looks like this:

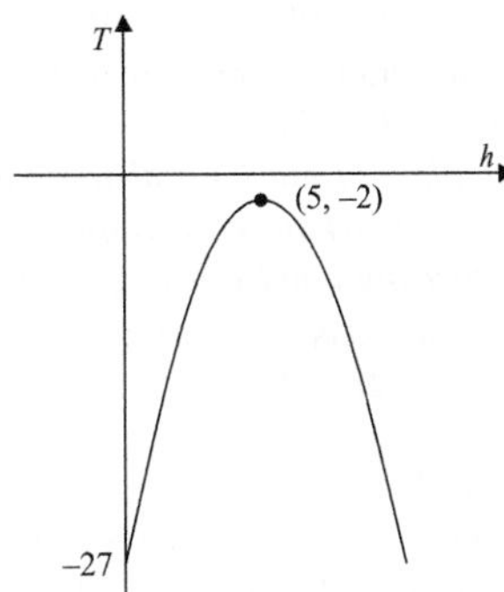

[2 marks available — 1 mark for drawing n-shaped curve that sits below the x-axis with the maximum roughly where shown (even if its position is not labelled), 1 mark for correct T-axis intercept (0, –27)]

6 Let $y = x^3$. Then $x^6 = 7x^3 + 8$ becomes $y^2 = 7y + 8$ ***[1 mark]***, so solve the quadratic in y:
$y^2 = 7y + 8 \Rightarrow y^2 - 7y - 8 = 0$
$(y - 8)(y + 1) = 0$, so $y = 8$ or $y = -1$ ***[1 mark]***.
Now replace y with x^3. So $x^3 = 8 \Rightarrow x = 2$ ***[1 mark]***
or $x^3 = -1 \Rightarrow x = -1$ ***[1 mark]***.
Here, you had to spot that the original equation was a quadratic of the form $x^2 + bx + c$, just in terms of x^3 not x.

7 When $f(x) = ax^2 + bx + c$ has no real roots, you know that $b^2 - 4ac < 0$ ***[1 mark]***. Here, $a = -j$, $b = 3j$ and $c = 1$.
Therefore $(3j)^2 - (4 \times -j \times 1) < 0 \Rightarrow 9j^2 + 4j < 0$ ***[1 mark]***
To find the values where $9j^2 + 4j < 0$, you need to start by solving $9j^2 + 4j = 0$: $j(9j + 4) = 0$, so $j = 0$ or $9j = -4 \Rightarrow j = -\frac{4}{9}$
[1 mark for both values of j]. Now sketch the graph:

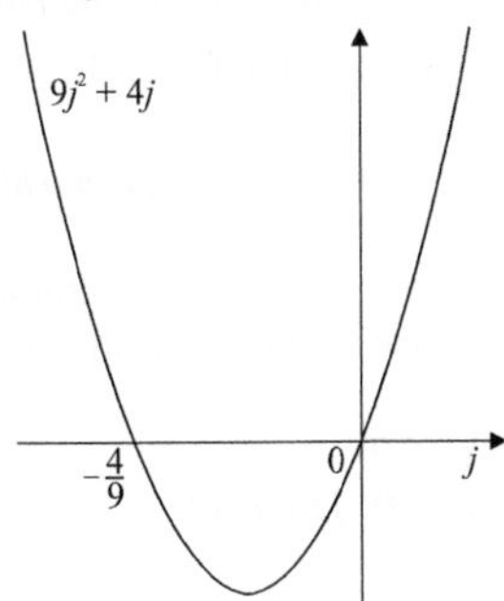

From the graph, you can see that $9j^2 + 4j < 0$ when $-\frac{4}{9} < j < 0$ ***[1 mark]***.

8 a) Complete the square by halving the coefficient of x to find the number in the brackets (m):
$x^2 - 7x + 17 = \left(x - \frac{7}{2}\right)^2 + n$
$\left(x - \frac{7}{2}\right)^2 = x^2 - 7x + \frac{49}{4}$, so $n = 17 - \frac{49}{4} = \frac{19}{4}$
So $x^2 - 7x + 17 = \left(x - \frac{7}{2}\right)^2 + \frac{19}{4}$
[3 marks available — 1 mark for the correct brackets, 1 mark for subtracting the correct value, 1 mark for the correct final answer]

b) The maximum value of $f(x)$ will be when the denominator is as small as possible — so you want the minimum value of $x^2 - 7x + 17$. Using the completed square above, you can see that the minimum value is $\frac{19}{4}$ ***[1 mark]*** because the squared part can equal but never be below 0.
So the maximum value of $f(x)$ is $\frac{1}{\left(\frac{19}{4}\right)} = \frac{4}{19}$ ***[1 mark]***.

9 If the function has two real roots, then $b^2 - 4ac > 0$ ***[1 mark]***.
For this equation, $a = 3k$, $b = k$ and $c = 2$.
Use the discriminant formula to find k:
$k^2 - (4 \times 3k \times 2) > 0$ ***[1 mark]***
$k^2 - 24k > 0$
$k(k - 24) > 0$
$k < 0$ or $k > 24$ ***[1 mark]***

10 Rearrange both equations:
$5x + y = 6$ (1)
$7x + 2y = 6$ (2)
(1) × 2: $10x + 2y = 12$ (3)
(3) – (2): $3x = 6 \Rightarrow x = 2$
Put $x = 2$ into (1): $(5 \times 2) + y = 6 \Rightarrow y = -4$
So the solution is $x = 2$, $y = -4$
[4 marks available — 1 mark for rearranging both equations, 1 mark for multiplying one equation and adding/subtracting to eliminate one variable, 1 mark for solving to find one variable, 1 mark for substituting into an equation to find the other variable]
For this question, you could have eliminated x first to find y, or used the substitution method instead.

11 a) $x^2 + y^2 = 13$ (1)
Rearrange the second equation: $x = 5y - 13$ (2)
Substitute (2) into (1):
$(5y - 13)^2 + y^2 = 13$
$\Rightarrow 25y^2 - 130y + 169 + y^2 - 13 = 0$ ***[1 mark]***
$\Rightarrow 26y^2 - 130y + 156 = 0$
$\Rightarrow y^2 - 5y + 6 = 0$ as required ***[1 mark]***

b) $y^2 - 5y + 6 = 0 \Rightarrow (y - 2)(y - 3) = 0$ ***[1 mark]***,
so $y = 2$ or $y = 3$ ***[1 mark]***
When $y = 2$, $x = 10 - 13 = -3$, and when $y = 3$, $x = 15 - 13 = 2$
So $x = -3$, $y = 2$ or $x = 2$, $y = 3$
[1 mark for both pairs of solutions]

12 a) At points of intersection,
$-2x + 4 = -x^2 + 3$ ***[1 mark]***
$x^2 - 2x + 1 = 0$
$(x - 1)^2 = 0$ ***[1 mark]***
so $x = 1$ ***[1 mark]***. When $x = 1$, $y = -2x + 4 = 2$, so there is one point of intersection at (1, 2) ***[1 mark]***.

b)

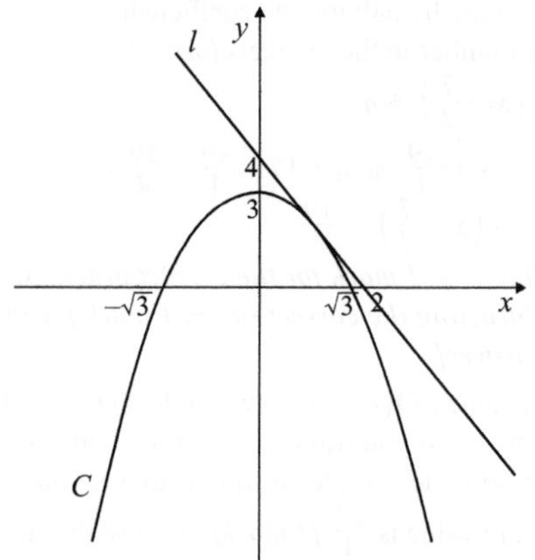

[5 marks available — 1 mark for drawing n-shaped curve, 1 mark for x-axis intercepts at $\pm\sqrt{3}$, 1 mark for maximum point of curve and y-axis intercept at (0, 3). 1 mark for line crossing the y-axis at (0, 4) and the x-axis at (2, 0). 1 mark for line and curve touching in one place at (1, 2).]

13 Rearrange the first equation to get y on its own:
$y + x = 7 \Rightarrow y = 7 - x$ ***[1 mark]***
Substitute the expression for y into the quadratic to get:
$7 - x = x^2 + 3x - 5$ ***[1 mark]***
Rearrange again to get everything on one side of the equation, and then factorise it:
$0 = x^2 + 4x - 12 \Rightarrow (x + 6)(x - 2) = 0$
So $x = -6$ and $x = 2$ ***[1 mark]***
Use these values to find the corresponding values of y:
When $x = -6$, $y = 7 - -6 = 13$
and when $x = 2$, $y = 7 - 2 = 5$ ***[1 mark for both y-values]***
So the solutions are $(-6, 13)$ or $(2, 5)$.

14 Draw the line $y = x + 2$, which has a gradient of 1, crosses the y-axis at (0, 2) and crosses the x-axis at (–2, 0). This should be a solid line.
Then draw the curve $y = 4 - x^2 = (2 + x)(2 - x)$. This is an n-shaped quadratic which crosses the x-axis at (–2, 0) and (2, 0) and the y-axis at (0, 4) (this is also the maximum point of the graph). This should be a dotted line.
Then test the point (0, 0) to see which side of the lines you want:
$0 \geq 0 + 2$ — this is false, so shade the other side of the line.
$4 - 0^2 > 0$ — this is true, so shade the region below the curve.
So the final region (labelled R) should look like this:

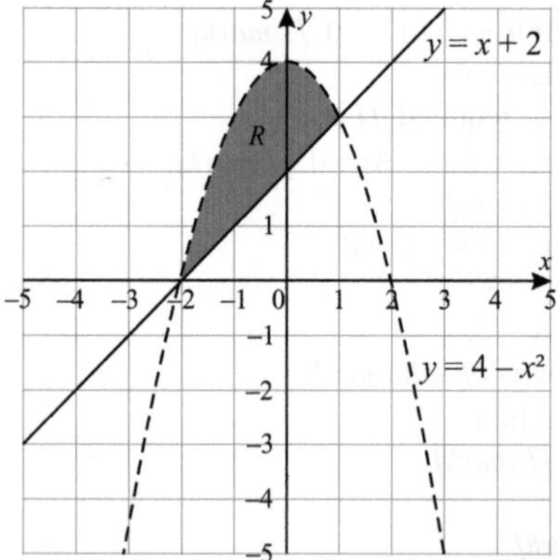

[3 marks available — 1 mark for drawing the line with correct gradient and intercepts, 1 mark for drawing the curve with correct intercepts, 1 mark for shading or indicating the correct region]

15 $x^2 - 8x + 15 > 0 \Rightarrow (x - 5)(x - 3) > 0$
Sketch a graph to see where the quadratic is greater than 0 — it'll be a u-shaped curve that crosses the x-axis at $x = 3$ and $x = 5$.

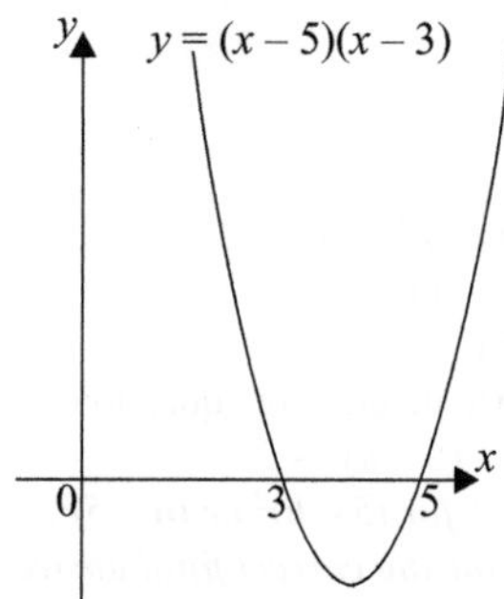

You can see from the graph that the function is positive when $x < 3$ and when $x > 5$. In set notation, this is $\{x : x < 3\} \cup \{x : x > 5\}$.
[4 marks available — 1 mark for factorising the quadratic, 1 mark for finding the roots, 1 mark for x < 3 and x > 5, 1 mark for the correct answer in set notation]

16 a) If $(x - 3)$ is a factor then $f(3) = 0$.
$f(3) = (3)^3 - 6(3)^2 - (3) + 30$ ***[1 mark]***
$= 27 - 54 - 3 + 30 = 0$,
so $(x - 3)$ is a factor of $f(x)$. ***[1 mark]***

b) $(x - 3)$ is a factor, so write $x^3 - 6x^2 - x + 30$ as a product of $x - 3$ and a quadratic factor and fill in the missing terms:
$x^3 - 6x^2 - x + 30 = (x - 3)(x^2 + ?x - 10)$
$= (x - 3)(x^2 - 3x - 10)$
Factorising the quadratic expression gives:
$f(x) = (x - 3)(x - 5)(x + 2)$
[3 marks available — 1 mark for dividing by x – 3 to find quadratic factor, 1 mark for correct quadratic factor, 1 mark for factorising quadratic to get correct final answer]

17 a) Multiply out the brackets and rearrange to get 0 on one side:
$(x - 1)(x^2 + x + 1) = 2x^2 - 17$
$x^3 + x^2 + x - x^2 - x - 1 = 2x^2 - 17$ ***[1 mark]***
$x^3 - 2x^2 + 16 = 0$ ***[1 mark]***

b) The factor theorem says that $(x - a)$ is a factor of a polynomial $f(x)$ if and only if $f(a) = 0$. So if $(x + 2)$ is a factor of $f(x)$, $f(-2) = 0$.
$f(x) = x^3 - 2x^2 + 16$
$f(-2) = (-2)^3 - 2(-2)^2 + 16 = -8 - 8 + 16 = 0$ ***[1 mark]***
$f(-2) = 0$, therefore $(x + 2)$ is a factor of $f(x)$ ***[1 mark]***.

c) From part b) you know that $(x + 2)$ is a factor of $f(x)$. Dividing $f(x)$ by $(x + 2)$ gives:
$x^3 - 2x^2 + 16 = (x + 2)(x^2 + ?x + 8) = (x + 2)(x^2 - 4x + 8)$
[2 marks available — 2 marks for all three correct terms in the quadratic, otherwise 1 mark for two terms correct]

d) From b) you know that $x = -2$ is a root. From c), $f(x) = (x + 2)(x^2 - 4x + 8)$. So for $f(x)$ to equal zero, either $(x + 2) = 0$ (so $x = -2$) or $(x^2 - 4x + 8) = 0$ ***[1 mark]***.
Completing the square of $(x^2 - 4x + 8)$ gives
$x^2 - 4x + 8 = (x - 2)^2 + 4$, which is always positive so has no real roots. So $f(x) = 0$ has no solutions other than $x = -2$, which means it only has one root ***[1 mark]***.
You could also have shown that $x^2 - 4x + 8$ has no real roots by finding the discriminant — the discriminant is $(-4)^2 - (4 \times 1 \times 8) = 16 - 32 = -16$, which is < 0 so the quadratic has no real roots.

18 If $(x - 1)$ is a factor of $f(x)$, then $f(1) = 0$ by the factor theorem ***[1 mark]***.
$f(1) = 1^3 - 4(1)^2 - a(1) + 10$, so $0 = 7 - a \Rightarrow a = 7$ ***[1 mark]***.
So $f(x) = x^3 - 4x^2 - 7x + 10$.
To solve $f(x) = 0$, first factorise $x^3 - 4x^2 - 7x + 10$. You know one factor, $(x - 1)$, so find the quadratic that multiplies with that factor to give the original equation:
$x^3 - 4x^2 - 7x + 10 = (x - 1)(x^2 + ?x - 10)$
$= (x - 1)(x^2 - 3x - 10)$ ***[1 mark]***

Then factorise the quadratic:

$= (x-1)(x-5)(x+2)$ ***[1 mark]***

Finally, solve $f(x) = 0$:

$x^3 - 4x^2 - 7x + 10 = 0 \Rightarrow (x-1)(x-5)(x+2) = 0$,

so $x = 1$, $x = 5$ or $x = -2$ ***[2 marks for all three x-values, otherwise 1 mark for either x = 5 or x = –2]***.

Pages 13-17: Algebra and Functions 3

1 a) The graph of $y = \frac{1}{x-3}$ is the graph of $y = f(x-3)$, where $f(x) = \frac{1}{x}$. $f(x)$ has asymptotes at $x = 0$ and $y = 0$, so $f(x-3)$ will have asymptotes at $x = 3$ and $y = 0$. When $x = 0$, $y = -\frac{1}{3}$, so the y-intercept is $(0, -\frac{1}{3})$.

The graph looks like this:

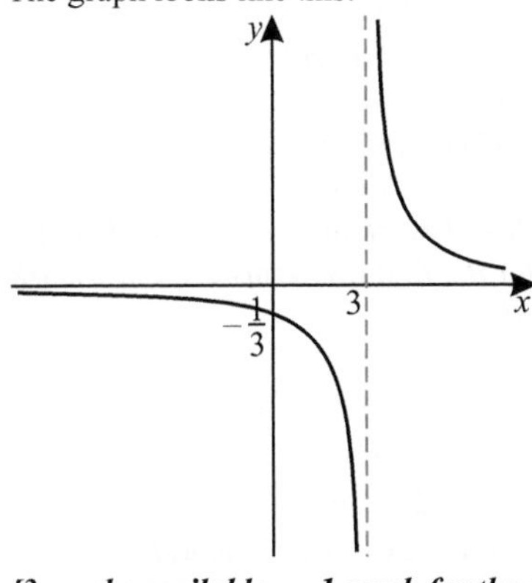

[3 marks available — 1 mark for the correct shape, 1 mark for asymptotes at x = 3 and y = 0, 1 mark for the correct y-intercept]

b) The cubic has already been factorised, so the curve crosses the x-axis at $(1, 0)$, $(-2, 0)$ and $(3, 0)$. When $x = 0$, $y = -6$, so the y-intercept is $(0, -6)$. The coefficient of the x^3 term is negative (-1), so the cubic goes from top left to bottom right.

The graph looks like this:

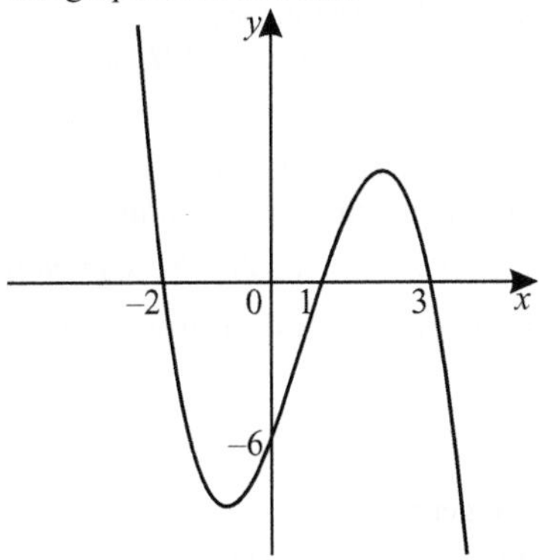

[3 marks available — 1 mark for the correct shape, 1 mark for the correct x-intercepts, 1 mark for the correct y-intercept]

c) The quartic has already been factorised — there are two double roots, one at $(2, 0)$ and the other at $(-3, 0)$. When $x = 0$, $y = (-2)^2(3^2) = 36$, so the y-intercept is $(0, 36)$. The coefficient of the x^4 term is positive, and as the graph only touches the x-axis but doesn't cross it, it is always above the x-axis.

The graph looks like this:

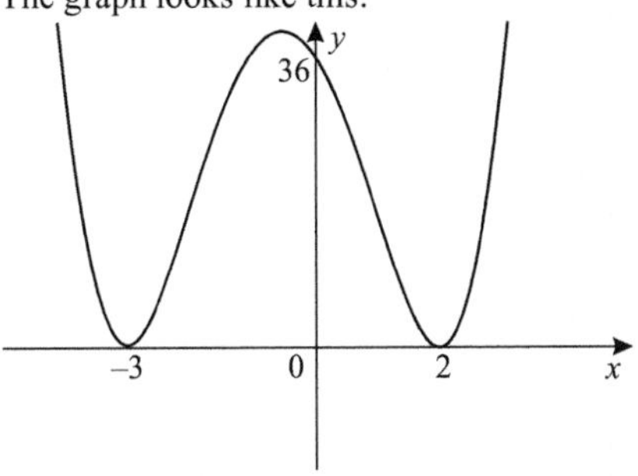

[3 marks available — 1 mark for the correct shape, 1 mark for the correct x-intercepts, 1 mark for the correct y-intercept]

2

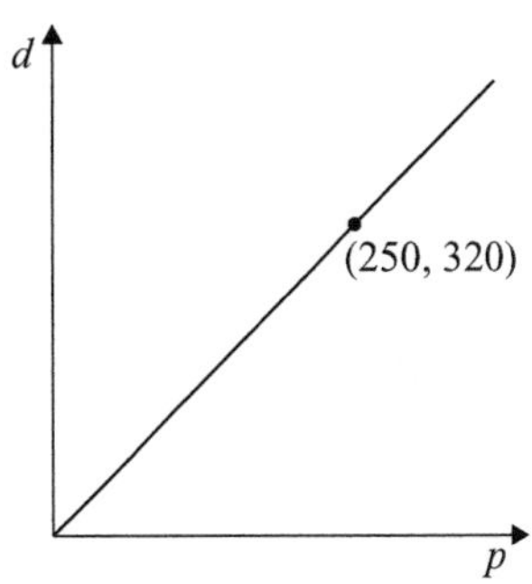

[1 mark for a straight line going through the origin]

Gradient = 320 ÷ 250 = 1.28 ***[1 mark]***

This gradient means that £1 is worth $1.28.

3 a) The curve is reflected in the x-axis ***[1 mark]***, and stretched vertically by a scale factor of 2 ***[1 mark]***.

b) $y = f(x) + 2$ ***[1 mark]***

4 a) Find where the curve cuts the axes:

When $y = 0$, $(x-1)^2(x+2) = 0 \Rightarrow x = 1$ or $x = -2$, so the curve cuts the x-axis at $(-2, 0)$ touches it at $(1, 0)$ (this is a double root — you can tell from the repeated factor).

When $x = 0$, $y = (-1)^2 \times 2 = 2$, so the curve cuts the y-axis at $(0, 2)$.

Put these with the basic shape of a cubic with a positive x^3 term and you can sketch the graph (shown below).

[3 marks available — 1 mark for correct shape, 1 mark for correct x-axis intercepts, 1 mark for correct y-axis intercept]

b) The graph of $f(x-a)$ is $f(x)$ translated to the right.

For $f(x-3)$, each x-intercept needs to translated 3 to the right (i.e. the x-values will be increased by 3), so the x-intercepts become $(1, 0)$ and $(4, 0)$ (see graph below).

[2 marks available — 1 mark for moving the graph to the right, 1 mark for correct new x-intercepts]

c) The graph of $af(x)$ is the graph of $f(x)$ stretched along the y-axis. For $2f(x)$, each y-value is doubled, so the y-intercept becomes $(0, 4)$ (the x-intercepts don't change).

[2 marks available — 1 mark for stretching, 1 mark for correct new x- and y- intercepts]

a)-c) The graphs should look like this:

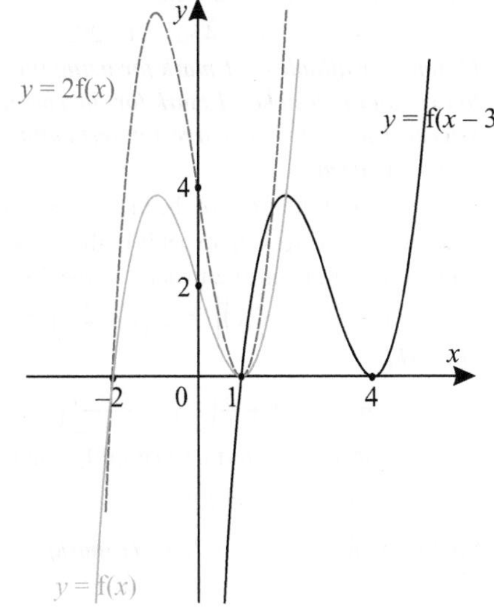

5 a)

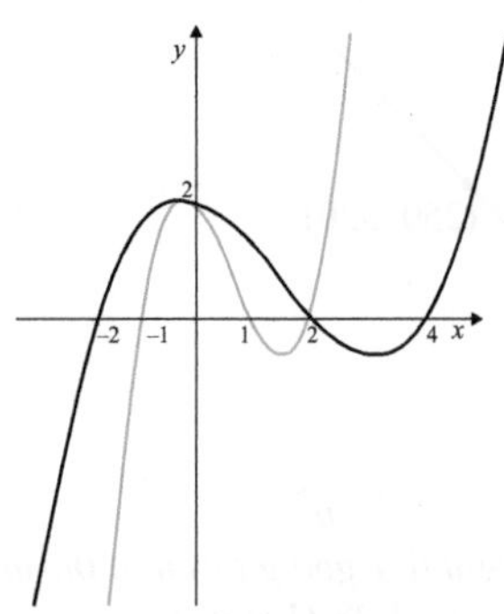

[3 marks available — 1 mark for horizontal stretch, 1 mark for x-axis intercepts at –2, 2 and 4, 1 mark for correct y-axis intercept at 2]

b)

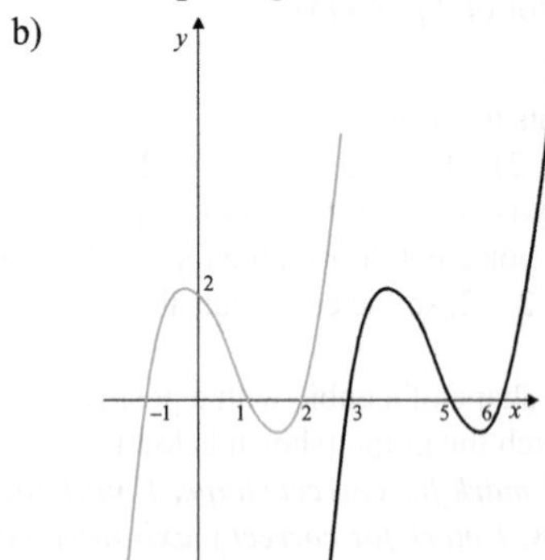

[2 marks available — 1 mark for horizontal translation to the right, 1 mark for x-axis intercepts at 3, 5 and 6]

6 The curve $y = x^3$ is translated ***[1 mark]*** by the vector $\begin{pmatrix}4\\0\end{pmatrix}$ ***[1 mark]***
Alternatively, you could describe this as a translation of 4 units right.

7 a) Using the binomial expansion formula:

$$(1+x)^n = 1 + \frac{n}{1}x + \frac{n(n-1)}{1\times 2}x^2 + \frac{n(n-1)(n-2)}{1\times 2\times 3}x^3 + \ldots + x^n$$

Expand the expression $(1 + ax)^{10}$ using this formula:

$$1 + \frac{10}{1}(ax) + \frac{10\times 9}{1\times 2}(ax)^2 + \frac{10\times 9\times 8}{1\times 2\times 3}(ax)^3 + \ldots$$

Then simplify each coefficient:

$$(1+ax)^{10} = 1 + 10ax + 45a^2x^2 + 120a^3x^3 + \ldots$$

[4 marks available — 1 mark for using the binomial formula to expand the bracket, 1 mark for the correct constant and x-term, 1 mark for the correct x^2 term and 1 mark for the correct x^3 term]

b) The number at the front of the bracket isn't 1, so you'll need to factorise the expression to get it in the correct form.
So first take a factor of 2 to get it in the form $(1 + ax)^n$:

$$(2+3x)^5 = \left[2\left(1+\frac{3}{2}x\right)\right]^5 = 2^5\left(1+\frac{3}{2}x\right)^5 = 32\left(1+\frac{3}{2}x\right)^5$$

[1 mark]

Now expand: $32\left[1 + \frac{5}{1}\left(\frac{3}{2}x\right) + \frac{5\times 4}{1\times 2}\left(\frac{3}{2}x\right)^2 + \ldots\right]$

You only need the x^2 term, so simplify that one:

$$32 \times \frac{20}{2} \times \left(\frac{3}{2}\right)^2 \times x^2 = 720x^2$$

So the coefficient of x^2 is 720 ***[1 mark]***
You could have used the formula for $(a + b)^n$ here, with $a = 2$ and $b = 3x$.

c) From part a), the x^2 term is $45a^2x^2$. This is equal to $720x^2$ so rearrange the formula to find a:
$45a^2 = 720$
$a^2 = 16$
$a = \pm 4$ ***[1 mark]***
Part a) tells you that $a > 0$, so $a = 4$. ***[1 mark]***

8 $(4+3x)^9 = 4^9 + {}^9C_1 4^8(3x) + {}^9C_2 4^7(3x)^2 + {}^9C_3 4^6(3x)^3 + {}^9C_4 4^5(3x)^4 + \ldots$ ***[1 mark]***

So: x coefficient $= 9 \times 4^8 \times 3 = 1\,769\,472$ ***[1 mark]***
x^2 coefficient $= 36 \times 4^7 \times 9 = 5\,308\,416$ ***[1 mark]***
x^3 coefficient $= 84 \times 4^6 \times 27 = 9\,289\,728$ ***[1 mark]***

9 a)

$$\left(1+\frac{x}{3}\right)^8 = 1 + {}^8C_1\left(\frac{x}{3}\right) + {}^8C_2\left(\frac{x}{3}\right)^2 + \ldots$$
$$= 1 + 8\left(\frac{x}{3}\right) + 28\left(\frac{x}{3}\right)^2 + \ldots$$
$$= 1 + \frac{8}{3}x + \frac{28}{9}x^2 + \ldots$$

[3 marks available —1 mark for a correct unsimplified x or x^2 term, 1 mark for the first two terms correct, 1 mark for the third term correct]

b) $\left(1+\frac{x}{3}\right)^8 = 1.002^8$ when $x = 0.006$, so find an approximation by putting $x = 0.006$ ***[1 mark]*** into the expansion of $\left(1+\frac{x}{3}\right)^8$.
Terms with higher powers of 0.006 can be ignored because 0.006 is small:

$$1.002^8 \approx 1 + \frac{8}{3}(0.006) + \frac{28}{9}(0.006)^2$$ ***[1 mark]***
$$= 1 + 0.016 + 0.000112$$
$$= 1.0161 \text{ to 4 d.p.}$$ ***[1 mark]***

10 a)

$$(1+3x)^6 = 1 + {}^6C_1(3x) + {}^6C_2(3x)^2 + \ldots$$
$$= 1 + 6(3x) + 15(3x)^2 + \ldots$$
$$= 1 + 18x + 135x^2 + \ldots$$

[3 marks available —1 mark for a correct unsimplified x or x^2 term, 1 mark for the first two terms correct, 1 mark for the third term correct]

b) $(1 - 2x)(1 + 3x)^6$
$= (1 - 2x)(1 + 18x + 135x^2 + \ldots)$
$\approx (1 - 2x)(1 + 18x + 135x^2)$
$= 1 + 18x + 135x^2 - 2x - 36x^2 - 270x^3$
$\approx 1 + 18x + 135x^2 - 2x - 36x^2$ ***[1 mark]***
$= 1 + 16x + 99x^2$ ***[1 mark]***

Pages 18-20: Coordinate Geometry

1 Find k to give you the coordinates of point A: at A, $x = 1$ and $y = k$, so $y + 2x - 5 = 0 \Rightarrow k + (2 \times 1) - 5 = 0 \Rightarrow k = 3$, so A is (1, 3) ***[1 mark]***
The gradient of l equals the coefficient of x when the equation of the line is in the form $y = mx + c$.
$y + 2x - 5 = 0 \Rightarrow y = -2x + 5$, so gradient $= -2$ ***[1 mark]***.
The line perpendicular to l has gradient $-1 \div -2 = \frac{1}{2}$ ***[1 mark]***.
Finally, find the equation of the new line using $y - y_1 = m(x - x_1)$ and A(1, 3), and rearrange it into the required form:
$y - 3 = \frac{1}{2}(x - 1) \Rightarrow 2y - 6 = x - 1 \Rightarrow x - 2y + 5 = 0$ ***[1 mark]***.

2 a) To find the coordinates of A, solve the equations of the lines simultaneously:
l_1: $x - y + 1 = 0$
l_2: $2x + y - 8 = 0$
Add the equations to get rid of y:
$3x - 7 = 0$ ***[1 mark]*** $\Rightarrow x = \frac{7}{3}$ ***[1 mark]***
Now put $x = \frac{7}{3}$ back into l_1 to find y:
$\frac{7}{3} - y + 1 = 0 \Rightarrow y = \frac{7}{3} + 1 = \frac{10}{3}$
So A is $\left(\frac{7}{3}, \frac{10}{3}\right)$ ***[1 mark]***

b) There's a lot of information here, so draw a quick sketch to make things a bit clearer:

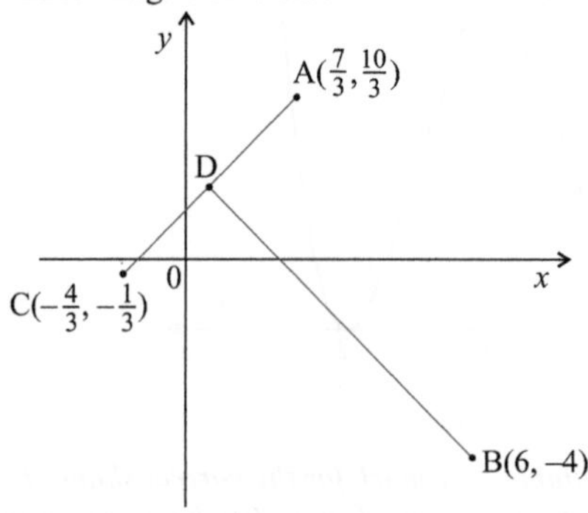

To find the equation of the line through B and D, you need its gradient. But before you can find the gradient, you need to find the coordinates of point D — the midpoint of AC. To find the midpoint of two points, find the average of the x-values and the average of the y-values:

$$D = \left(\frac{x_A + x_C}{2}, \frac{y_A + y_C}{2}\right) = \left(\frac{\frac{7}{3} + \frac{-4}{3}}{2}, \frac{\frac{10}{3} + \frac{-1}{3}}{2}\right)$$ ***[1 mark]***

$D = \left(\frac{1}{2}, \frac{3}{2}\right)$ ***[1 mark]***

To find the gradient (m) of the line through B and D, use this rule: $m_{BD} = \frac{y_D - y_B}{x_D - x_B}$

$$m = \frac{\frac{3}{2} - -4}{\frac{1}{2} - 6} = \frac{\frac{3}{2} + \frac{8}{2}}{\frac{1}{2} - \frac{12}{2}} = \frac{3+8}{1-12} = -1$$ ***[1 mark]***

Now you can find the equation of the line. Input the known values of x and y at B(6, −4) and the gradient (−1) into $y - y_1 = m(x - x_1)$, which gives:
$y - (-4) = -1(x - 6)$ ***[1 mark]***
$\Rightarrow y + 4 = -x + 6 \Rightarrow x + y - 2 = 0$ ***[1 mark]***

c) Look at the sketch above. To prove triangle ABD is a right-angled triangle, you need to prove that lines AD and BD are perpendicular — in other words, prove the product of their gradients equals −1.
You already know the gradient of BD = −1.
Use the same rule to find the gradient of AD:
$m_{AD} = \frac{y_D - y_A}{x_D - x_A}$

$$m = \frac{\frac{3}{2} - \frac{10}{3}}{\frac{1}{2} - \frac{7}{3}} = \frac{\frac{9}{6} - \frac{20}{6}}{\frac{3}{6} - \frac{14}{6}} = \frac{9-20}{3-14} = 1$$ ***[1 mark]***

$m_{BD} \times m_{AD} = -1 \times 1 = -1$ ***[1 mark]***, so triangle ABD is a right-angled triangle ***[1 mark]***.

3 a) To find the equation of the line through points A and B, you need to find its gradient and the coordinates of a point on the line. Start with the gradient:
The gradient of the line through B and C equals the coefficient of x when the equation of the line is in the form $y = mx + c$.
$-3x + 5y = 16 \Rightarrow 5y = 3x + 16 \Rightarrow y = \frac{3}{5}x + \frac{16}{5}$,
so gradient = $\frac{3}{5}$ ***[1 mark]***.
AB and BC are perpendicular, so the gradient of the line through A and B equals $-1 \div \frac{3}{5} = -\frac{5}{3}$ ***[1 mark]***.
Point B has coordinates (3, k), so you can find k by substituting $x = 3$ and $y = k$ into the equation of the line through B and C:
$-3x + 5y = 16 \Rightarrow (-3 \times 3) + 5k = 16 \Rightarrow 5k = 25 \Rightarrow k = 5$,
so point B = (3, 5) ***[1 mark]***.
Now you can input the values of x and y at B(3, 5) and the gradient ($-\frac{5}{3}$) into $y - y_1 = m(x - x_1)$, which gives:
$y - 5 = -\frac{5}{3}(x - 3) \Rightarrow y - 5 = -\frac{5}{3}x + 5$
$3y - 15 = -5x + 15 \Rightarrow 3y + 5x = 30$ ***[1 mark]***

b) To find the area, you need to know the length of one side — say AB. So start by finding the coordinates of point A:
A lies on the y-axis, so $x = 0$ and, using your equation from part a), $3y + (5 \times 0) = 30 \Rightarrow 3y = 30$, so $y = 10$, and A is the point (0, 10) ***[1 mark]***.
Now find the length AB using Pythagoras' theorem:
$(AB)^2 = (10 - 5)^2 + (0 - 3)^2$ ***[1 mark]*** $= 25 + 9 = 34$,
so AB = $\sqrt{34}$
Area = $(AB)^2 = (\sqrt{34})^2 = 34$ units^2 ***[1 mark]***

c) Two lines are parallel if they have the same gradient.
$5x + 3y - 6 = 0 \Rightarrow 3y = -5x + 6 \Rightarrow y = -\frac{5}{3}x + 2$, so the gradient is $-\frac{5}{3}$ ***[1 mark]***.
The line with equation $5x + 3y - 6 = 0$ has the same gradient as the line through points A and B, so the lines are parallel ***[1 mark]***.

4 a) The centre of the circle must be the midpoint of AB, since AB is a diameter. Midpoint of AB is:
$\left(\frac{2+0}{2}, \frac{1+-5}{2}\right) = (1, -2)$ ***[1 mark]***
The radius is the distance from the centre (1, −2) to point A:
radius = $\sqrt{(2-1)^2 + (1-(-2))^2}$ ***[1 mark]*** $= \sqrt{10}$ ***[1 mark]***
You could have used the coordinates of B instead of A here.

b) The general equation for a circle with centre (a, b) and radius r is: $(x - a)^2 + (y - b)^2 = r^2$. So for a circle with centre (1, −2) and radius $\sqrt{10}$, that gives $(x - 1)^2 + (y + 2)^2 = 10$ ***[1 mark]***.
To show that the point (4, −1) lies on the circle, show that it satisfies the equation of the circle:
$(4 - 1)^2 + (-1 + 2)^2 = 9 + 1 = 10$, so (4, −1) lies on the circle ***[1 mark]***.

c) Start with your equation from part b) and multiply out to get the form given in the question:
$(x - 1)^2 + (y + 2)^2 = 10$ ***[1 mark]***
$(x - 1)(x - 1) + (y + 2)(y + 2) = 10$
$x^2 - 2x + 1 + y^2 + 4y + 4 = 10$
$x^2 + y^2 - 2x + 4y - 5 = 0$ ***[1 mark]***

d) The radius at A has the same gradient as the diameter AB, so gradient of radius = $\frac{1 - -5}{2 - 0} = 3$ ***[1 mark]***.
The tangent at point A is perpendicular to the radius at point A, so the tangent has gradient $-1 \div 3 = -\frac{1}{3}$ ***[1 mark]***.
Put the gradient $-\frac{1}{3}$ and point A(2, 1) into the formula for the equation of a straight line and rearrange:
$y - y_1 = m(x - x_1) \Rightarrow y - 1 = -\frac{1}{3}(x - 2)$
$\Rightarrow y - 1 = -\frac{1}{3}x + \frac{2}{3} \Rightarrow y = -\frac{1}{3}x + \frac{5}{3}$ ***[1 mark]***

5 a) The line through the centre P bisects the chord, and so is perpendicular to the chord AB at the midpoint M.
Gradient of AB = Gradient of AM = $\frac{(7-10)}{(11-9)} = -\frac{3}{2}$.
Gradient of PM = $-1 \div -\frac{3}{2} = \frac{2}{3}$
Gradient of PM = $\frac{(7-3)}{(11-p)} = \frac{2}{3}$
$\Rightarrow 3(7 - 3) = 2(11 - p) \Rightarrow 12 = 22 - 2p \Rightarrow p = 5$.
[5 marks available — 1 mark for identifying that PM and AB are perpendicular, 1 mark for correct gradient of AB (or AM), 1 mark for correct gradient of PM, 1 mark for substitution of the y-coordinate of P into the equation for the gradient or equation of the line PM, and 1 mark for correct final answer]

b) The equation of a circle is $(x - a)^2 + (y - b)^2 = r^2$.
The centre of the circle is P(5, 3), so $a = 5$ and $b = 3$ ***[1 mark]***.
r^2 is the square of the radius. The radius equals the length of AP, so you can find r^2 using Pythagoras' theorem:
$r^2 = (AP)^2 = (9 - 5)^2 + (10 - 3)^2 = 65$ ***[1 mark]***.
So the equation of the circle is:
$(x - 5)^2 + (y - 3)^2 = 65$ ***[1 mark]***.

6 a) A is on the y-axis, so the x-coordinate is 0.
Just put $x = 0$ into the equation and solve:
$0^2 - (6 \times 0) + y^2 - 4y = 0$ ***[1 mark]***
$\Rightarrow y^2 - 4y = 0 \Rightarrow y(y - 4) = 0 \Rightarrow y = 0$ or $y = 4$
$y = 0$ is the origin, so A is at (0, 4) ***[1 mark]***

b) Complete the square for the terms involving x and y separately:
Completing the square for $x^2 - 6x$ means you have to start with $(x - 3)^2$, but $(x - 3)^2 = x^2 - 6x + 9$, so you need to subtract 9:
$(x - 3)^2 - 9$ ***[1 mark]***
Now the same for $y^2 - 4y$: $(y - 2)^2 = y^2 - 4y + 4$,
so subtract 4 which gives: $(y - 2)^2 - 4$ ***[1 mark]***
Put these new expressions back into the original equation:
$(x - 3)^2 - 9 + (y - 2)^2 - 4 = 0$
$\Rightarrow (x - 3)^2 + (y - 2)^2 = 13$ ***[1 mark]***

c) In the general equation for a circle $(x - a)^2 + (y - b)^2 = r^2$, the centre is (a, b) and the radius is r.
So for the equation in part b), $a = 3$, $b = 2$, $r = \sqrt{13}$.
Hence, the centre is (3, 2) ***[1 mark]***
and the radius is $\sqrt{13}$ ***[1 mark]***

d) The tangent at point A is perpendicular to the radius at A. The radius between A(0, 4) and the centre(3, 2) has gradient:
$\frac{y_2 - y_1}{x_2 - x_1} = \frac{2-4}{3-0} = -\frac{2}{3}$ ***[1 mark]***
So the gradient of the tangent at A $= -1 \div -\frac{2}{3} = \frac{3}{2}$ ***[1 mark]***
Put $m = \frac{3}{2}$ and A = (0, 4) into $y - y_1 = m(x - x_1)$ to find the equation of the tangent to the circle at point A:
$y - 4 = \frac{3}{2}(x - 0) \Rightarrow y - 4 = \frac{3}{2}x \Rightarrow y = \frac{3}{2}x + 4$ ***[1 mark]***
Point B lies on the line with equation $y = \frac{3}{2}x + 4$.
B also lies on the x-axis, so substitute $y = 0$ into the equation of the line to find the x-coordinate of B:
$0 = \frac{3}{2}x + 4 \Rightarrow x = -\frac{8}{3}$, so B is the point $\left(-\frac{8}{3}, 0\right)$ ***[1 mark]***
Now find AB using Pythagoras' theorem:
$(AB)^2 = \left(0 - -\frac{8}{3}\right)^2 + (4-0)^2$ ***[1 mark]*** $= \frac{64}{9} + 16$,
so AB $= \sqrt{\frac{64}{9} + 16} = \sqrt{\frac{208}{9}} = \frac{4\sqrt{13}}{3}$ ***[1 mark]***

Pages 21-23: Trigonometry

1 Consider the following triangle:

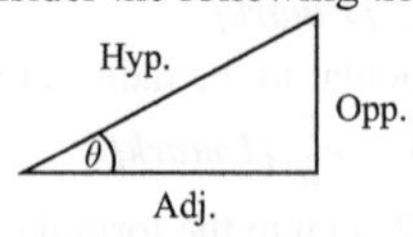

You are given that $\cos\theta = \frac{5}{6}$, which, using trigonometry, means that $\frac{\text{Adj.}}{\text{Hyp.}} = \frac{5}{6}$, and so Adj. = 5 and Hyp. = 6 ***[1 mark]***.
Now using Pythagoras:
Opp. $= \sqrt{6^2 - 5^2} = \sqrt{36 - 25} = \sqrt{11}$.***[1 mark]***
And so $\sin\theta = \frac{\text{Opp.}}{\text{Hyp.}} = \frac{\sqrt{11}}{6}$ ***[1 mark]***
and $\tan\theta = \frac{\text{Opp.}}{\text{Adj.}} = \frac{\sqrt{11}}{5}$ ***[1 mark]***

2 The graph of $y = \sin x$ is mapped onto the graph of $y = \sin\frac{x}{2}$ via a stretch parallel to the x-axis of scale factor 2.
The graphs should appear as follows:

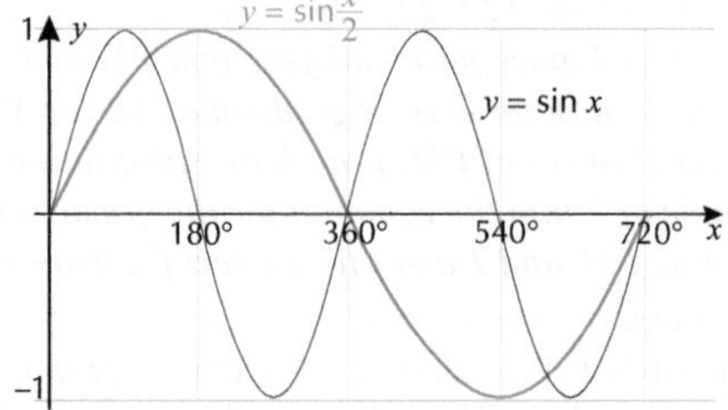

[3 marks available — 1 mark for sin x correct, 1 mark for sin $\frac{x}{2}$ correct, 1 mark for correct axis labelling]

3 Use the cosine rule: $a^2 = b^2 + c^2 - 2bc\cos A$, where $b = 10$, $c = 7$ and angle $A = 60°$:
$a^2 = 10^2 + 7^2 - 2 \times 10 \times 7 \times \cos 60°$ ***[1 mark]***
$= 149 - 140\cos 60°$
$= 149 - 140(0.5)$
$= 79$
So $a = \sqrt{79} = 8.89$ cm to 3 s.f. ***[1 mark]***
Now use the sine rule to find θ:
$\frac{a}{\sin A} = \frac{b}{\sin B} = \frac{c}{\sin C}$
θ is the angle opposite the 10 cm side, so if the 10 cm side is 'side b', then θ = angle B.
$\frac{\sqrt{79}}{\sin 60°} = \frac{10}{\sin\theta}$ ***[1 mark]***
$\sin\theta = \frac{10 \times \sin 60°}{\sqrt{79}} = 0.9743...$
$\Rightarrow \theta = \sin^{-1}0.9743... = 77.0°$ to 3 s.f. ***[1 mark]***

4 a) Use the cosine rule:
e.g. $\cos A = \frac{50^2 + 70^2 - 90^2}{2 \times 50 \times 70}$ ***[1 mark]***
$\cos A = -0.1$ ***[1 mark]***
$A = 95.739...°$ ***[1 mark]***
Now use this value of A to find the area:
Area $= \frac{1}{2} \times 50 \times 70 \times \sin 95.739...°$ ***[1 mark]***
$= 1741.228... = 1741$ m^2 (nearest m^2) ***[1 mark]***
If you've allocated your values of a, b, c etc. differently, or found a different angle, then the numbers in your working will be different. You should still get the same final answer though.

b) E.g. the model is unlikely to give an area accurate to the nearest square metre as the given side lengths are most likely rounded, at least to the nearest metre, possibly to the nearest 5 m or 10 m. This means that there is a large range of possible areas. / The sides are unlikely to be perfectly straight, so the model will not be accurate ***[1 mark for a sensible comment]***.

5 a) Substituting $t = 35.26...°$ into both sides of the equation gives:
LHS: $\sin(2 \times 35.26...°) = 0.94$ (2 s.f)
RHS: $\sqrt{2}\cos(2 \times 35.26...°) = 0.47$ (2 s.f.)
$0.94 \neq 0.47$, so Adam's solutions is incorrect ***[1 mark]***.

b) Adam has incorrectly divided by 2:
$\tan 2t = \sqrt{2} \not\Rightarrow \tan t = \frac{\sqrt{2}}{2}$ ***[1 mark]***

c) $t = -27.36...°$ is not a solution of the original equation ***[1 mark]***. The error has appeared because Bethan squared the equation and then taken roots ***[1 mark]***.

6 Rearrange the equation to get in terms of one trig function:
$4\sin 2x - \cos 2x = 0 \Rightarrow 4\sin 2x = \cos 2x$
$\Rightarrow \frac{\sin 2x}{\cos 2x} = \frac{1}{4} \Rightarrow \tan 2x = \frac{1}{4}$
So solve $\tan 2x = \frac{1}{4}$ in the range $0° \leq 2x \leq 720°$:
$2x = \tan^{-1}\frac{1}{4} = 14.036...°, 194.036...°, 374.036...°, 554.036...°$
So $x = 7.0°, 97.0°, 187.0°, 277.0°$ (all to 1 d.p.)
[4 marks available — 1 mark for rewriting the equation in terms of tan 2x, 1 mark for solving for 2x over an appropriate interval, 2 marks for all 4 answers correct, otherwise 1 mark for 2-3 answers correct. Lose 1 mark if solutions outside the specified range are included.]
tan x repeats every 180°, so keep adding on 180° to the original solution to find the other solutions in the interval.

7 a) Use the trig identity $\tan\theta \equiv \frac{\sin\theta}{\cos\theta}$:
$\tan^2\theta + \frac{\tan\theta}{\cos\theta} = 1 \Rightarrow \frac{\sin^2\theta}{\cos^2\theta} + \frac{\sin\theta}{\cos^2\theta} = 1$ ***[1 mark]***
Put over a common denominator: $\frac{\sin^2\theta + \sin\theta}{\cos^2\theta} = 1$
$\Rightarrow \sin^2\theta + \sin\theta = \cos^2\theta$ ***[1 mark]***
Now use the identity $\cos^2\theta \equiv 1 - \sin^2\theta$ to give:
$\sin^2\theta + \sin\theta = 1 - \sin^2\theta$ ***[1 mark]***
$\Rightarrow 2\sin^2\theta + \sin\theta - 1 = 0$ ***[1 mark]***.

b) Factorising the quadratic from a) gives:
$(2\sin\theta - 1)(\sin\theta + 1) = 0$ ***[1 mark]***
$\Rightarrow \sin\theta = \frac{1}{2}$ or $\sin\theta = -1$ ***[1 mark]***
$\sin\theta = \frac{1}{2} \Rightarrow \theta = 30°$
or $\theta = (180° - 30°) = 150°$
$\sin\theta = -1 \Rightarrow \theta = 270°$, but this value is excluded.
So the solutions are $\theta = 30°$ and $150°$ ***[1 mark]***

8 $7 - 3\cos x = 9\sin^2 x$, and $\sin^2 x \equiv 1 - \cos^2 x$
$\Rightarrow 7 - 3\cos x = 9(1 - \cos^2 x)$
$\Rightarrow 7 - 3\cos x = 9 - 9\cos^2 x$
$\Rightarrow 9\cos^2 x - 3\cos x - 2 = 0$
Substitute y for $\cos x$ and solve $9y^2 - 3y - 2 = 0$ by factorising:
$(3y - 2)(3y + 1) = 0 \Rightarrow y = \frac{2}{3}$ or $y = -\frac{1}{3}$
So $\cos x = \frac{2}{3}$ or $\cos x = -\frac{1}{3}$
For $\cos x = \frac{2}{3}$, $x = 48.189...° = 48.2°$ (1 d.p.).
For $\cos x = -\frac{1}{3}$, $x = 109.471...° = 109.5°$ (1 d.p).
[5 marks available — 1 mark for correct substitution using trig identity, 1 mark for forming a quadratic in cos x, 1 mark for finding correct values of cos x, 1 mark for each of the 2 correct solutions]

Pages 24-27: Exponentials and Logarithms

1 Rewrite the expression using the laws of logs:
$\log_a 4 + 3\log_a 2 = \log_a 4 + \log_a 2^3$ ***[1 mark]***
$= \log_a (4 \times 2^3) = \log_a 32$
Therefore $\log_a x = \log_a 32$, so $x = 32$ ***[1 mark]***

2 Rewrite all the terms as powers of p and use the laws of logs to simplify:
$\log_p(p^4) + \log_p(p^{\frac{1}{2}}) - \log_p(p^{-\frac{1}{2}})$ ***[1 mark]***
$= 4\log_p p + \frac{1}{2}\log_p p - \left(-\frac{1}{2}\right)\log_p p$ ***[1 mark]***
$= 4 + \frac{1}{2} - \left(-\frac{1}{2}\right) = 4 + 1 = 5$ (as $\log_p p = 1$) ***[1 mark]***

3 a) $2^x = 9$, so taking logs to base 2 of both sides gives:
$\log_2 2^x = \log_2 9 \Rightarrow x = \log_2 9$ ***[1 mark]***
So $x = 3.17$ to 2 d.p. ***[1 mark]***
If your calculator can't do logs of any base, you could take $\log_{10}$ of both sides. You'd use the log laws to get $x \log_{10} 2 = \log_{10} 9$, then divide both sides by $\log_{10} 2$ to find the value of x.

b) $2^{2x} = (2^x)^2$ (from the power laws), so let $y = 2^x$, then $y^2 = 2^{2x}$.
This gives a quadratic in y: $y^2 - 13y + 36 = 0$ ***[1 mark]***
$(y - 9)(y - 4) = 0$ ***[1 mark]***, so $y = 9$ or $y = 4$
$\Rightarrow 2^x = 9$ or $2^x = 4$ ***[1 mark for both]***
From a), $2^x = 9 \Rightarrow x = 3.17$ to 2 d.p. ***[1 mark]***
and for $2^x = 4$, $x = 2$ (since $2^2 = 4$) ***[1 mark]***.

4 $3^{y^2 - 4} = 7^{(y+2)}$, so taking logs of both sides gives:
$(y^2 - 4)\log 3 = (y + 2)\log 7$ ***[1 mark]***
$\Rightarrow (y + 2)(y - 2)\log 3 - (y + 2)\log 7 = 0$ ***[1 mark]***
$\Rightarrow (y + 2)[(y - 2)\log 3 - \log 7] = 0$ ***[1 mark]***
$\Rightarrow y + 2 = 0$ or $(y - 2)\log 3 - \log 7 = 0$
$\Rightarrow y = -2$ or $y = \frac{\log 7 + 2\log 3}{\log 3}$
$\Rightarrow y = -2$ ***[1 mark]*** or $y = 3.77$ (3 s.f.) ***[1 mark]***

5 a) $\log_4 p - \log_4 q = \frac{1}{2}$, so using the log laws:
$\log_4\left(\frac{p}{q}\right) = \frac{1}{2}$
Taking exponentials of base 4 gives:
$\frac{p}{q} = 4^{\frac{1}{2}} = \sqrt{4} = 2 \Rightarrow p = 2q$
[3 marks available — 1 mark for combining the two logs, 1 mark for taking exponentials of base 4 of each side, 1 mark for the correct final working.]

b) Since $p = 2q$ (from a)), the equation can be written:
$\log_2(2q) + \log_2 q = 7$ ***[1 mark]***
This simplifies to: $\log_2(2q^2) = 7$ ***[1 mark]***
Taking exponentials of base 2 gives: $2q^2 = 2^7 = 128$ ***[1 mark]***
$\Rightarrow q^2 = 64 \Rightarrow q = 8$ (since p and q are positive) ***[1 mark]***
$p = 2q \Rightarrow p = 16$ ***[1 mark]***

6 For $3\ln x - \ln 3x = 0$, use the log laws to simplify to:
$\ln x^3 - \ln 3x = 0 \Rightarrow \ln\frac{x^3}{3x} = 0 \Rightarrow \ln\frac{x^2}{3} = 0$ ***[1 mark]***
Taking exponentials of both sides gives:
$\frac{x^2}{3} = e^0 = 1 \Rightarrow x^2 = 3 \Rightarrow x = \sqrt{3}$ ***[1 mark]***
You can ignore the negative solution as $x > 0$.

7 a) A is the point where the curve crosses the y-axis, so $x = 0$.
When $x = 0$, $y = e^{k \times 0} = 1$, so the coordinates are (0, 1) ***[1 mark]***.

b) The gradient of $y = e^{kx}$ is ke^{kx}.
At A, $x = 0 \Rightarrow 4 = ke^{k \times 0} \Rightarrow k = 4$ ***[1 mark]***.

c) When $x = -1$, the gradient $= ke^{kx} = 4e^{4 \times -1} = 4e^{-4}$ ***[1 mark]***.

d) At B, $4e^8 = 4e^{4x} \Rightarrow x = 2$ ***[1 mark]***
When $x = 2$, $y = e^{4 \times 2} = e^8$ ***[1 mark]***
So the coordinates of B are $(2, e^8)$.

8 a) You need to find t such that:
$2100 - 1500e^{-0.15t} > 5700e^{-0.15t}$ ***[1 mark]***
$2100 > 7200e^{-0.15t}$
$\frac{7}{24} > e^{-0.15t}$
$\ln\frac{7}{24} > -0.15t$ ***[1 mark]***
$\ln\frac{7}{24} \div -0.15 < t$
$t > 8.21429...$ ***[1 mark]***
So the population of Q first exceeds the population of P when $t > 8.21$ (3 s.f.), i.e. in the year 2018 ***[1 mark]***.
Don't forget to flip the inequality sign when you divide by −0.15.

b)

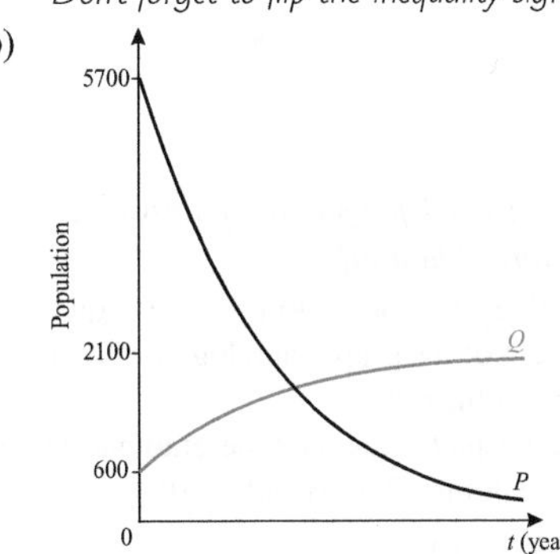

[2 marks available — 1 mark for correct shape of graph, 1 mark for (0, 5700) labelled]

c) Bird of prey:
E.g. Any one of:
- The model predicts the population of the birds of prey will increase, but will tend to a limit. This seems realistic, as the bird of prey will have to compete for the available sources of food as one source decreases.
- The population grows quite slowly (especially compared to the rate of decrease of the other species) — this seems more realistic than a rapid population growth.
- The rate of growth slows over time, which would be expected as food supplies dwindle.

[1 mark for a sensible comment about the birds of prey]
Endangered species:
E.g. Any one of:
- The model predicts the population will decrease, which seems realistic as the birds of prey will hunt them.
- The model predicts a very rapid decline at first, which does not seem realistic — you'd expect the rate of decrease to be slower at first.

[1 mark for a sensible comment about the endangered species]

d) When $P = 1000$: $1000 = 5700e^{-0.15t} \Rightarrow 1000 = \frac{5700}{e^{0.15t}}$
$\Rightarrow e^{0.15t} = \frac{5700}{1000} = 5.7$ ***[1 mark]***. Take ln of both sides:
$0.15t = \ln 5.7 \Rightarrow t = \frac{\ln 5.7}{0.15} = 11.6031...$ years.
So the population will drop below 1000 in the year 2021 ***[1 mark]***.

e) E.g. The function could be refined so that from 2021, the population is predicted to stop decreasing — it could either level out or start increasing ***[1 mark for a sensible comment]***.

9 a) $y = ab^t$

Take logs of both sides: $\log_{10} y = \log_{10} ab^t$

Then use the laws of logs:

$\log_{10} y = \log_{10} a + \log_{10} b^t$ ***[1 mark]***

$\log_{10} y = \log_{10} a + t\log_{10} b$ ***[1 mark]***

or: $\log_{10} y = t\log_{10} b + \log_{10} a$, as required.

b)

t	1	2	3	4	5
$\log_{10} y$	0	0.301	0.602	0.903	1.146

[1 mark for all three correct values]

c) 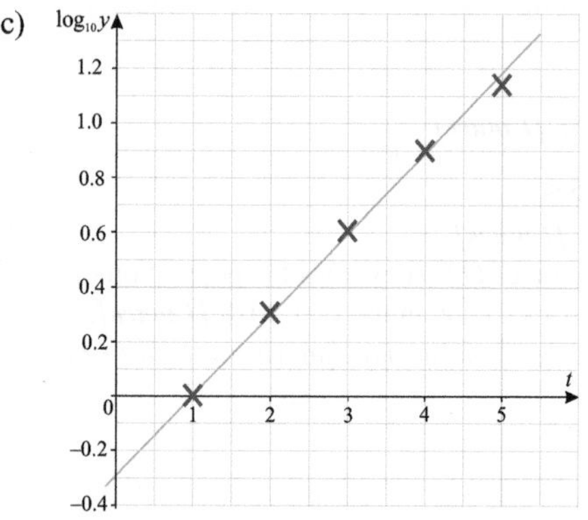

[2 marks available — 1 mark for plotting points correctly, 1 mark for drawing line of best fit]

Comparing $\log_{10} y = t\log_{10} b + \log_{10} a$ to $y = mx + c$ gives $\log_{10} b = m$, the gradient of the graph, and $\log_{10} a = c$, the vertical-axis intercept of the graph.

Use points from your graph to calculate the gradient, m:

For example, using the points (2, 0.3) and (1, 0):

$$m = \frac{y_2 - y_1}{x_2 - x_1} = \frac{0.3 - 0}{2 - 1} = 0.3$$

So $\log_{10} b = 0.3 \Rightarrow b = 2.0$ (2 s.f.) ***[1 mark]***

Now estimate the vertical-axis intercept to find $\log_{10} a$:

$\log_{10} a = -0.29 \Rightarrow a = 0.51$ (2 s.f.) ***[1 mark]***.

Don't worry if your values of a and b are slightly different — it depends on your line of best fit.

d) From part c), the equation modelling the increase in attendance is $y = 0.51(2.0)^t$. y is the average attendance in hundreds, so an attendance of 5000 gives a y-value of 50.

Use your equation to find the corresponding t-value:

$50 = 0.51(2.0)^t$ ***[1 mark]***

$98.039... = 2.0^t$

$\log(98.039...) = \log(2.0^t)$

$\log(98.039...) = t\log(2.0)$

$t = \log(98.039...) \div \log(2.0) = 6.6$ (2 s.f.) ***[1 mark]***

Pages 28-32: Differentiation

1 a) Rewrite all the terms as powers of x: $y = x^7 + \frac{2}{x^3} = x^7 + 2x^{-3}$

and then differentiate each term:

$$\frac{dy}{dx} = 7x^6 + (-3)2x^{-4} = 7x^6 - \frac{6}{x^4}$$

[2 marks available — 1 mark for each correct term]

b) This is a second-order derivative, so differentiate your answer to part a):

$$\frac{d^2y}{dx^2} = \frac{d}{dx}(7x^6 - 6x^{-4}) = 6(7x^5) - 4(-6x^{-5}) = 42x^5 + \frac{24}{x^5}$$

[2 marks available — 1 mark for each correct term]

2 To find the gradient of the curve, differentiate $y = 3x + 4 + x^4$:

$$\frac{dy}{dx} = 3 + 4x^3$$

To find the gradient at point A, substitute $x = 2$ into the derivative:

At A, gradient $= 3 + 4 \times 2^3 = 35$

[4 marks available — 1 mark for differentiating, 1 mark for the correct derivative, 1 mark for substituting in x = 2, 1 mark for the correct answer]

3 a) The gradient of the tangent is the same as the gradient of the curve, so differentiate:

$$\frac{dy}{dx} = 6x^2 - 20x - 2x^{-\frac{1}{2}} = 6x^2 - 20x - \frac{2}{\sqrt{x}}$$

Now put $x = 4$ into your derivative:

$$6(4^2) - 20(4) - \frac{2}{\sqrt{4}} = 96 - 80 - 1 = 15$$

[4 marks available — 1 mark for differentiating, 1 mark for the correct derivative, 1 mark for substituting in x = 4, 1 mark for the correct answer]

b) The gradient of the normal is $-1 \div$ the gradient of the tangent $= -1 \div 15 = -\frac{1}{15}$ ***[1 mark]***.

At $x = 4$, the y-value is $2(4^3) - 10(4^2) - 4(\sqrt{4}) + 12$ $= 128 - 160 - 8 + 12 = -28$ ***[1 mark]***.

Putting these values into the formula $y - y_1 = m(x - x_1)$ gives:

$y - -28 = -\frac{1}{15}(x - 4)$ ***[1 mark]***

$\Rightarrow y + 28 = -\frac{1}{15}x + \frac{4}{15}$

$\Rightarrow 15y + 420 = -x + 4$

$\Rightarrow x + 15y + 416 = 0$ ***[1 mark]***

4 a) Differentiate f(x) to find f'(x):

$f'(x) = 3x^2 - 14x + 8$

So the graph of f'(x) is a positive quadratic (i.e. u-shaped).

It crosses the y-axis when $x = 0$, which gives a y-value of 8.

It crosses the x-axis when $3x^2 - 14x + 8 = 0$

$\Rightarrow (3x - 2)(x - 4) = 0$, so $x = \frac{2}{3}$ and $x = 4$.

Now sketch the graph:

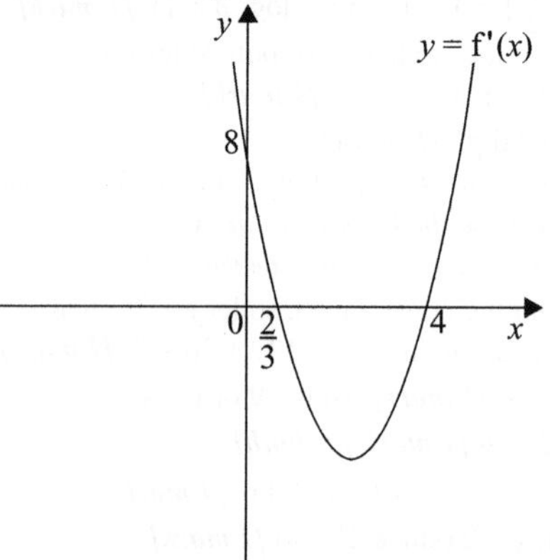

[4 marks available — 1 mark for attempting to differentiate, 1 mark for the correct function for y = f'(x), 1 mark for the correct shape of the graph, 1 mark for the correct x- and y-intercepts]

b) The x-intercepts are where $f'(x) = 0$, so they are where the stationary points of the graph of $y = f(x)$ occur ***[1 mark]***.

5 a) The gradient of the normal at R is the same as the gradient of the line $4y + x = 24$. Rearrange this equation to find the gradient:

$4y + x = 24 \Rightarrow 4y = 24 - x \Rightarrow y = 6 - \frac{1}{4}x$,

so gradient of normal at R $= -\frac{1}{4}$

Gradient of curve at R $= -1 \div -\frac{1}{4} = 4$

Find an expression for the gradient of the curve by differentiating $y = kx^2 - 8x - 5$:

$$\frac{dy}{dx} = 2kx - 8$$

At R, gradient $= 2k(2) - 8 = 4k - 8$

Put this expression equal to the value of the gradient at R to find k:

$4k - 8 = 4 \Rightarrow 4k = 12 \Rightarrow k = 3$

[5 marks available — 1 mark for finding the gradient of the normal at R, 1 mark for finding the gradient of the curve at R, 1 mark for attempting to differentiate y, 1 mark for forming an equation for k, 1 mark for the correct value of k]

b) Gradient of tangent at R = gradient of curve = 4.
At R, $x = 2$, so $y = 3(2^2) - 8(2) - 5 = -9$ ***[1 mark]***
Use these values in $y - y_1 = m(x - x_1)$ to find the equation of the tangent:
$y + 9 = 4(x - 2) \Rightarrow y + 9 = 4x - 8 \Rightarrow y = 4x - 17$ ***[1 mark]***
Equate $y = 4x - 17$ and $y = 4x - \frac{1}{x^3} - 9$ to find S:
$4x - 17 = 4x - \frac{1}{x^3} - 9$ ***[1 mark]***
$-8 = -\frac{1}{x^3} \Rightarrow x = \frac{1}{2}$ and $y = 4(\frac{1}{2}) - 17 = -15$
So at S, $x = \frac{1}{2}$ ***[1 mark]*** and $y = -15$ ***[1 mark]***

6 $\frac{dy}{dx} = 5x^4 - 12x^2 - \frac{1}{x^2}$
At $x = a$, $\frac{dy}{dx} = 5a^4 - 12a^2 - \frac{1}{a^2}$
At $x = -a$, $\frac{dy}{dx} = 5(-a)^4 - 12(-a)^2 - \frac{1}{(-a)^2} = 5a^4 - 12a^2 - \frac{1}{a^2}$
The gradient of the curve is the same at $x = a$ and $x = -a$, therefore the gradients of the tangents are the same at $x = a$ and $x = -a$. Lines with the same gradient are parallel, so the tangents at $x = a$ and $x = -a$ are parallel for all values of a.
[3 marks available — 1 mark for differentiating, 1 mark for finding the gradients at a and –a, 1 mark for a correct conclusion]

7 $f'(x) = \lim_{h\to 0}\left(\frac{(8(x+h)^2 - 1) - (8x^2 - 1)}{h}\right)$ ***[1 mark]***
$= \lim_{h\to 0}\left(\frac{(8(x^2 + 2xh + h^2) - 1) - (8x^2 - 1)}{h}\right)$
$= \lim_{h\to 0}\left(\frac{8x^2 + 16xh + 8h^2 - 1 - 8x^2 + 1}{h}\right)$ ***[1 mark]***
$= \lim_{h\to 0}\left(\frac{16xh + 8h^2}{h}\right)$
$= \lim_{h\to 0}(16x + 8h)$ ***[1 mark]***
As $h \to 0$, $16x + 8h \to 16x$, so $f'(x) = 16x$
[1 mark for letting h → 0 and obtaining the correct limit]

8 $f'(x) = \lim_{h\to 0}\left(\frac{5(x+h)^3 - 5x^3}{h}\right)$ ***[1 mark]***
$= \lim_{h\to 0}\left(\frac{5(x^3 + 3hx^2 + 3h^2x + h^3) - 5x^3}{h}\right)$
$= \lim_{h\to 0}\left(\frac{5x^3 + 15hx^2 + 15h^2x + 5h^3 - 5x^3}{h}\right)$ ***[1 mark]***
$= \lim_{h\to 0}\left(\frac{15hx^2 + 15h^2x + 5h^3}{h}\right)$
$= \lim_{h\to 0}(15x^2 + 15hx + 5h^2)$ ***[1 mark]***
As $h \to 0$, $15x^2 + 15hx + 5h^2 \to 15x^2$, so $f'(x) = 15x^2$
[1 mark for letting h → 0 and obtaining the correct limit]

9 a) Find $\frac{dy}{dx}$ then input the known value of x at the stationary point and set the derivative equal to zero:
$\frac{dy}{dx} = 6x^2 + a$ ***[1 mark]***
When $x = 3$, $6(3^2) + a = 0$ ***[1 mark]*** $\Rightarrow 54 + a = 0$
$\Rightarrow a = -54$ ***[1 mark]***
$y = b$ when $x = 3$, so $b = 2(3^3) + (-54 \times 3) - 5$ ***[1 mark]***
$= 54 - 162 - 5 = -113$ ***[1 mark]***

b) Find $\frac{d^2y}{dx^2}$ then input $x = 3$ to find if it gives a negative or positive value:
$\frac{d^2y}{dx^2} = 12x$ ***[1 mark]***
So when $x = 3$, $\frac{d^2y}{dx^2} = 12 \times 3 = 36$
This is positive, so it's a minimum ***[1 mark]***.

10 f(x) is an increasing function for all values of x if $f'(x) > 0$ for all x.
Differentiate f(x) to find f'(x):
$3x^3 + 9x^2 + 25x \Rightarrow f'(x) = 9x^2 + 18x + 25$ ***[1 mark for differentiating, 1 mark for the correct derivative]***
Complete the square to show that $f'(x) > 0$:
$f'(x) = 9x^2 + 18x + 25 \Rightarrow f'(x) = 9(x^2 + 2x) + 25$
$\Rightarrow f'(x) = 9(x + 1)^2 - 9 + 25$
$\Rightarrow f'(x) = 9(x + 1)^2 + 16$ ***[1 mark]***
$(x + 1)^2 \geq 0$, so f'(x) has a minimum value of 16.
So $f'(x) > 0$ for all x ***[1 mark]***, which means that f(x) is an increasing function for all values of x.

11 a) Differentiate f(x) and set the derivative equal to zero:
$f'(x) = 8x^3 + 27$ ***[1 mark]***
$8x^3 + 27 = 0 \Rightarrow x^3 = -\frac{27}{8} \Rightarrow x = \sqrt[3]{-\frac{27}{8}} = -\frac{3}{2} = -1.5$
[1 mark]
When $x = -1.5$, $f(x) = 2(-1.5)^4 + 27(-1.5) = -30.375$
So the stationary point is at (–1.5, –30.375) ***[1 mark]***

b) The function is increasing if the gradient is positive.
$f'(x) > 0$ if $8x^3 + 27 > 0 \Rightarrow x^3 > -\frac{27}{8} \Rightarrow x > \sqrt[3]{-\frac{27}{8}}$
$\Rightarrow x > -1.5$
The function is decreasing if the gradient is negative.
$f'(x) < 0$ if $8x^3 + 27 < 0 \Rightarrow x^3 < -\frac{27}{8} \Rightarrow x < \sqrt[3]{-\frac{27}{8}}$
$\Rightarrow x < -1.5$
[2 marks available — 1 mark for forming at least one correct inequality, 1 mark for both ranges of values correct]

c) You know from parts a) and b) that the function has a stationary point at (–1.5, –30.375) and that this is a minimum point because the function is decreasing to the left of this point and increasing to the right of it.
Find where the curve crosses the y-axis:
When $x = 0$, $f(x) = 0$, so the curve goes through the origin.
Find where the curve crosses the x-axis:
When $f(x) = 0$, $2x^4 + 27x = 0 \Rightarrow x(2x^3 + 27) = 0$
$\Rightarrow x = 0$ or $2x^3 + 27 = 0$
$\Rightarrow x^3 = -\frac{27}{2} \Rightarrow x = \sqrt[3]{-\frac{27}{2}} = -2.381$ (3 d.p.),
so the curve crosses the x-axis at $x = 0$ and $x = -2.381$.
Now use the information you've found to sketch the curve:

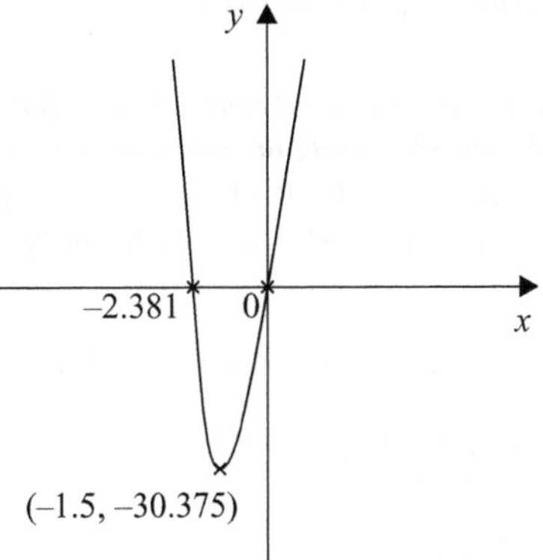

[3 marks available — 1 mark for a curve with the correct shape, 1 mark for the correct minimum point, 1 mark for the correct intercepts]

12 a) Surface area of the container = sum of the areas of all 5 sides $= x^2 + x^2 + xy + xy + xy = 2x^2 + 3xy$ ***[1 mark]***
40 litres = 40 000 cm^3
Volume of the container = length × width × height
$= x^2y = 40\,000$ cm^3 ***[1 mark]*** $\Rightarrow y = \frac{40\,000}{x^2}$
Put this into the formula for the area:
$A = 2x^2 + 3xy = 2x^2 + 3x\left(\frac{40\,000}{x^2}\right)$ ***[1 mark]***
$= 2x^2 + \frac{120\,000}{x}$ ***[1 mark]***

b) To find stationary points, first find $\frac{dA}{dx}$:
$\frac{dA}{dx} = 4x - \frac{120\,000}{x^2}$ ***[1 mark for each term]***
Then find the value of x where $\frac{dA}{dx} = 0$:
$4x - \frac{120\,000}{x^2} = 0$ ***[1 mark]*** $\Rightarrow x^3 = 30\,000$
$\Rightarrow x = 31.07... = 31.1$ cm (3 s.f.) ***[1 mark]***
To check if it's a minimum, find $\frac{d^2A}{dx^2}$:
$\frac{d^2A}{dx^2} = 4 + \frac{240\,000}{x^3} = 12$ at $x = 31.07...$ ***[1 mark]***.
The second derivative is positive, so it's a minimum ***[1 mark]***

c) Put the value of x found in part b) into the formula for the area given in part a):
$A = 2(31.07...)^2 + \frac{120\,000}{31.07...}$ ***[1 mark]*** $= 5792.936...$
$= 5790$ cm^2 (3 s.f.) ***[1 mark]***

d) E.g. the model does not take into account the thickness of the steel, so the minimum area needed is likely to be slightly greater than this to create the required capacity ***[1 mark for a sensible comment]***.

Pages 33-35: Integration

1 $\int (4x^3 + 6x + 3)\,dx = \frac{4x^4}{4} + \frac{6x^2}{2} + 3x + C = x^4 + 3x^2 + 3x + C$

[3 marks available — 1 mark for increasing the power of one term by 1, 1 mark for the first two terms correct, 1 mark for the third term and adding C]

2 $\int \left(2\sqrt{x} + \frac{1}{x^3}\right) dx = \int (2x^{\frac{1}{2}} + x^{-3})\,dx = \frac{2x^{\frac{3}{2}}}{\left(\frac{3}{2}\right)} + \frac{x^{-2}}{-2} + C$

$= \frac{4}{3}x^{\frac{3}{2}} - \frac{x^{-2}}{2} + C = \frac{4}{3}\sqrt{x^3} - \frac{1}{2x^2} + C$

[3 marks available — 1 mark for writing both terms as powers of x, 1 mark for increasing the power of one term by 1, 1 mark for the correct integrated terms and adding C]

3 $\int \left(\frac{x^2 + 3}{\sqrt{x}}\right) dx = \int (x^{\frac{3}{2}} + 3x^{-\frac{1}{2}})\,dx = \frac{x^{\frac{5}{2}}}{\left(\frac{5}{2}\right)} + \frac{3x^{\frac{1}{2}}}{\left(\frac{1}{2}\right)} + C$

$= \frac{2}{5}x^{\frac{5}{2}} + 6x^{\frac{1}{2}} + C = \frac{2}{5}\sqrt{x^5} + 6\sqrt{x} + C$

[3 marks available — 1 mark for writing both terms as powers of x, 1 mark for increasing the power of one term by 1, 1 mark for the correct integrated terms and adding C]

4 Integrate the derivative to find the equation of the curve:

$y = \int (3x^2 + 6x - 4)\,dx = \frac{3x^3}{3} + \frac{6x^2}{2} - 4x + C$

$= x^3 + 3x^2 - 4x + C$

[2 marks for all four terms correct, otherwise 1 mark for attempting to integrate by increasing the power of one term by 1]

Use the point (0, 0) to find C: $0 = 0 + 0 - 0 + C \Rightarrow C = 0$ ***[1 mark]***

So the equation of the curve is $y = x^3 + 3x^2 - 4x$ ***[1 mark]***.

5 To find f(x), integrate f'(x):

$f(x) = \int \left(2x + 5\sqrt{x} + \frac{6}{x^2}\right) dx = \int (2x + 5x^{\frac{1}{2}} + 6x^{-2})\,dx$

$= \frac{2x^2}{2} + 5\left(\frac{x^{\frac{3}{2}}}{\left(\frac{3}{2}\right)}\right) + \left(\frac{6x^{-1}}{-1}\right) + C$

$f(x) = x^2 + \frac{10\sqrt{x^3}}{3} - \frac{6}{x} + C$

[4 marks available for the above working — 1 mark for writing all terms as powers of x, 1 mark for increasing the power of one term by 1, 1 mark for two correct simplified terms, 1 mark for the third correct integrated term and adding C]

You've been given a point on the curve so calculate the value of C:
If $y = 7$ when $x = 3$, then

$3^2 + \frac{10\sqrt{3^3}}{3} - \frac{6}{3} + C = 7$ ***[1 mark]***

$9 + 10\sqrt{3} - 2 + C = 7$

$7 + 10\sqrt{3} + C = 7 \Rightarrow C = -10\sqrt{3}$

$f(x) = x^2 + \frac{10\sqrt{x^3}}{3} - \frac{6}{x} - 10\sqrt{3}$ ***[1 mark]***

6 $\int_p^{4p} \left(\frac{1}{\sqrt{x}} - 4x^3\right) dx = \int_p^{4p} (x^{-\frac{1}{2}} - 4x^3)\,dx = \left[\frac{x^{\frac{1}{2}}}{\frac{1}{2}} - \frac{4x^4}{4}\right]_p^{4p}$

$= [2x^{\frac{1}{2}} - x^4]_p^{4p} = [2\sqrt{x} - x^4]_p^{4p}$

$= (2\sqrt{4p} - (4p)^4) - (2\sqrt{p} - p^4)$

$= (4\sqrt{p} - 256p^4) - (2\sqrt{p} - p^4)$

$= 2\sqrt{p} - 255p^4$

[4 marks available — 1 mark for increasing the power of one term by 1, 1 mark for the correct integrated terms, 1 mark for correct handling of the limits, 1 mark for simplifying to get the final answer]

7 To find the area of region A, you need to integrate the function between $x = 2$ and $x = 4$:

Area $= \int_2^4 \frac{2}{\sqrt{x^3}}\,dx = \int_2^4 2x^{-\frac{3}{2}}\,dx = [-2(2x^{-\frac{1}{2}})]_2^4 = \left[\frac{-4}{x^{\frac{1}{2}}}\right]_2^4 = \left[\frac{-4}{\sqrt{x}}\right]_2^4$

$= \left(\frac{-4}{\sqrt{4}}\right) - \left(\frac{-4}{\sqrt{2}}\right) = \frac{-4}{2} + \frac{4}{\sqrt{2}} = -2 + \frac{4\sqrt{2}}{2}$

$= 2\sqrt{2} - 2$ as required

[5 marks available — 1 mark for writing down the correct integral to find, 1 mark for integrating correctly, 1 mark for correct handling of the limits, 1 mark for rationalising the denominator, 1 mark for rearranging to give the answer in the correct form]

8 Evaluate the integral, treating k as a constant:

$\int_{\sqrt{2}}^2 (8x^3 - 2kx)\,dx = \left[\frac{8x^4}{4} - \frac{2kx^2}{2}\right]_{\sqrt{2}}^2 = [2x^4 - kx^2]_{\sqrt{2}}^2$

$= (2(2)^4 - k(2)^2) - (2(\sqrt{2})^4 - k(\sqrt{2})^2)$

$= (32 - 4k) - (8 - 2k) = 24 - 2k$

You know that the value of this integral is $2k^2$, so set this expression equal to $2k^2$ and solve to find k:

$24 - 2k = 2k^2$

$0 = 2k^2 + 2k - 24 \Rightarrow k^2 + k - 12 = 0 \Rightarrow (k + 4)(k - 3) = 0$

So $k = -4$ or $k = 3$

[5 marks available — 1 mark for increasing the power of one term by 1, 1 mark for the correct integrated terms, 1 mark for substituting in the limits and setting equal to $2k^2$, 1 mark for factorising quadratic, 1 mark for both values of k]

9 a) Integrate the derivative to find the equation of the curve:

$y = \int 4(1 - x)\,dx = 4\int (1 - x)\,dx = 4\left(x - \frac{x^2}{2}\right) + C$

$= 4x - 2x^2 + C$

[2 marks for all three terms correct, otherwise 1 mark for attempting to integrate by increasing the power of one term by 1]

Substitute the known values of x and y at point A to find C:

$6 = (4 \times 2) - (2 \times 2^2) + C$

$6 = 8 - 8 + C$

$6 = C$ ***[1 mark]***

So the equation of the curve is $y = 4x - 2x^2 + 6$ ***[1 mark]***

b) Quickly sketch the curve to see the area you're trying to find. The curve crosses the x-axis when $y = 0$, so

$0 = 4x - 2x^2 + 6$

$x^2 - 2x - 3 = 0$

$(x + 1)(x - 3) = 0$

It crosses the x-axis at (–1, 0) and (3, 0). The coefficient of x^2 is negative, so it's an n-shaped quadratic which looks like this:

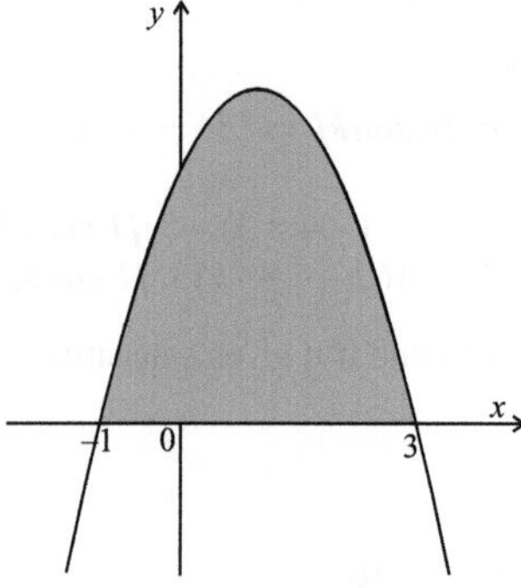

So the area you're trying to find is the shaded area, which is

$\int_{-1}^3 (4x - 2x^2 + 6)\,dx = \left[\frac{4x^2}{2} - \frac{2x^3}{3} + 6x\right]_{-1}^3 = \left[2x^2 - \frac{2x^3}{3} + 6x\right]_{-1}^3$

$= \left(2(3^2) - \frac{2(3^3)}{3} + 6(3)\right) - \left(2(-1^2) - \frac{2(-1^3)}{3} + 6(-1)\right)$

$= (18 - 18 + 18) - \left(2 + \frac{2}{3} - 6\right) = 18 - \left(-\frac{10}{3}\right) = \frac{64}{3}$

[6 marks available — 1 mark for a correct method to find the limits to integrate between (using a graph or otherwise), 1 mark for both limits correct, 1 mark for attempting to integrate, 1 mark for the three correct terms after integrating, 1 mark for correct handling of the limits, 1 mark for the correct answer]

10 To find the shaded area, you need to integrate the function between –1 and 0.5 and add it to the integral of the function between 0.5 and 2 (making this value positive first).

$$\int_{-1}^{0.5}(2x^3-3x^2-11x+6)\,dx=\left[\frac{2x^4}{4}-\frac{3x^3}{3}-\frac{11x^2}{2}+6x\right]_{-1}^{0.5}$$
$$=\left[\frac{x^4}{2}-x^3-\frac{11}{2}x^2+6x\right]_{-1}^{0.5}$$
$$=\left(\frac{(0.5)^4}{2}-(0.5)^3-\frac{11}{2}(0.5)^2+6(0.5)\right)-\left(\frac{(-1)^4}{2}-(-1)^3-\frac{11}{2}(-1)^2+6(-1)\right)$$
$$=1.53125-(-10)=11.53125$$

So the area between –1 and 0.5 is 11.53125.

$$\int_{0.5}^{2}(2x^3-3x^2-11x+6)\,dx=\left[\frac{x^4}{2}-x^3-\frac{11}{2}x^2+6x\right]_{0.5}^{2}$$
$$=\left(\frac{(2)^4}{2}-(2)^3-\frac{11}{2}(2)^2+6(2)\right)-1.53125$$
$$=-10-1.53125=-11.53125$$

So the area between 0.5 and 2 is 11.53125.
So area = 11.53125 + 11.53125 = 23.0625
[6 marks available — 1 mark for considering the area above and below the x-axes separately, 1 mark for increasing the power of at least one term by 1, 1 mark for the correct integral, 1 mark for finding the area between –1 and 0.5, 1 mark for finding the area between 0.5 and 2, 1 mark for adding the areas to get the correct answer]
If you'd just integrated between –1 and 2, you'd have ended up with an answer of 0, as the areas cancel each other out. You had to realise you have to split the area into two parts and find each one separately.

Pages 36-38: Vectors

1 a) $\overrightarrow{AB}=\overrightarrow{OB}-\overrightarrow{OA}=(6\mathbf{i}-3\mathbf{j})-(4\mathbf{i}+2\mathbf{j})$ ***[1 mark]***
$=2\mathbf{i}-5\mathbf{j}$ ***[1 mark]***

b) Magnitude $=\sqrt{2^2+(-5)^2}$ ***[1 mark]***
$=\sqrt{29}$ ***[1 mark]***

2 a) $\overrightarrow{AB}=\overrightarrow{OB}-\overrightarrow{OA}=(5\mathbf{i}-3\mathbf{j})-(-\mathbf{i}+7\mathbf{j})=6\mathbf{i}-10\mathbf{j}$ ***[1 mark]***
$\overrightarrow{AM}=\frac{1}{2}\overrightarrow{AB}=3\mathbf{i}-5\mathbf{j}$ ***[1 mark]***
Magnitude $=\sqrt{3^2+(-5)^2}=\sqrt{34}$ ***[1 mark]***

b) $\overrightarrow{BD}=\overrightarrow{OD}-\overrightarrow{OB}\Rightarrow\overrightarrow{OD}=\overrightarrow{BD}+\overrightarrow{OB}$ ***[1 mark]***
$\overrightarrow{BD}=\overrightarrow{AC}=(8\mathbf{i}+4\mathbf{j})-(-\mathbf{i}+7\mathbf{j})=9\mathbf{i}-3\mathbf{j}$ ***[1 mark]***
So $\overrightarrow{OD}=(9\mathbf{i}-3\mathbf{j})+(5\mathbf{i}-3\mathbf{j})=14\mathbf{i}-6\mathbf{j}$ ***[1 mark]***

3 $\overrightarrow{AB}=\overrightarrow{OB}-\overrightarrow{OA}=\begin{pmatrix}-3\\5\end{pmatrix}-\begin{pmatrix}1\\4\end{pmatrix}=\begin{pmatrix}-4\\1\end{pmatrix}$ ***[1 mark]***
C is $\frac{1}{4}$ of the way along $\overrightarrow{AB}$, so $\overrightarrow{AC}=\frac{1}{4}\overrightarrow{AB}=\begin{pmatrix}-1\\\frac{1}{4}\end{pmatrix}$ ***[1 mark]***
$\overrightarrow{OC}=\overrightarrow{OA}+\overrightarrow{AC}=\begin{pmatrix}1\\4\end{pmatrix}+\begin{pmatrix}-1\\\frac{1}{4}\end{pmatrix}$ ***[1 mark]***
$=\begin{pmatrix}0\\\frac{17}{4}\end{pmatrix}$ ***[1 mark]***

4 $\mathbf{a}+\mathbf{b}+\mathbf{c}=(4\mathbf{i}+6\mathbf{j})+(\mathbf{i}-2\mathbf{j})+(-3\mathbf{j})=(5\mathbf{i}+\mathbf{j})$ ***[1 mark]***
magnitude $=\sqrt{5^2+1^2}$ ***[1 mark]***
$=\sqrt{26}$ ***[1 mark]***
(= 5.099... = 5.10 (3 s.f.))
$\theta=\tan^{-1}\left(\frac{1}{5}\right)$ ***[1 mark]***
= 11.309...° = 11.3° (3 s.f.) above **i** ***[1 mark]***

5 a)
Use trigonometry to find the horizontal and vertical components of the magnitude $4\sqrt{2}$ vector:
Horizontal component: $4\sqrt{2}\cos 315°=4\mathbf{i}$
Vertical component: $4\sqrt{2}\sin 315°=-4\mathbf{j}$
Resultant, $\mathbf{r}=7\mathbf{j}+(4\mathbf{i}-4\mathbf{j})$
So $\mathbf{r}=4\mathbf{i}+3\mathbf{j}$
[2 marks available — 1 mark for finding the horizontal and vertical components and 1 mark for correct expression for r]
Remember — angles are normally measured anticlockwise from the positive x-axis, so here, 360° – 45° = 315°

b) $|\mathbf{r}|=\sqrt{4^2+3^2}=5$
$\Rightarrow\mathbf{s}=7\mathbf{r}$
So $\mathbf{s}=7(4\mathbf{i}+3\mathbf{j})=28\mathbf{i}+21\mathbf{j}$
[3 marks available — 1 mark for finding magnitude of r, 1 mark for correct working to find s, 1 mark for correct expression for s]

6 a)

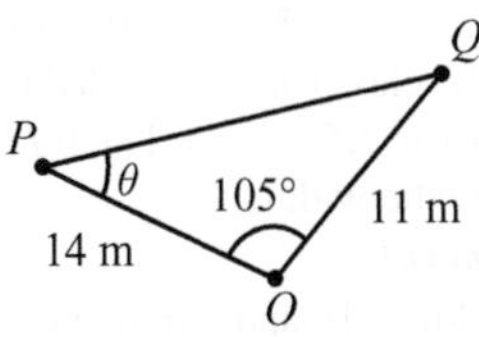

Using the cosine rule:
$PQ^2=14^2+11^2-(2\times14\times11)\cos 105°$
$PQ^2=396.716...$
$\Rightarrow PQ=19.917...=19.9$ m (3 s.f.)
[2 marks available — 1 mark for correct use of cosine rule, 1 mark for correct value of PQ]

b) Using the sine rule:
$\frac{\sin 105°}{19.917...}=\frac{\sin\theta}{11}$
$\Rightarrow\sin\theta=11\times\frac{\sin 105°}{19.917...}=0.533...$
$\Rightarrow\theta=\sin^{-1}(0.533...)$
$=32.239...°=32.2°$ (3 s.f.)
[2 marks available — 1 mark for correct use of sine rule, 1 mark for correct value for angle]

7 $\overrightarrow{AB}=(\mathbf{i}-4\mathbf{j})-(5\mathbf{i}+2\mathbf{j})=(-4\mathbf{i}-6\mathbf{j})$ m ***[1 mark]***
$\overrightarrow{AC}=(19\mathbf{i}+2\mathbf{j})-(5\mathbf{i}+2\mathbf{j})=14\mathbf{i}$ m ***[1 mark]***
The perimeter of the parallelogram is $2|\overrightarrow{AB}|+2|\overrightarrow{AC}|$ ***[1 mark]***
This is because length AC = BD and AB = CD
$|\overrightarrow{AB}|=\sqrt{(-4)^2+(-6)^2}=\sqrt{52}$ m ***[1 mark]***
$|\overrightarrow{AC}|=14$ m ***[1 mark]***
So perimeter $=(28+2\sqrt{52})$ m ***[1 mark]***
$=(28+4\sqrt{13})$ m
Make sure to leave the surd in your answer — the question asks for the exact length.

8 $\overrightarrow{PR}=\overrightarrow{PQ}+\overrightarrow{QR}=\begin{pmatrix}2\\-9\end{pmatrix}+\begin{pmatrix}14\\6\end{pmatrix}=\begin{pmatrix}16\\-3\end{pmatrix}$ ***[1 mark]***
$|\overrightarrow{PQ}|=\sqrt{2^2+(-9)^2}=\sqrt{85}$
$|\overrightarrow{QR}|=\sqrt{14^2+6^2}=\sqrt{232}$
$|\overrightarrow{PR}|=\sqrt{16^2+(-3)^2}=\sqrt{265}$
[1 mark for attempting to find magnitudes using Pythagoras, 1 mark for all 3 magnitudes correct]
Find angle QPR using the cosine rule:
$\cos QPR=\frac{85+265-232}{2\times\sqrt{85}\times\sqrt{265}}=0.3931...$ ***[1 mark]***
angle $QPR=\cos^{-1}0.3931$
$=66.851...°=66.9°$ (3 s.f.) ***[1 mark]***
There's more than one way to do this question — as long as you show all your working and end up with the correct final answer, you'll get the marks.

Section Two — Statistics

Pages 39-45: Data Presentation and Interpretation

1 a) mean = $\frac{\sum x}{n} = \frac{500}{10} = 50$ ***[1 mark]***

variance = $\frac{\sum x^2}{10} - 50^2 = \frac{25\,622}{10} - 2500$ ***[1 mark]*** $= 62.2$

So standard deviation = $\sqrt{62.2} = 7.89$ ***[1 mark]***

b) (i) The mean will be unchanged ***[1 mark]***, because the new value is equal to the original mean ***[1 mark]***.

(ii) The standard deviation will decrease ***[1 mark]***. This is because the standard deviation measures the deviation of values from the mean. So by adding a new value that's equal to the mean, you're not adding to the total deviation from the mean, but as you have an extra reading, you now have to divide by 11 (not 10) when you work out the variance ***[1 mark]***.

2 The area of the $24.0 \le t < 25.0$ bar is $0.5 \times 4 = 2$ cm^2.
The frequency of the $24.0 \le t < 25.0$ class is 8,
so 1 cm^2 = $8 \div 2 = 4$ days ***[1 mark]***.
The frequency of the $25.0 \le t < 27.5$ class is also 8, so it must also have an area of 2 cm^2. The class width of the $24.0 \le t < 25.0$ class is 1 °C, and the width for this bar is 0.5 cm, so the width of the bar (in cm) is the width of the class (in °C) divided by 2.
The width of the $25.0 \le t < 27.5$ bar is $2.5 \div 2 = 1.25$ cm ***[1 mark]*** and its height is the area divided by the width,
so height = $2 \div 1.25 = 1.6$ cm ***[1 mark]***.

3 a) The $0 \le b < 10$ class has a width of 10 and a frequency of 12, so its frequency density is $12 \div 10 = 1.2$. Use this to label the vertical axis and draw the missing bars:
$10 \le b < 15$ class: frequency density = $23 \div 5 = 4.6$
$25 \le b < 35$ class: frequency density = $6 \div 10 = 0.6$

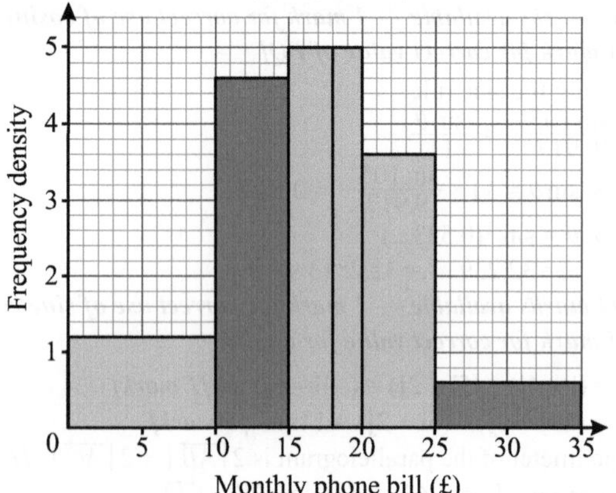

Then use the frequency density axis and the formula
frequency = frequency density × class width
to work out the missing values in the table:

Monthly phone bill, £b	Frequency
$0 \le b < 10$	12
$10 \le b < 15$	23
$15 \le b < 18$	$5 \times 3 = 15$
$18 \le b < 20$	$5 \times 2 = 10$
$20 \le b < 25$	18
$25 \le b < 35$	6

[4 marks available — 1 mark for using the frequency density and the 0 ≤ b < 10 bar or the 20 ≤ b < 25 bar to work out the scale on the vertical axis, 1 mark for both bars correct, 1 mark for using frequency = frequency density × class width, 1 mark for both entries in table correct]

b) £12.50 is halfway through the $10 \le b < 15$ class, so there are approximately $23 \div 2 = 11.5$ students that pay between £12.50 and £15. £17.50 is $\frac{5}{6}$ of the way through the $15 \le b < 18$ class, so there are $\frac{5}{6} \times 15 = 12.5$ students that pay between £15 and £17.50. So an estimate for the number of students that have a monthly phone bill of between £12.50 and £17.50 is $11.5 + 12.5 = 24$.
[2 marks available — 1 mark for a correct method, 1 mark for the correct answer]

c) Add columns to the table showing the class midpoint and the midpoint × frequency:

Monthly phone bill, £b	Frequency, f	Class midpoint, x	$f \times x$
$0 \le b < 10$	12	5	60
$10 \le b < 15$	23	12.5	287.5
$15 \le b < 18$	15	16.5	247.5
$18 \le b < 20$	10	19	190
$20 \le b < 25$	18	22.5	405
$25 \le b < 35$	6	30	180

There are $12 + 23 + 15 + 10 + 18 + 6 = 84$ students in total, and $\sum fx = 60 + 287.5 + 247.5 + 190 + 405 + 180 = 1370$.

So mean = $\frac{\sum fx}{\sum f} = \frac{1370}{84} = 16.309... = £16.31$ to 2 d.p.

[3 marks available — 1 mark for use of class midpoints, 1 mark for $\sum fx$, 1 mark for the correct answer]

d) Add columns for x^2 and fx^2:

Monthly phone bill, £b	Frequency, f	x^2	$f \times x^2$
$0 \le b < 10$	12	25	300
$10 \le b < 15$	23	156.25	3593.75
$15 \le b < 18$	15	272.25	4083.75
$18 \le b < 20$	10	361	3610
$20 \le b < 25$	18	506.25	9112.5
$25 \le b < 35$	6	900	5400

$\sum fx^2 = 26\,100$

Standard deviation = $\sqrt{\frac{\sum fx^2}{\sum f} - \bar{x}^2} = \sqrt{\frac{26\,100}{84} - 16.309...^2}$

$= 6.68683... = £6.69$ (2 d.p.)

[3 marks available — 1 mark for calculating $\sum fx^2$, 1 mark for substituting into the formula for standard deviation, 1 mark for the correct answer]

e) The 20th percentile is in the $\frac{20}{100} \times 84 = 16.8 = 17$th position.
This lies in the class $10 \le b < 15$.
So 20th percentile = $10 + 5 \times \frac{17 - 12}{23} = 10 + 1.0869...$
$= £11.09$ (2 d.p.)

[3 marks available — 1 mark for calculating the position of the 20th percentile, 1 mark for substituting into the formula for linear interpolation, 1 mark for the correct answer]

4 a) There are $5 + 12 + 10 + 3 = 30$ giraffes in total.
The median is in position $30 \div 2 = 15$, which lies in the interval $3 < h \le 4$. This class has 12 giraffes, and width 1 m.

So median = $3 + \left(1 \times \frac{15 - 5}{12}\right) = 3 + 0.833... = 3.83$ m (3 s.f.)

[3 marks available — 1 mark for finding the class the median lies in, 1 mark for a correct method to find the median, 1 mark for the correct answer]

b)

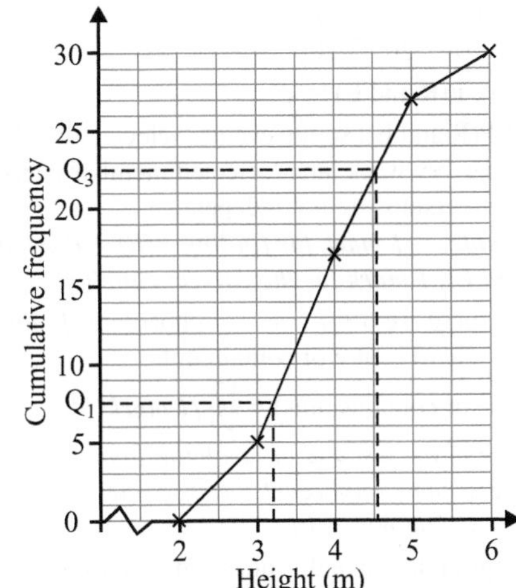

[1 mark for all points plotted correctly and 1 mark for a correctly drawn line or curve]

c) Q_1 position is $30 \div 4 = 7.5$.
Q_3 position is $(3 \times 30) \div 4 = 22.5$.
So, using the graph (see above), $Q_1 \approx 3.2$ m ***[1 mark]*** and $Q_3 \approx 4.55$ m ***[1 mark]***.
The interquartile range is $4.55 - 3.2 = 1.35$ m ***[1 mark]***.

d) The giraffes in the zoo are generally taller, as they have a higher median ***[1 mark]***. Two giraffes in the game reserve have extreme heights that are outliers, but there are no outliers in the zoo ***[1 mark]***. The two populations seem similarly varied, since they have similar ranges (the range for the zoo is 2.86 m and, ignoring the outliers, the range for the game reserve is 2.8 m), although the IQR for the giraffes in the zoo is slightly greater than for the giraffes in the game reserve ***[1 mark]***.

5 a) The ordered list of the 12 data points is:
3.8, 4.1, 4.2, 4.6, 4.9, 5.5, 5.8, 5.9, 6.0, 6.2, 6.4, 9.1.
n is even and $\frac{n}{2} = 6$, so take the average of the 6th and 7th values. So the median (Q_2) is:
$\frac{1}{2}(5.5 + 5.8) = 5.65$, which represents £5650 ***[1 mark]***.
Since $12 \div 4 = 3$, the lower quartile is the average of the 3rd and 4th values. So the lower quartile (Q_1) is:
$\frac{1}{2}(4.2 + 4.6) = 4.4$, which represents £4400 ***[1 mark]***.
Since $12 \div 4 \times 3 = 9$, the upper quartile is the average of the 9th and 10th values. So the upper quartile (Q_3) is:
$\frac{1}{2}(6.0 + 6.2) = 6.1$, which represents £6100 ***[1 mark]***.

b) The lower fence is given by:
$Q_1 - 1.5 \times (Q_3 - Q_1) = 4.4 - 1.5 \times (6.1 - 4.4) = 1.85$.
So there are no outliers below the lower fence ***[1 mark]***.
The upper fence is given by:
$Q_3 + 1.5 \times (Q_3 - Q_1) = 6.1 + 1.5 \times (6.1 - 4.4) = 8.65$.
So there is one outlier — the value of 9.1 ***[1 mark]***.

c) E.g. the manager should not include this outlier in his analysis as it might be caused by an outside factor, e.g. Christmas, so including it would not accurately reflect normal sales. / The manager should include this outlier in his analysis as it accurately reflects actual sales for this period, even if one week was unusually high. ***[1 mark for a sensible comment]***

d)

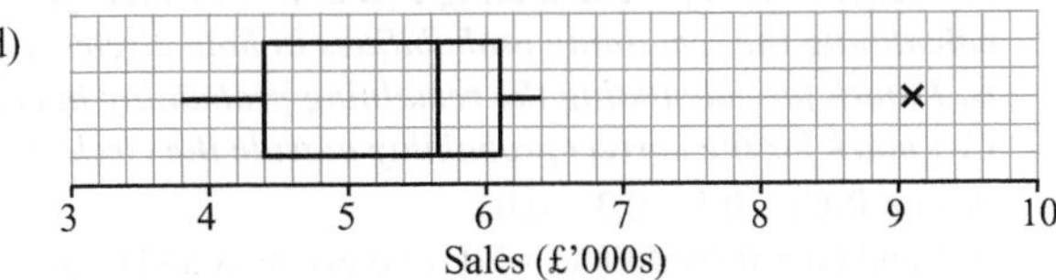

[2 marks available — 1 mark for drawing the box correctly, 1 mark for the whiskers and outlier drawn correctly]

e) E.g. the mean and standard deviation are affected by outliers, whereas the median and IQR are not. So as this set of data includes an outlier, the median and IQR are more useful. / The mean and standard deviation take into account all data values, so are more useful as they reflect the actual data.
[2 marks available — 1 mark for stating which values are more useful, 1 mark for a sensible explanation]

6 a) Town A = Hurn — the data points are generally closer together, which means a smaller standard deviation ***[1 mark]***.
Town B = Heathrow — the line for Town B has more variation, which means a larger standard deviation ***[1 mark]***.

b) Hurn (Town A):
Outliers are below $7.73 - (3 \times 7.85) = -15.82$ mm (impossible) or above $7.73 + (3 \times 7.85) = 31.28$ mm. The highest value for Hurn is roughly 25 mm, so there are no outliers for Hurn ***[1 mark]***.
Heathrow (Town B):
Outliers are below $8.31 - (3 \times 13.2) = -31.29$ mm (impossible) or above $8.31 + (3 \times 13.2) = 47.91$ mm. There is one value above this point for Heathrow, so the point for the 9th October (roughly 53 mm) is an outlier and should be circled ***[1 mark]***.
If you'd made a mistake in part a) and got the towns the wrong way round, you'd still get the marks for doing the calculations for the outliers.

c) E.g. On this day, there was also a peak in rainfall for Town A, so there appears to have been unusually heavy rainfall on that day ***[1 mark for a sensible comment]***.
Although outliers can be down to recording errors, in this case it wouldn't appear to be an error as it corresponds to a peak in rainfall in the other town.

7 Mean of $q = \frac{104}{10} = 10.4$ hPa ***[1 mark]***
So mean of $p = (2 \times 10.4) + 1000 = 1020.8$ hPa ***[1 mark]***
Standard deviation of $q = \sqrt{\frac{1492}{10} - 10.4^2} = 6.406...$ hPa ***[1 mark]***
So standard deviation of $p = 2 \times 6.406... = 12.8$ hPa (3 s.f.) ***[1 mark]***
Remember, adding or subtracting a value when coding has no effect on the standard deviation (but multiplying or dividing will affect it).

8 a) E.g. The diagram does show negative correlation overall, so Jiao's claim seems reasonable ***[1 mark]***. However, the data is clearly grouped into two clusters (possibly one for rural locations and one for urban locations), with little correlation within each cluster ***[1 mark]***.

b) E.g. Although correlation doesn't necessarily mean causation, in this case it seems reasonable that Killian is correct, as a habitat where reindeer thrive (e.g. a woodland) will not be densely populated — if it were, it would no longer be woodland so the deer population would decrease. / No, Killian is not likely to be correct — there could be a third factor affecting both populations (e.g. climate — reindeer prefer a colder climate, whereas population density for people is higher in more temperate regions.) ***[1 mark for a suitable statement, 1 mark for a sensible explanation]***

9 a)

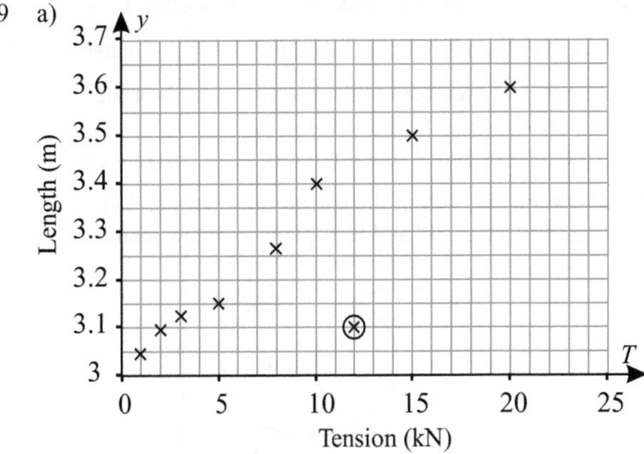

[2 marks for all points correctly plotted, or 1 mark if at least 4 points are correctly plotted]

b) See graph above ***[1 mark for correct point circled]***

c) Strong positive correlation — as the tension (T) increases, the length of the cable (y) also increases ***[1 mark]***.

d) a represents the length of the cable when it is not under tension, so when $T = 0$, the cable is 3 m long ***[1 mark]***.
b represents the extension of the cable, so for every 1 kN increase in tension, the length of the cable increases by 0.03 m ***[1 mark]***.

e) $y = 3 + 0.03T$, so when $T = 30$,
$y = 3 + 0.03 \times 30 = 3.9$ m ***[1 mark]***

f) This estimate may be unreliable as it involves extrapolating beyond the range of the experimental data ***[1 mark]***.

Pages 46-49: Probability

1 a) P(neither is a tenor) = P(not tenor) × P(not tenor)
$= (1 - 0.22) \times (1 - 0.22) = 0.78 \times 0.78 = 0.6084$
[2 marks available — 1 mark for a correct method, 1 mark for the correct answer]

b) P(same type of voice) = P(S, S) + P(A, A) + P(T, T) + P(B, B)
$= (0.36 \times 0.36) + (0.27 \times 0.27) + (0.22 \times 0.22) + (0.15 \times 0.15)$
$= 0.1296 + 0.0729 + 0.0484 + 0.0225 = 0.2734$
[3 marks available — 1 mark for finding the correct products, 1 mark for adding the probabilities, 1 mark for the correct answer]

2 a) Draw a tree diagram. Let C = 'pick a heart from the complete pack':

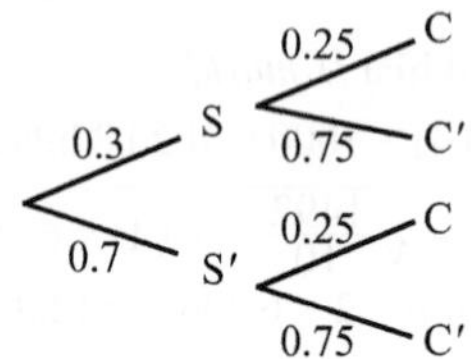

You want to find P(S or C). Now, either at least one of the cards is a heart or neither of them are,
so P(S or C) = 1 – P(S' and C') ***[1 mark]***
$= 1 - (0.7 \times 0.75) = 1 - 0.525 = 0.475$ ***[1 mark]***

b) The only results that have exactly one heart card picked are (S and C') and (S' and C).
P(S and C') = 0.3 × 0.75 = 0.225 and
P(S' and C) = 0.7 × 0.25 = 0.175
[1 mark for at least one correct product]
so P(exactly one card is a heart) = 0.225 + 0.175 ***[1 mark]***
= 0.4 ***[1 mark]***

3 a) The number of people who do not play badminton is
$5 + 3 + 4 + 4 = 16$, so P(does not play badminton) = $\frac{16}{30}$ ***[1 mark]***
The number of people who do archery or chess is
$5 + 2 + 2 + 3 + 1 + 4 = 17$, so P(does archery or chess) = $\frac{17}{30}$ ***[1 mark]***.
Riyad is not correct since P(does archery or chess) = $\frac{17}{30}$ is greater than P(does not play badminton) = $\frac{16}{30}$ ***[1 mark]***.

b) The number of members of the badminton club or the chess club but not both is $9 + 2 + 3 + 4 = 18$,
so P(member of B or C but not both) = $\frac{18}{30} = \frac{3}{5}$ ***[1 mark]***

4 a) Draw a Venn diagram of the known information. Let E = 'goes every week' and R = 'plans to renew membership':

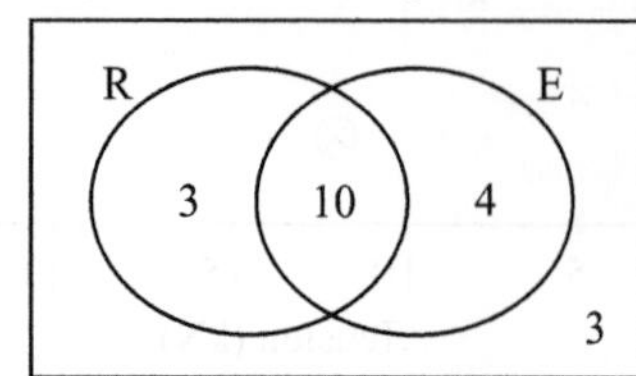

Using the Venn diagram, the number of people that go every week and plan to renew their membership is shown in the intersection. So 10 people go every week and plan to renew their membership, so P(R and E) = $\frac{10}{20} = \frac{1}{2}$
[2 marks available — 1 mark for a correct method, 1 mark for the correct answer]

b) $P(R) \times P(E) = \frac{13}{20} \times \frac{14}{20} = \frac{91}{200}$
But from part a), P(R and E) = $\frac{1}{2}$
P(R) × P(E) ≠ P(R and E), so the events 'selected member goes to the club every week' and 'selected member plans to renew their membership' are not independent.
[2 marks available — 1 mark for finding P(R) × P(E) and stating P(R and E), 1 mark for the correct conclusion]

5 a) From the table, there are $6 + 7 + 4 = 17$ chocolates ***[1 mark]*** that either have a hard centre or contain nuts.
So P(hard centre or contains nuts) = $\frac{17}{20}$ ***[1 mark]***
Be careful here — if you just add up the totals from the 'nuts' row and 'hard centre' column, you'll count the chocolates that have a hard centre and contain nuts twice.

b) Draw a tree diagram to make this question easier (you only need to fill in the branches you're going to use):

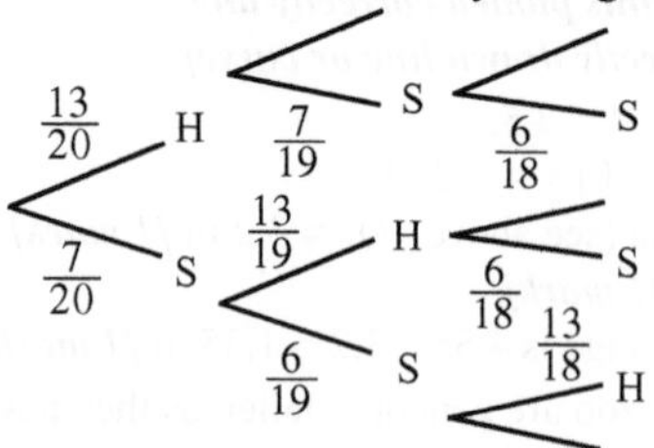

P(Pick hard centre first) =
$\frac{13}{20} \times \frac{7}{19} \times \frac{6}{18} = \frac{546}{6840} = \frac{91}{1140}$ ***[1 mark]***
P(Pick hard centre second) = $\frac{91}{1140}$
P(Pick hard centre third) = $\frac{91}{1140}$
So P(pick exactly one hard centre) = $3 \times \frac{91}{1140}$ ***[1 mark]***
$= \frac{91}{380}$ or 0.239 (3 s.f.) ***[1 mark]***

6 As L and M are independent, P(L and M) = P(L) × P(M) ***[1 mark]***
P(L) = 0.1 + 0.4 = 0.5 and P(M) = $2x + 0.4$ ***[1 mark]***
P(L and M) = 0.4 = 0.5 × $(2x + 0.4) = x + 0.2 \Rightarrow x = 0.2$ ***[1 mark]***
So this means P(L or M) = 0.1 + 0.4 + 0.4 = 0.9
⇒ P(L' and M') = 1 – 0.9 = 0.1 ***[1 mark]***

7 a) A and B are mutually exclusive, so P(A and B) = 0.
This means the circles don't intersect.
B and C are independent, so
P(B and C) = P(B) × (P(C) = 0.4 × 0.3 = 0.12
P(A and C) = 0.06
Use this to fill in the Venn diagram:

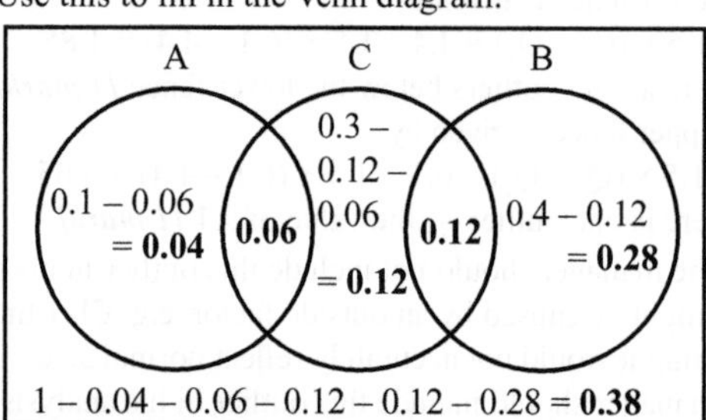

[5 marks available — 1 mark for circles overlapping correctly, 1 mark for calculating P(B and C), 1 mark for calculating the remaining probabilities in both circles A and B, 1 mark for calculating the remaining probability in circle C, 1 mark for the correct probability outside the circles]

b) P(A) × P(C) = 0.1 × 0.3 = 0.03
P(A and C) = 0.06 ≠ P(A) × P(C), so events A and C are not independent.
[2 marks available — 1 mark for finding P(A) × P(C) and stating P(A and C), 1 mark for the correct conclusion]

c) P(B or C not both) = 0.28 + 0.12 + 0.06 = 0.46 ***[1 mark]***

d) P(not A and not B) = 0.12 + 0.38 = 0.5 ***[1 mark]***

Pages 50-52: Statistical Distributions

1 a) The total probability must be 1, so go through all the possible values of x and add the probabilities:

$$\frac{k}{6}+\frac{2k}{6}+\frac{3k}{6}+\frac{3k}{6}+\frac{2k}{6}+\frac{k}{6}=\frac{12k}{6}=2k$$ ***[1 mark].***

This must equal 1, so k must be $\frac{1}{2}$ ***[1 mark].***

b) $P(1 < X \leq 4) = P(X = 2) + P(X = 3) + P(X = 4)$ ***[1 mark]***

$= \frac{1}{6}+\frac{1}{4}+\frac{1}{4}=\frac{2}{3}$ ***[1 mark]***

c) Every value of y has the same probability, and there are no other possible values as these add up to 1, so Y follows a discrete uniform distribution ***[1 mark].***

2 Using $\sum_{\text{all } x} P(X = x) = 1$:

$0.4 + 0.3 + a + b = 1$ ***[1 mark]*** $\Rightarrow 0.7 + a + b = 1 \Rightarrow a + b = 0.3$

A contestant is twice as likely to be awarded 2 points as 3 points, so you also know that $a = 2b$. Substitute this in the above to get:

$2b + b = 0.3 \Rightarrow 3b = 0.3 \Rightarrow b = 0.1$ and $a = 2b = 0.2$

[1 mark for both correct]

P(one contestant scores 2 and the other scores 3)

= P(1st scores 2 and 2nd scores 3 or 1st scores 3 and 2nd scores 2)

$= (0.2 \times 0.1) + (0.1 \times 0.2)$ ***[1 mark]***

$= 0.04$ ***[1 mark]***

3 a) The probability of getting 3 heads is:

$\frac{1}{2}\times\frac{1}{2}\times\frac{1}{2}=\frac{1}{8}$

The probability of getting 2 heads is: $3\times\frac{1}{2}\times\frac{1}{2}\times\frac{1}{2}=\frac{3}{8}$

(multiply by 3 because any of the three coins could be the tail — the order in which the heads and the tail occur isn't important).

The probability of getting 1 or 0 heads

$= 1 - P(\text{2 heads}) - P(\text{3 heads}) = 1-\frac{3}{8}-\frac{1}{8}=\frac{1}{2}$

Hence the probability distribution of X is:

x	20p	10p	nothing
$P(X = x)$	$\frac{1}{8}$	$\frac{3}{8}$	$\frac{1}{2}$

[3 marks for a completely correct table, otherwise 1 mark for drawing a table with the correct values of x and 1 mark for any one correct probability]

b) You need the probability that the player wins more than 20p over the two games. There are three ways to do this: win 20p and 10p, win 10p and 20p, or win 20p and 20p.

So P(profit over 2 games)

$=\left(\frac{1}{8}\times\frac{3}{8}\right)+\left(\frac{3}{8}\times\frac{1}{8}\right)+\left(\frac{1}{8}\times\frac{1}{8}\right)$ ***[1 mark]***

$=\frac{3}{64}+\frac{3}{64}+\frac{1}{64}=\frac{7}{64}$ ***[1 mark]***

4 a) 1) The probability P(chocolate bar contains a golden ticket) must be constant.

2) The trials must be independent (i.e. whether or not a chocolate bar contains a golden ticket must be independent of other chocolate bars).

[1 mark for each correct condition]

b) $P(X > 1) = 1 - P(X \leq 1)$ ***[1 mark]***

$= 1 - 0.3991 = 0.6009$ (4 d.p.) ***[1 mark].***

c) If more than 35 bars do not contain a golden ticket, then the student finds 4 or fewer golden tickets.

So find $P(X \leq 4)$ ***[1 mark]*** $= 0.9520$ (4 d.p.) ***[1 mark]***

5 a) Let the random variable X represent the number of cars in the sample of 20 that develop the rattle.

Then $X \sim B(20, 0.65)$ ***[1 mark],***

and you need to find $P(12 \leq X < 15)$.

$P(12 \leq X < 15) = P(X \leq 14) - P(X \leq 11)$

$= 0.7546... - 0.2376...$ ***[1 mark for either]***

$= 0.5170$ (4 d.p.) ***[1 mark]***

b) $P(X > 10) = 1 - P(X \leq 10)$ ***[1 mark]***

$= 1 - 0.1217...$

$= 0.8782$ (4 d.p.) ***[1 mark].***

c) The probability of more than half of a sample of 20 cars having the rattle is 0.8782 (from part b).

Let Q be the number of samples containing more than 10 rattling cars. Then $Q \sim B(5, 0.8782)$ ***[1 mark].***

$P(Q = 3) = \binom{5}{3}\times 0.8782^3\times(1-0.8782)^2$ ***[1 mark]***

$= 0.1005$ (to 4 d.p.) ***[1 mark]***

You could use your calculator's binomial distribution functions to find P(Q = 3).

6 a) Let X be the number of customers in the sample of 20 who chose a sugar cone. Then $X \sim B(n, p)$ where $n = 20$, but you need to find p (the probability of choosing a sugar cone).

p is equal to the proportion of customers on the 1st July who chose a sugar cone, so:

$p = \frac{880}{1100} = 0.8$ ***[1 mark],*** so $X \sim B(20, 0.8)$ ***[1 mark]***

$P(X = 12) = \binom{20}{12} \times 0.8^{12} \times 0.2^8 = 0.0222$ (4 d.p.) ***[1 mark]***

Or you could use your calculator's binomial distribution functions here.

b) Let Y be the number of customers who choose at least one scoop of chocolate ice cream.

Then $Y \sim B(75, 0.42)$ ***[1 mark].***

$P(Y > 30) = 1 - P(Y \leq 30)$ ***[1 mark]***

$= 1 - 0.4099... = 0.5901$ (4 d.p.) ***[1 mark]***

You need to use your calculator c.d.f. function for this one.

c) E.g. it is not reasonable to assume that the customers' choices of ice cream are independent of each other, e.g. one person might see another person with a chocolate ice cream and decide to get one too, so the 75 trials are not independent. / The probability of choosing chocolate ice cream may not be constant, e.g. it might run out. Therefore the model may not be valid ***[1 mark for a sensible comment].***

Pages 53-56: Statistical Hypothesis Testing

1 a) If the whole population was tested, every camera would be destroyed by water and there would be none left to sell ***[1 mark].***

b) E.g. match each camera's product code to a unique 3-digit number between 001 and 300 ***[1 mark].*** Generate a sequence of random 3-digit numbers (e.g. using a calculator or random number table), ignoring numbers outside the range 001-300 and any repeats ***[1 mark]*** until 15 different numbers between 001 and 300 are obtained. Select the 15 cameras with the corresponding numbers ***[1 mark].***

2 a) All the pupils in her school ***[1 mark].***

b) One of the following: the data would be an accurate representation of the population / the data wouldn't be affected by sampling bias / the data wouldn't be affected by natural variability of samples. ***[1 mark]***

c) Opportunity (or convenience) sampling ***[1 mark]***

d) It is unlikely to be representative because, e.g: the students in the sample are all in the same age group, so won't represent the whole school / GCSE music students might be biased towards certain types of music / groups of friends in the music class might like the same type of music / all the pupils who aren't in Josie's GCSE music class are excluded from the sample.

[1 mark for a sensible explanation]

3 a) Total population of working adults
$= 1200 + 2100 + 3500 + 3200 + 1500 = 11\,500$

18-27 years: $\frac{1200}{11\,500} \times 50 = 5.217... \approx 5$

28-37 years: $\frac{2100}{11\,500} \times 50 = 9.130... \approx 9$

38-47 years: $\frac{3500}{11\,500} \times 50 = 15.217... \approx 15$

48-57 years: $\frac{3200}{11\,500} \times 50 = 13.913... \approx 14$

Over 57 years: $\frac{1500}{11\,500} \times 50 = 6.521... \approx 7$

[4 marks available — 1 mark for the correct method, 1 mark for using the correct total in the calculations, 1 mark for at least 2 correct values, 1 mark for all 5 correct values]

b) Jamila can't use her data to draw conclusions about the whole population because, e.g: she only has data for one small town in one location / the types of employment in her town might not be representative of the whole of the UK / the age distribution of the working adults in Jamila's town might not be representative of the whole of the UK.
[1 mark for a sensible explanation]

4 a) If p = proportion of residents against the plan, then H_0: $p = 0.1$ and H_1: $p > 0.1$ ***[1 mark]***.

b) Let X = number of sampled residents who are against the plan. Under H_0, $X \sim B(50, 0.1)$ ***[1 mark]***.
Find the probability of a value of X at least as extreme as the observed value (the p-value):
$P(X \geq 6) = 1 - P(X < 6) = 1 - P(X \leq 5)$ ***[1 mark]***
$= 1 - 0.6161... = 0.3839$ (4 d.p.) ***[1 mark]***
$0.3839 > 0.01$ ***[1 mark]***, so the result is not significant.
There is insufficient evidence at the 1% level of significance to reject H_0 in favour of the campaigners' claim that the proportion has increased ***[1 mark]***.

5 a) If p = proportion of students who have done judo for at least two years, then H_0: $p = 0.2$ and H_1: $p \neq 0.2$ ***[1 mark for both]***.

b) Let X = number of students in the sample of 20 who have done judo for at least two years. Under H_0, $X \sim B(20, 0.2)$.
It's a two-tailed test, so the critical region is split into two, with a probability of ≤ 0.025 in each tail.
For the lower tail: $P(X \leq 0) = 0.0115$ and $P(X \leq 1) = 0.0692$
For the upper tail:
$P(X \geq 9) = 1 - 0.9900 = 0.0100$ and
$P(X \geq 8) = 1 - 0.9679 = 0.0321$
So CR is $X = 0$ or $X \geq 9$.
[3 marks available — 1 mark for finding probabilities using the correct distribution, 1 mark for the correct lower limit and 1 mark for the correct upper limit]
You might be able to use your calculator to generate a table of values for the distribution.

c) Actual significance level $= P(X = 0) + P(X \geq 9)$
$= 0.0115 + 0.0100 = 0.0215$ or 2.15% ***[1 mark]***

d) 7 does not lie in the critical region, so do not reject H_0 ***[1 mark]***. There is insufficient evidence at the 5% level to suggest that the proportion who have done judo for at least two years has changed ***[1 mark]***.

e) E.g. The binomial model is unlikely to be valid since the sample members have not been selected randomly, which means they are unlikely to be independent. All the sample members will attend either a 'basic' class or an 'advanced' class, so using a binomial model with $p = 0.2$ is unlikely to be valid.
[2 marks for saying that the model is unlikely to be valid with a sensible explanation of why, otherwise 1 mark for making one sensible comment]

6 a) If p = proportion of days with a maximum temperature of less than 19 °C, then H_0: $p = 0.5$ and H_1: $p \neq 0.5$ ***[1 mark]***.
Let X = number of sampled days with a maximum temperature of less than 19 °C. Under H_0, $X \sim B(30, 0.5)$. ***[1 mark]***
Under H_0, you'd expect there to be $30 \times 0.5 = 15$ days with a maximum temperature of less than 19 °C. The observed value of 14 is less than this, so you're interested in the lower tail.
Find the p-value of obtaining 14 or less:
$P(X \leq 14) = 0.4278$ (4 d.p.) ***[1 mark]***
It's a two-tailed test, so there's a probability of 0.05 in each tail.
$0.4278 > 0.05$ ***[1 mark]***, so the result is not significant ***[1 mark]***.
There is insufficient evidence at the 10% level to suggest that the proportion of days with a maximum temperature of less than 19 °C was different for 2015 ***[1 mark]***.
If you prefer, you can carry out the test in part b) by finding the critical region. You get a critical region of $X \leq 10$ or $X \geq 20$.

b) E.g. the temperatures vary quite a lot for the different months, so using simple random sampling you might just happen to select a large proportion of days with colder/hotter temperatures. The data is listed in time order, so a systematic sample should include a good spread of days from each month, including colder and hotter temperatures.
[1 mark for a sensible reason]

7 a) If p = proportion of gym members who use the pool, then H_0: $p = 0.45$ and H_1: $p < 0.45$ ***[1 mark]***.
Let X = number of people in sample of 16 who use the pool.
Under H_0, $X \sim B(16, 0.45)$ ***[1 mark]***.
Find the p-value of obtaining a value of X at least as extreme as the observed value, using your calculator:
$P(X \leq 3) = 0.0281$ (4 d.p.) ***[1 mark]***
$0.0281 < 0.05$ ***[1 mark]***, so the result is significant ***[1 mark]***.
There is evidence at the 5% level of significance to suggest that the popularity of the pool has decreased ***[1 mark]***.

b) For the second test:
Let X be the number of people in a sample of 50 who use the pool. Then under H_0, $X \sim B(50, 0.45)$ ***[1 mark]***.
The result of the test is that the manager rejects H_0, so you're looking for the biggest possible value x such that $P(X \leq x) \leq 0.05$.
Using the binomial tables, $P(X \leq 16) = 0.0427$ ***[1 mark]*** and $P(X \leq 17) = 0.0765$ ***[1 mark]***.
So the maximum possible number in the sample who use the pool is 16 ***[1 mark]***.
You might be able to use your calculator to generate a table of values for the distribution, rather than using the binomial tables.

Section Three — Mechanics

Pages 57-60: Kinematics

1 a) $u = 15$, $v = 40$, $a = ?$, $t = 4$, $s = ?$
You need to find a, so use '$v = u + at$':
$$a = \frac{v - u}{t} = \frac{40 - 15}{4} = 6.25 \text{ ms}^{-2}$$
[2 marks available — 1 mark for using '$v = u + at$' or equivalent and 1 mark for correct value of a]

b) $u = 40$, $v = 26$, $a = -2.8$, $t = ?$, $s = ?$
You need t, so it's '$v = u + at$'. Rearrange and substitute:
$$t = \frac{v - u}{a} = \frac{26 - 40}{-2.8} = 5 \text{ s}$$
[2 marks available — 1 mark for using '$v = u + at$' or equivalent and 1 mark for correct value of a]

c) Using '$s = \frac{1}{2}(u + v)t$':
A to B: $s = \frac{1}{2}(u + v)t = \frac{1}{2}(15 + 40) \times 4 = 110$ m
B to C: $s = \frac{1}{2}(u + v)t = \frac{1}{2}(40 + 26) \times 5 = 165$ m
$AC = 275$ m
[3 marks available — 1 mark for using '$s = \frac{1}{2}(u + v)t$' or equivalent, 1 mark for either intermediate distance correct, 1 mark for the correct value of AC]

2 a)

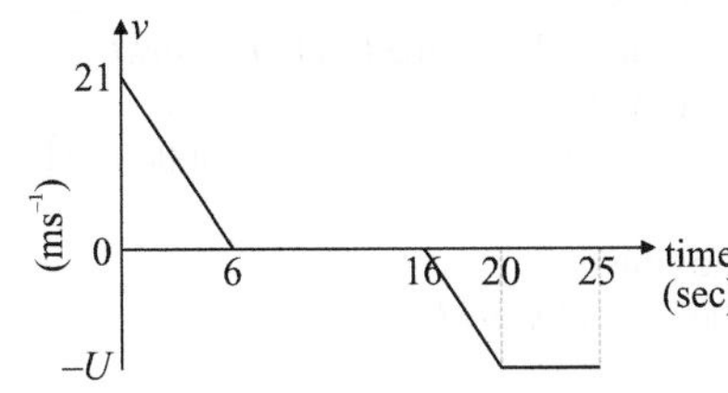

[3 marks available — 1 mark for the correct shape, 1 mark for the correct times, 1 mark for the correct velocities]

b) Gradient of graph while van is decelerating $= -\frac{21}{6} = -3.5$

So the van decelerates at a rate of 3.5 ms^{-2}

[2 marks available — 1 mark for using gradient = acceleration, 1 mark for correct value of deceleration]

You could also do this using $v = u + at$ with $v = 0$, $u = 21$ and $t = 6$.

c) Area under graph = distance

Area under graph $= \frac{21 \times 6}{2} + \frac{U \times 4}{2} + (U \times 5) = 63 + 7U$

$63 + 7U = 161 \Rightarrow U = 98 \div 7 = 14$ ms^{-1}

[2 marks available — 1 mark for using area under graph = distance, 1 mark for correct value of U]

d) Displacement = (distance travelled in positive direction) – (distance travelled in negative direction)

Displacement $= \frac{21 \times 6}{2} - \left[\frac{U \times 4}{2} + (U \times 5)\right]$

$= 63 - 7U = 63 - 7(14) = -35$ m

So the van is 35 m from its initial position, in the negative direction.

[2 marks available — 1 mark for correct workings, 1 mark for correct value of displacement]

3 a) a = gradient of graph

$t = 0 - 2$ s: $a = 6 \div 2 = 3$ ms^{-2}

$t = 17 - 18$ s: $a = -6 \div 1 = -6$ ms^{-2}

$t = 23 - 27$ s: $a = 30 \div 4 = 7.5$ ms^{-2}

Greatest acceleration is 7.5 ms^{-2}.

[3 marks available — 1 mark for finding gradients or equivalent, 1 mark for correct workings, 1 mark for correct statement of greatest acceleration]

b) Distance, d = area under the graph

$t = 0 - 2$ s: $d = \frac{1}{2}(6)2 = 6$ m (triangle: area $= \frac{1}{2}bh$)

$t = 2 - 17$ s: $d = 6 \times 15 = 90$ m (rectangle)

$t = 17 - 18$ s: $d = \frac{1}{2}(6)1 = 3$ m (triangle)

$t = 18 - 23$ s: $d = 0 \times 5 = 0$ m

$t = 23 - 27$ s: $d = \frac{1}{2}(30)4 = 60$ m (triangle)

Total distance = 6 + 90 + 3 + 0 + 60 = 159 m

[3 marks available — 1 mark for using distance = area under graph, 1 mark for correct workings, 1 mark for correct value of total distance]

4 a) $u = 5, v = 0, a = -9.8, t = ?$

Using $v = u + at$: $0 = 5 - 9.8t \Rightarrow t = 5 \div 9.8 = 0.5102...$

$t = 0.510$ s (3 s.f.)

[3 marks available — 1 mark for using appropriate equation, 1 mark for correct workings, 1 mark for correct value of t]

b) $u = 5, a = -9.8, s = -2, v = ?$

Using $v^2 = u^2 + 2as$:

$v^2 = 5^2 + 2(-9.8 \times -2) = 64.2 \Rightarrow v = -8.0124...$

$= -8.01$ ms^{-1} (3 s.f.)

The velocity is negative when it reaches B as the ball is travelling in the negative direction (you can also see this from the graph).

[3 marks available — 1 mark for using appropriate equation, 1 mark for correct workings, 1 mark for correct value of v]

5 a) From A to B:

$s = ut + \frac{1}{2}at^2 \Rightarrow 1.5 = 3u + \frac{1}{2}(a \times 3^2)$ ***[1 mark]***

$\Rightarrow 1.5 = 3u + \frac{9}{2}a$ ① ***[1 mark]***

From A to C:

$s = ut + \frac{1}{2}at^2 \Rightarrow 6.5 = 7u + \frac{1}{2}(a \times 7^2)$ ***[1 mark]***

$\Rightarrow 6.5 = 7u + \frac{49}{2}a$ ② ***[1 mark]***

3 × ② – 7 × ① gives: $9 = 42a$ ***[1 mark]***

$\Rightarrow a = 0.2142... = 0.214$ ms^{-2} (3 s.f.) ***[1 mark]***

b) Use $s = vt - \frac{1}{2}at^2$ for the motion between A and B: ***[1 mark]***

$1.5 = 3v - \frac{1}{2}(0.2142... \times 3^2)$

$\Rightarrow v = 0.8214... = 0.821$ ms^{-1} (3 s.f.) ***[1 mark]***

6 a) $s = \int v \, dt = \frac{11}{2}t^2 - \frac{2}{3}t^3 + c$ for $0 \le t \le 5$.

When $t = 0$, $s = 0 \Rightarrow c = 0$, so $s = \frac{11}{2}t^2 - \frac{2}{3}t^3$

So when $t = 5$:

$s = \frac{11}{2}(25) - \frac{2}{3}(125) = 54.16... = 54.2$ m (3 s.f.)

[4 marks available — 1 mark for integrating with respect to time, 1 mark for obtaining an expression for s, 1 mark for finding c, 1 mark for correct final answer]

b) $s = \int v \, dt = 25t - 2t^2 + k$ for $t > 5$ ***[1 mark]***

When $t = 5$, $s = 54.16...$ (from part a)) — use this to find k:

$54.16... = 25(5) - 2(25) + k$. So, $k = -20.83...$ ***[1 mark]***

Need to find t when $s = 0$, i.e. when:

$2t^2 - 25t + 20.83... = 0$ ***[1 mark]***

Solve using quadratic formula:

$t = 0.898$ or 11.6 s ***[1 mark]***

$t = 0.898$ can be ignored, as it is outside the interval for which the equation is valid.

So P is back at the origin after 11.6 s (3 s.f.) ***[1 mark]***

7 a) At $t = 9$ s, the acceleration is 0 ms^{-2} ***[1 mark]***, so the rocket is travelling at its maximum velocity at this time ***[1 mark]***.

b) Integrate acceleration with respect to time to find an expression for the rocket's velocity:

$v = \int a \, dt = \int 3t^2 - \frac{t^3}{3} \, dt = t^3 - \frac{t^4}{12} + C$.

From the question, when $t = 0$ s, $v = 0$ ms^{-1} $\Rightarrow C = 0$.

So $v = t^3 - \frac{t^4}{12}$

Integrate velocity with respect to time to find an expression for displacement:

$s = \int v \, dt = \int \left(t^3 - \frac{t^4}{12}\right) dt = \frac{t^4}{4} - \frac{t^5}{60} + C$.

When $t = 0$, $s = 0 \Rightarrow C = 0$.

So $s = \frac{t^4}{4} - \frac{t^5}{60}$.

$t = 5 \text{ s} \Rightarrow s = \frac{5^4}{4} - \frac{5^5}{60} = 104$ m (3 s.f.)

So, according to the model, it would take the rocket less than 5 seconds to reach a height of 75 m. This indicates that the student's model is inaccurate.

[7 marks available — 1 mark for integrating to find an expression for velocity, 1 mark for a correct expression for the velocity, 1 mark for integrating to find an expression for displacement, 1 mark for a correct expression for the displacement, 1 mark for substituting t = 5, 1 mark for finding the displacement at 5 seconds, 1 mark for a sensible conclusion about the model]

c) E.g. The rocket has been modelled as a light particle, so the model could be improved to take the rocket's weight and/or air resistance could be taken into account. ***[1 mark for any sensible improvement]***

8 a) Differentiate the equation for displacement to get an expression for the velocity: ***[1 mark]*** $v = \frac{dx}{dt} = 4t^3 - 12t^2 - 16t$ ***[1 mark]***

$v = 0 \Rightarrow 4t^3 - 12t^2 - 16t = 0 \Rightarrow t^3 - 3t^2 - 4t = 0$

$t(t^2 - 3t - 4) = 0 \Rightarrow t(t + 1)(t - 4) = 0$ ***[1 mark]***

$\Rightarrow$ Particle is stationary at $t = 0$ ***[1 mark]*** and $t = 4$ ***[1 mark]***

Notice that $t = -1$ is not included as time can't be negative (you're told $t \ge 0$ in the question).

b) The particle is stationary at $t = 4$ (which means the particle could change direction at this point), so you need to consider the motion for $0 \le t \le 4$ and the motion for $4 < t \le 5$ separately. You need to find the two displacements and add them together ***[1 mark]***.
The displacement from $t = 0$ to $t = 4$ is given by:
$x(4) - x(0) = -127 - 1 = -128$ m ***[1 mark]***
The displacement from $t = 4$ to $t = 5$ is given by:
$x(5) - x(4) = -74 + 127 = 53$ m ***[1 mark]***
So the total distance travelled is: $128 + 53 = 181$ m ***[1 mark]***.
Remember, you're looking to find the total distance travelled here, not overall displacement. So even though one of the values of displacement is negative, you need to add together the magnitude of the two displacements to find the total distance travelled.

c) Differentiate the equation for velocity to get an expression for the acceleration: ***[1 mark]***
$a = \frac{dv}{dt} = 12t^2 - 24t - 16$ ***[1 mark]***
$a = 0 \Rightarrow 12t^2 - 24t - 16 = 0 \Rightarrow 3t^2 - 6t - 4 = 0$ ***[1 mark]***
Use the quadratic formula to solve for t:
$t = \frac{6 + \sqrt{36 - (4 \times 3 \times -4)}}{6}$ ***[1 mark]***
$t = 2.53$ s (3 s.f.) ***[1 mark]***
You don't need to worry about the other t-value that the formula gives you, as it is negative, and you're told t ≥ 0 in the question

Pages 61-64: Forces and Newton's Laws

1 a) E.g. Shinji has assumed the table is smooth ***[1 mark]***.
Shinji has assumed that the horizontal force acts parallel to the top of the table ***[1 mark]***.

b) Using $F = ma$ ***[1 mark]***:
$12 = 2m \Rightarrow m = 6$ ***[1 mark]***, so $x = 6g = 58.8$ ***[1 mark]***.

2 a) Using $a = \frac{F}{m}$:
$a = \frac{34\,000\,000}{1\,400\,000}$ ***[1 mark]*** $= 24.3$ ms^{-2} ***[1 mark]***

b) Using $F = ma$: $34\,000\,000 - R = 1\,400\,000 \times 12$ ***[1 mark]***
so $R = 34\,000\,000 - 16\,800\,000 = 17\,200\,000$ N ***[1 mark]***

c) E.g. The force of gravity acting on the rocket is constant.
[1 mark for any suitable assumption]

3 It's usually a good idea to draw a diagram to make it clear what's going on:

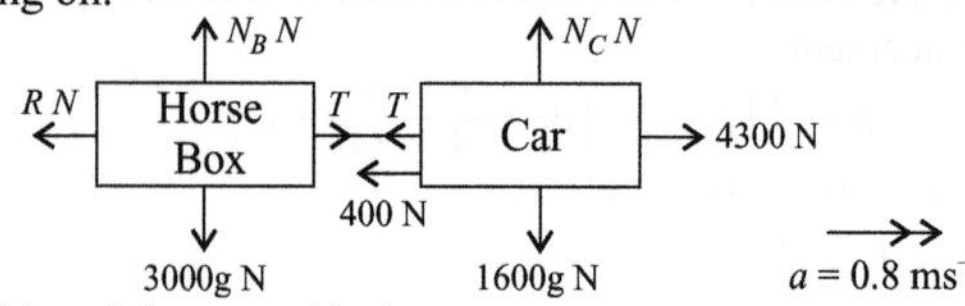

(Taking right as positive)

a) Resolve forces acting on the car only:
$F_{net} = ma$
$\Rightarrow 4300 - 400 - T = 1600 \times 0.8$
[1 mark for LHS, 1 mark for RHS]
$\Rightarrow T = 4300 - 400 - (1600 \times 0.8) = 2620$ N ***[1 mark]***.

b) Resolve forces acting on the horse box only:
$F_{net} = ma$
$T - R = 3000 \times 0.8$ ***[1 mark]***
$\Rightarrow R = 2620 - (3000 \times 0.8)$ ***[1 mark]*** $= 220$ N ***[1 mark]***.

c) $F_{net} = ma \Rightarrow -220 = 3000a$ ***[1 mark]***
$\Rightarrow a = -220 \div 3000 = -0.0733$ ms^{-2} (3 s.f.) .
So the deceleration of the horse box is 0.0733 ms^{-2} ***[1 mark]***.

d) Use $v^2 = u^2 + 2as$: ***[1 mark]***
$0 = 7^2 + (2 \times -0.0733 \times s)$ ***[1 mark]***
$\Rightarrow s = -49 \div (2 \times -0.0733) = 334$ m (3 s.f.) ***[1 mark]***.

4 Find the resultant of $\mathbf{F}_1$ and $\mathbf{F}_2$:
$\mathbf{F}_1 + \mathbf{F}_2 = (3\mathbf{i} + 2\mathbf{j}) + (2\mathbf{i} - \mathbf{j}) = (3 + 2)\mathbf{i} + (2 - 1)\mathbf{j} = 5\mathbf{i} + \mathbf{j}$.
Using $\mathbf{F} = m\mathbf{a}$:
$5\mathbf{i} + \mathbf{j} = 0.5\mathbf{a} \Rightarrow \mathbf{a} = 10\mathbf{i} + 2\mathbf{j}$.
[3 marks available — 1 mark for correct resultant, 1 mark for using vector form of F = ma and 1 mark for correct acceleration]

5 a) Because the pulley is smooth, the tension in the rope T will be the same for both the rock and the truck. ***[1 mark]***
Using $F = ma$ for the truck:
$10000 - (800 + T) = 3000a \Rightarrow 9200 - T = 3000a$ ①
[1 mark]
Using $F = ma$ for the rock:
$T - 500g = 500a$ ② ***[1 mark]***
① + ② gives:
$9200 - T + T - 500g = 3500a$ ***[1 mark]*** $\Rightarrow 4300 = 3500a$
So, $a = 1.2285... = 1.23$ ms^{-2} (3 s.f.) ***[1 mark]***

b) E.g. The rock is accelerating more slowly than the model predicts. This could be because the model does not include the friction of the pulley, so could be improved by modelling the pulley as rough.
[1 mark for a valid assessment of the model, 1 mark for a sensible suggestion to improve the model]

6 Call the mass of the woman W.
Drawing two force diagrams will really help:

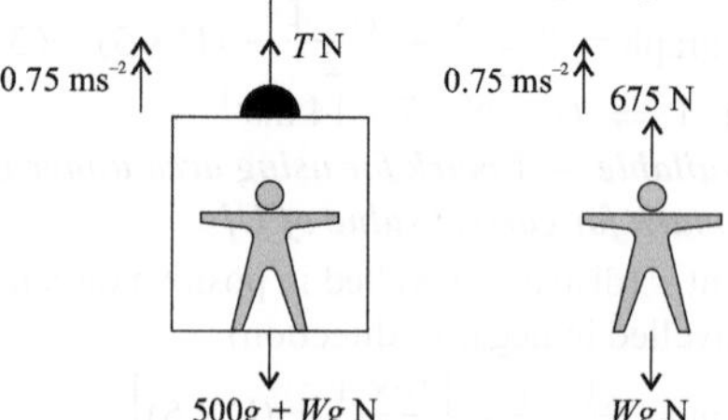

First, use $F = ma$ for the woman in the lift to find her mass:
$675 - Wg = 0.75W \Rightarrow 675 = 0.75W + Wg \Rightarrow W = 63.981...$ kg
Now use $F = ma$ for the whole connected system:
$T - (500 + 63.981...)g = 0.75(500 + 63.981...) \Rightarrow T = 5950$ N
[4 marks available — 1 mark for using F = ma for the woman, 1 mark for finding the mass of the woman, 1 mark for using F = ma on the whole system, 1 mark for the correct answer]

7 a)

If mass of $A = 0.2$ kg, mass of $W = 1.5 \times 0.2 = 0.3$ kg
For W, $F = ma$:
$0.3g - T = 0.3(4) \Rightarrow T = 2.94 - 1.2 = 1.74$
For A, $F = ma$:
$T - F = 4(0.2) = 0.8 \Rightarrow F = 1.74 - 0.8 = 0.94$ N
[4 marks available — 1 mark for treating each side of the pulley as a separate system, 1 mark for using F = ma, 1 mark for correct value of T, 1 mark for correct value of R]

b) Speed of A at h = speed of W at h (where it impacts ground)
Calculate speed of A at h using $v^2 = u^2 + 2as$:
$v^2 = 0^2 + 2(4 \times h)$ ***[1 mark]*** $\Rightarrow v^2 = 8h$ ①
Distance travelled by A beyond $h = \frac{3}{4}h$ ***[1 mark]***
Using $F = 0.94$ from part a) with $F = ma$:
$a = -0.94 \div 0.2 = -4.7$ ***[1 mark]***
Speed of A at h using $u^2 = v^2 - 2as$:
$u^2 = 3^2 - 2(-4.7 \times \frac{3}{4}h) = 9 + 7.05h$ ② ***[1 mark]***
Substituting ① into ② (where $v^2 = u^2$):
$8h = 9 + 7.05h$ so $h = 9.47$ m ***[1 mark]***
Tricky. The thing to realise is that when W has moved a distance of h and hits the ground, A has also moved a distance of h. A then carries on moving, but is slowed down by friction, so you can calculate the speed of A when it's moved a distance of h in two different ways. This gives you two simultaneous equations that you can solve to find h.

c) Time taken to reach h using $s = ut + \frac{1}{2}at^2$:
$9.47 = (0 \times t) + \frac{1}{2}(4 \times t^2) = 2t^2$ ***[1 mark]***
so $t^2 = 4.74$ and $t = 2.18$ s ***[1 mark]***

c) E.g. It means that A and W have the same acceleration when W is falling.
[1 mark for correct explanation]

Practice Exam Paper 1: Pure Mathematics

1 a) Gradient of graph (m) = $\frac{10-7}{1-5} = -0.75$
So using $y = mx + c$, $y = -0.75x + c$
Substitute $x = 1$, $y = 10$ to find c:
$10 = -0.75(1) + c \Rightarrow c = 10.75$
So equation is: $y = -0.75x + 10.75$
[3 marks available — 1 mark for using the given data to calculate the gradient, 1 mark for working to find the y-intercept, 1 mark for correct equation]

b) The gradient represents the increase in height per hour. Because the gradient is negative, the height is decreasing ***[1 mark]***. The y-intercept represents the height of the candle when it was lit ***[1 mark]***.

2 $\sqrt{2} \times 32^3 \div 2^{-6} = 2^{\frac{1}{2}} \times (2^5)^3 \div 2^{-6}$
$= 2^{\frac{1}{2}} \times 2^{15} \div 2^{-6} = 2^{\frac{1}{2}+15-(-6)} = 2^{21\frac{1}{2}} (= 2^{\frac{43}{2}})$
[1 mark for converting $\sqrt{2}$ to $2^{\frac{1}{2}}$ and 32 to 2^5, 1 mark for adding and subtracting powers, 1 mark for correct final answer]

3 Let A be the area of the triangle and x the length of the short side to be found.
$A = \frac{1}{2} \times \text{base} \times \text{height} \Rightarrow 4 + \sqrt{2} = \frac{1}{2}(2 - \sqrt{2})x$
$x = \frac{2(4+\sqrt{2})}{2-\sqrt{2}}$ ***[1 mark]***
Rationalise the denominator:
$x = \frac{(8+2\sqrt{2})(2+\sqrt{2})}{(2-\sqrt{2})(2+\sqrt{2})}$ ***[1 mark]*** $= \frac{20+12\sqrt{2}}{2}$ ***[1 mark]***
$= 10 + 6\sqrt{2} = 2(5 + 3\sqrt{2})$ ***[1 mark]***
So $a = 5$ and $b = 3$

4 a) Position vector of $M = \overrightarrow{OM} = 3\mathbf{i} + 7\mathbf{j}$
$\overrightarrow{ON} = \overrightarrow{OM} + \overrightarrow{MN} = \overrightarrow{OM} - \overrightarrow{NM}$
$= (3\mathbf{i} + 7\mathbf{j}) - (-4\mathbf{i} + 3\mathbf{j})$ ***[1 mark]*** $= 7\mathbf{i} + 4\mathbf{j}$ ***[1 mark]***

b) $|\overrightarrow{NM}| = \sqrt{4^2 + 3^2}$ ***[1 mark]***
$|\overrightarrow{NM}| = 5$
radius = 2.5 units ***[1 mark]***

5 $y = 8x^{\frac{1}{2}} - x$
$\frac{dy}{dx} = 4x^{-\frac{1}{2}} - 1$
When $x = 4$, $\frac{dy}{dx} = (4)\left(\frac{1}{\sqrt{4}}\right) - 1 = 1$, so the gradient of the tangent is 1.
When $x = 4$, $y = 8\sqrt{4} - 4 = 12$, so the tangent passes through (4, 12).
Equation of a straight line is $y = mx + c$, so the equation of the tangent is $y = x + c$.
Substitute (4, 12) into $y = x + c$ to find c:
$12 = 4 + c \Rightarrow c = 8$
So the equation of the tangent is $y = x + 8$.
[6 marks available — 1 mark for attempting to differentiate, 1 mark for finding $\frac{dy}{dx}$, 1 mark for substituting x = 4 into $\frac{dy}{dx}$, 1 mark for finding the gradient of the tangent, 1 mark for finding the coordinates (4, 12), 1 mark for the equation of the tangent]

6 a) Factorise to get in the form $(1 + ax)^n$:
$(2+x)^6 = \left(2\left(1+\frac{x}{2}\right)\right)^6 = 2^6\left(1+\frac{x}{2}\right)^6$
$= 2^6\left(1 + 6\left(\frac{x}{2}\right) + \frac{6 \times 5}{1 \times 2}\left(\frac{x}{2}\right)^2 + ...\right)$
$= 64\left(1 + 3x + \frac{15x^2}{4} + ...\right)$
$= 64 + 192x + 240x^2 + ...$
[4 marks available — 1 mark for correct substitution into binomial expansion formula and 1 mark for each correct term in the final answer]
You could have used the $(a + b)^n$ formula instead.

b) Substitute $x = 0.001$ into the equation ***[1 mark]***:
$2.001^6 = (2 + 0.001)^6 \approx 64 + 192(0.001) + 240(0.001^2)$
$2.001^6 \approx 64.19224$ ***[1 mark]***

c) To find an approximation for 3.001^6, you would need to substitute $x = 1.001$ into the equation in a). $x > 1$, so larger powers of x are increasing. The first three terms in the binomial expansion would therefore not provide a good approximation to 3.001^6, because the following terms in the expansion are also significant so cannot be ignored. ***[1 mark]***

7 At point P, $2^{3x+2} = 19$ — solve this equation using logarithms:
$\log 2^{3x+2} = \log 19$ ***[1 mark]***
$(3x + 2)\log 2 = \log 19$ ***[1 mark]***
$3x + 2 = \frac{\log 19}{\log 2} = 4.2479...$ ***[1 mark]***
$x = \frac{4.2479... - 2}{3} = 0.7493... = 0.749$ (3 s.f.) ***[1 mark]***
You could have taken logs of base 2 if your calculator can do logs of any base. $\log_2 2 = 1$, so you'd get $3x + 2$ on the LHS and $\log_2 19$ on the RHS (you'll end up with the same answer though).

8 a) f(x) crosses the x-axis when f(x) = 0.
$\sqrt{x} - 10 + \frac{21}{\sqrt{x}} = 0$
Multiplying each term by $\sqrt{x}$:
$x - 10\sqrt{x} + 21 = 0$ ***[1 mark]***
Substituting $u = \sqrt{x}$:
$u^2 - 10u + 21 = 0$ ***[1 mark]***
$(u - 3)(u - 7) = 0$
$u = 3$ or $u = 7$ ***[1 mark]***
Substituting $\sqrt{x}$ back in:
$\sqrt{x} = 3$ or $\sqrt{x} = 7$
$x = 9$ or $x = 49$
So the coordinates are (9, 0) and (49, 0)
[1 mark for each correct set of coordinates]

b) g(x) = f($2x$), so f(x) is stretched by a factor of 0.5 in the x-direction to produce g(x). g(x) crosses the x-axis at (4.5, 0) and (24.5, 0).
[2 marks available — 1 mark for correct transformation, 1 mark for correct coordinates]

9 Let the shorter sides have lengths x m and y m.
Using Pythagoras, $x^2 + y^2 = 18^2$ — call this equation (1)
$x + y + 18 = 40 \Rightarrow x + y = 22$ — call this equation (2)
Solve the simultaneous equations:
Substitute $x = (22 - y)$ into equation (1):
$(22 - y)^2 + y^2 = 324$
$484 - 44y + y^2 + y^2 = 324$
$2y^2 - 44y + 160 = 0$
$y^2 - 22y + 80 = 0$
Using the quadratic formula:
$y = \frac{22 \pm \sqrt{(-22)^2 - (4 \times 1 \times 80)}}{2 \times 1}$
$y = \frac{22 \pm \sqrt{484 - 320}}{2} = \frac{22 \pm \sqrt{164}}{2}$
$y = 17.40$ m or $y = 4.60$ m
If $y = 17.40$ m, $x = 22 - 17.40 = 4.60$ m
If $y = 4.60$ m, $x = 22 - 4.60 = 17.40$ m
So the sides are 4.60 m and 17.40 m long.
[6 marks available — 2 marks for setting up equations 1 and 2, 1 mark for attempting to solve simultaneous equations by substitution, 1 mark for forming a quadratic, 1 mark for attempting to solve the quadratic equation, 1 mark for both correct lengths]

10 a) $f(x) = x^3 - 8x^2 + 9x + 18$
If $f(a) = 0$, then $(x - a)$ is a factor of $f(x)$ (by the factor theorem). So try integer values of a in the range $0 < a < 5$:
$f(3) = 3^3 - 8(3^2) + 9(3) + 18 = 27 - 72 + 27 + 18 = 0$
$f(3) = 0$ so $(x - 3)$ is a factor of $f(x)$, and $a = 3$.
[2 marks available — 1 mark for using the factor theorem, 1 mark for finding a = 3]
You might have to try a few different values before you find $a = 3$.

b) $(x - 3)$ is a factor, so use this to fully factorise f(x):
$f(x) = x^3 - 8x^2 + 9x + 18 = (x - 3)(x^2 + ... - 6)$
$= (x - 3)(x^2 - 5x - 6)$
Factorising the quadratic gives:
$f(x) = (x - 3)(x - 6)(x + 1)$
So $y = f(x)$ crosses the x-axis at $(-1, 0)$, $(3, 0)$ and $(6, 0)$.
When $x = 0$, $f(x) = 18$, so f(x) crosses the y-axis at $(0, 18)$.

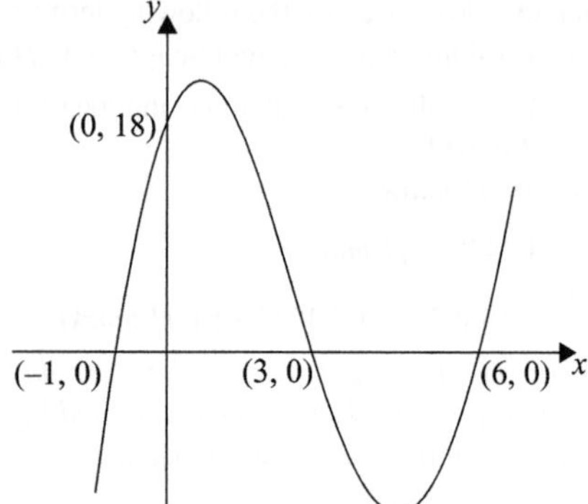

[4 marks available — 1 mark for correct quadratic factor, 1 mark for correct full factorisation of equation, 1 mark for correct shape of curve, 1 mark for correct x-and y-intercepts]

You're not asked anything about the position of the turning points of the graph, so don't worry too much about exactly where you've drawn the maximum or minimum points.

c) If the polynomial has only one real root, that means the quadratic factor has no real roots, so the discriminant must be less than 0 ***[1 mark]***.
$b^2 - 4ac < 0$
$k^2 - (4 \times 1 \times 9) < 0$
$k^2 - 36 < 0$ ***[1 mark]***
$k^2 < 36 \Rightarrow -6 < k < 6$ ***[1 mark]***

11 Substituting $\tan x \equiv \frac{\sin x}{\cos x}$:
$$6\frac{\sin^2 x}{\cos^2 x} - \frac{19\sin x}{\cos^2 x} + \frac{10}{\cos^2 x} = 0$$
$6\sin^2 x - 19\sin x + 10 = 0$
Factorise: $(2\sin x - 5)(3\sin x - 2) = 0$
$\sin x = \frac{2}{3}$ (or $\sin x = \frac{5}{2}$ but ignore this value as $-1 \leq \sin x \leq 1$)
$x = \sin^{-1}\left(\frac{2}{3}\right) = 41.810...\ 41.8°$ (1 d.p.)
This is the only solution between −90° and 90°.
[5 marks available — 1 mark for substituting for tan x, 1 mark for forming a quadratic in sin x, 1 mark for factorising the quadratic, 1 mark for solving for sin x, 1 mark for the correct value of x]

12 Rewrite the quadratic part of the expression in completed-square form:
$x^2 - 4x + 6 = (x - 2)^2 + 2$ ***[1 mark]***
$(x - 2)^2 \geq 0$, so $(x - 2)^2 + 2 \geq 2$ ***[1 mark]***
$-1 \leq \sin x \leq 1$, so when $\sin x$ takes its smallest possible value:
$\sin x + (x - 2)^2 + 2 \geq -1 + 2 = 1$ ***[1 mark]***
Hence $\sin x + x^2 - 4x + 6 > 0$ ***[1 mark]***

13 a) $2\log_6 x + \log_6 (x^2 - 25) - \log_6 (x^2 + 5x)$
$= \log_6 x^2 + \log_6 (x^2 - 25) - \log_6 (x^2 + 5x)$ ***[1 mark]***
$= \log_6 x^2(x^2 - 25) - \log_6 (x^2 + 5x)$ ***[1 mark]***
$= \log_6 \frac{x^2(x^2 - 25)}{(x^2 + 5x)}$ ***[1 mark]***

b) $2\log_6 x + \log_6 (x^2 - 25) - \log_6 (x^2 + 5x) \leq 2$
$\Rightarrow \log_6 \frac{x^2(x^2 - 25)}{(x^2 + 5x)} \leq 2 \Rightarrow \frac{x^2(x^2 - 25)}{(x^2 + 5x)} \leq 6^2$ ***[1 mark]***
$\frac{x^2(x + 5)(x - 5)}{x(x + 5)} \leq 36$ ***[1 mark]***
$x(x - 5) \leq 36$
$x^2 - 5x - 36 \leq 0$ ***[1 mark]***
$(x - 9)(x + 4) \leq 0$
The graph of $f(x) = x^2 - 5x - 36$ is a u-shaped quadratic and $f(x) \leq 0$ when $-4 \leq x \leq 9$ ***[1 mark]***.
You're told in the question that $x > 5$, so $5 < x \leq 9$ ***[1 mark]***

14 a) $\int (2x^3 + x^2 - 7x - 6)\,dx = \frac{1}{2}x^4 + \frac{1}{3}x^3 - \frac{7}{2}x^2 - 6x + C$
[3 marks available — 1 mark for increasing the power of one term by 1, 1 mark for the first two terms correct, 1 mark for the remaining terms, including C]

b) To find the shaded area, you need to integrate the function between −1.5 and −1 and add it to the integral of the curve between −1 and 1 (making this value positive first).
$$\int_{-1.5}^{-1} (2x^3 + x^2 - 7x - 6)\,dx = \left[\frac{1}{2}x^4 + \frac{1}{3}x^3 - \frac{7}{2}x^2 - 6x\right]_{-1.5}^{-1}$$
$$= \left(\frac{(-1)^4}{2} + \frac{(-1)^3}{3} - \frac{7(-1)^2}{2} - 6(-1)\right) - \left(\frac{(-1.5)^4}{2} + \frac{(-1.5)^3}{3} - \frac{7(-1.5)^2}{2} - 6(-1.5)\right)$$
$$= \left(\frac{1}{2} - \frac{1}{3} - \frac{7}{2} + 6\right) - \left(\frac{81}{32} - \frac{9}{8} - \frac{63}{8} + 9\right) = \frac{13}{96}$$
So area between −1.5 and −1 is $\frac{13}{96}$
$$\int_{-1}^{1} (2x^3 + x^2 - 7x - 6)\,dx = \left[\frac{1}{2}x^4 + \frac{1}{3}x^3 - \frac{7}{2}x^2 - 6x\right]_{-1}^{1}$$
$$= \left(\frac{1^4}{2} + \frac{1^3}{3} - \frac{7(1)^2}{2} - 6(1)\right) - \left(\frac{(-1)^4}{2} + \frac{(-1)^3}{3} - \frac{7(-1)^2}{2} - 6(-1)\right)$$
$$= \left(\frac{1}{2} + \frac{1}{3} - \frac{7}{2} - 6\right) - \left(\frac{1}{2} - \frac{1}{3} - \frac{7}{2} + 6\right) = -\frac{34}{3}$$
So area between −1 and 1 is $\frac{34}{3}$
Total shaded area $= \frac{13}{96} + \frac{34}{3} = 11.468... = 11.5$ units^2 (3 s.f.)
[4 marks available — 1 mark for a correct method to find the area, 1 mark for finding the area between −1.5 and −1, 1 mark for finding the area between −1 and 1, 1 mark for adding the areas to get the correct answer]

15 a) Let l be the length of the pen.
$4w + 2l = 200$, so $l = 100 - 2w$
$A = wl = w(100 - 2w)$
$A = 100w - 2w^2$
[3 marks available — 1 mark for equation 4w + 2l = 200, 1 mark for rearranging to make l the subject, 1 mark for correctly substituting l into area equation]

b) $\frac{dA}{dw} = 100 - 4w$
At the maximum, $\frac{dA}{dw} = 0$, so $w = 25$.
[2 marks available — 1 mark for differentiation, 1 mark for final answer]
You can check this is a maximum by differentiating again — the second derivative is −4, which is negative for all values of x, so w = 25 is a maximum.

c) Maximum area occurs when $w = 25$:
$A = 100w - 2w^2 = (100 \times 25) - (2 \times 25^2)$
$A = 1250$ m^2
[2 marks available — 1 mark for substituting w into the area equation, 1 mark for correct final answer]

16 a) Take the natural log of both sides of the equation:
$I = ae^{bt}$
$\ln I = \ln (ae^{bt})$
$= \ln a + \ln e^{bt}$
$= \ln a + bt \ln e$
$= bt + \ln a$
So m = b and c = $\ln a$
[2 marks available — 1 mark for taking ln of both sides, 1 mark for the correct values for m and c]

b) From the first point given:
$4.012 = 5b + \ln a$ (1)
From the second point given:
$4.072 = 8b + \ln a$ (2) ***[1 mark for both equations]***
Solving simultaneously:
$8(1) - 5(2)$: $11.736 = 3 \ln a \Rightarrow \ln a = 3.912$
$\Rightarrow a = e^{3.912} = 49.9988... = 50.0$ (3 s.f.) ***[1 mark]***
Substitute this value back into (1) to find b:
$4.012 = 5b + \ln 49.9988...$
$\Rightarrow b = (4.012 - \ln 49.9988...) \div 5 = 0.02$ ***[1 mark]***
You could also find the value of b by finding the gradient of the line segment between the two given points.

c) The model to use is $I = 50.0e^{0.02t}$
When $t = 15$, $I = 50.0e^{0.02 \times 15} = 67.4929... = 67.5$ g (3 s.f.) ***[1 mark]***

d) E.g. the model is unlikely to be very realistic for large values of t, as it predicts the mass of iron filings will continue rising infinitely, whereas there is likely to be a finite amount of iron filings ***[1 mark for a sensible comment]***.

17 First, find the centre of the circle. Do this by finding the perpendicular bisectors of any two sides:
Midpoint of AB $= \left(\frac{3+0}{2}, \frac{1+2}{2}\right) = \left(\frac{3}{2}, \frac{3}{2}\right)$,
gradient of AB $= \frac{y_A - y_B}{x_A - x_B} = \frac{1-2}{3-0} = \frac{-1}{3} = -\frac{1}{3}$
[1 mark for midpoint and gradient]
So the perpendicular bisector of AB has gradient $-1 \div -\frac{1}{3} = 3$ and goes through $\left(\frac{3}{2}, \frac{3}{2}\right)$, so has equation
$y - \frac{3}{2} = 3(x - \frac{3}{2}) \Rightarrow y = 3x - 3$ ***[1 mark]***.
Midpoint of AC $= \left(\frac{3+1}{2}, \frac{1+5}{2}\right) = (2, 3)$,
gradient of AC $= \frac{y_A - y_C}{x_A - x_C} = \frac{1-5}{3-1} = \frac{-4}{2} = -2$
[1 mark for midpoint and gradient]
So the perpendicular bisector of AC has gradient $-1 \div -2 = \frac{1}{2}$ and goes through (2, 3), so has equation
$y - 3 = \frac{1}{2}(x - 2) \Rightarrow y = \frac{1}{2}x + 2$ ***[1 mark]***.
Find the centre of the circle by setting these equations of the perpendicular bisectors equal to one another and solving:
$3x - 3 = \frac{1}{2}x + 2 \Rightarrow \frac{5}{2}x = 5 \Rightarrow x = 2$, so $y = (3 \times 2) - 3 = 3$
So the centre is (2, 3) ***[1 mark]***.
The distance from the centre to point B (0, 2) is the radius:
$r = \sqrt{(2-0)^2 + (3-2)^2} = \sqrt{4+1} = \sqrt{5}$ ***[1 mark]***, so $r^2 = (\sqrt{5})^2 = 5$
So the equation of the circumcircle is
$(x - 2)^2 + (y - 3)^2 = 5$ ***[1 mark]***.
You might have noticed that the centre of the circle is the same as the midpoint of AC — so AC is a diameter of the circle.

Practice Exam Paper 2: Statistics and Mechanics

1 a) Opportunity (or convenience) sampling ***[1 mark]***.
E.g. People in the same waiting room are likely to be waiting for the same trains / the sample might exclude people who aren't waiting because their train is on time, so the sample is unlikely to be an accurate representation of all the people using the station ***[1 mark for a sensible comment]***.

b) Read off the cumulative frequencies from the graph to fill in the table:

Delay time (t, mins)	Frequency	Cumulative frequency
$0 \le t < 10$	15	15
$10 \le t < 20$	45	60
$20 \le t < 40$	30	90
$40 \le t < 60$	10	100

[2 marks for all six correct values, or 1 mark for at least three correct values]

c) $\frac{n}{2} = 50$, so the median is in the $10 \le t < 20$ class.
Lower class boundary is 10 and class width is 10,
so estimate for median $= 10 + 10 \times \frac{50 - 15}{45}$ ***[1 mark]***
$= 17.8$ minutes (3 s.f.) ***[1 mark]***

2 a) P(all three attend) = 0.04 goes in the middle of the circles and P(none of them) = 0.16 goes outside the circles.
P(J and K) = 0.12, so P(J and K and H') = 0.12 – 0.04 = 0.08
P(H and J) = 0.2, so P(J and H and K') = 0.2 – 0.04 = 0.16
The probabilities of J and K attending are independent, so P(J) × P(K) = P(J and K) ⇒ P(K) = 0.12 ÷ 0.6 = 0.2
The probabilities of H and K attending are independent, so P(H and K) = P(H) × P(K) = 0.4 × 0.2 = 0.08,
so P(H and K and J') = 0.08 – 0.04 = 0.04
P(J and H' and K') = 0.6 – (0.16 + 0.04 + 0.08) = 0.32
P(H and J' and K') = 0.4 – (0.16 + 0.04 + 0.04) = 0.16
P(K and J' and H') = 0.2 – (0.08 + 0.04 + 0.04) = 0.04

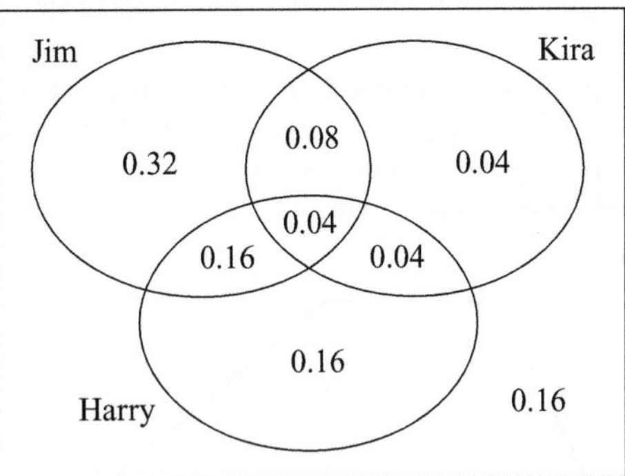

[4 marks for a completely correct Venn diagram, otherwise 1 mark for P(J and K and H') and P(J and H and K') both correct, 1 mark for P(K) correct and 1 mark for P(H and K and J') correct]
You can check your answer by making sure your Venn diagram agrees with each of the statements in the question, and by checking that all of the probabilities add together to make 1.

b) Statistical independence is shown if P(J) × P(H) = P(J and H).
0.6 × 0.4 = 0.24 ≠ 0.2, so they are not statistically independent ***[1 mark]***.

c) 0.04 × 0.04 = 0.0016 ***[1 mark]***

3 a) Let X be the number of batches of T-shirts that pass the quality checks during the week.
p = probability that a batch passes the checks = 0.85,
so $X \sim B(25, 0.85)$ ***[1 mark]***.
$P(X = 25) = \binom{25}{25} \times 0.85^{25} \times 0.15^0 = 0.0172$ (4 d.p.) ***[1 mark]***

b) £500 ÷ £120 = 4.166..., so the target will be exceeded if 5 or more batches fail the checks ***[1 mark]***.
If there are 5 or more failures, then that means there must be 20 or fewer passes.
So find $P(X \le 20) = 0.3179$ (4 d.p.) ***[1 mark]***
Use the binomial functions on your calculator for this question.

c) If p = proportion of batches that pass the quality check, then $H_0: p = 0.85$ and $H_1: p > 0.85$ ***[1 mark]***
Let Y be the number of batches that pass, out of 50 batches.
Under H_0, $Y \sim B(50, 0.85)$ ***[1 mark]***
3 batches failed the checks, so there must have been 47 passes.
Find the probability of a value of Y at least as extreme as the observed value:
$P(Y \ge 47) = 1 - P(Y \le 46)$ ***[1 mark]***
$= 1 - 0.953953... = 0.0460$ (4 d.p.) ***[1 mark]***
$0.0460 < 0.1$ ***[1 mark]***, so the result is significant.
There is evidence at the 10% level to suggest that the proportion of quality check passes is higher than the production manager states ***[1 mark]***.

4 a) $(\text{Standard deviation})^2 = \frac{\sum M^2}{n} - (\overline{M})^2$

$\Rightarrow 2.36^2 = \frac{9466.98}{30} - (\overline{M})^2$

$\Rightarrow (\overline{M})^2 = \frac{9466.98}{30} - 2.36^2 = 309.9964$

$\Rightarrow \overline{M} = 17.61$ °C (2 d.p.)

[2 marks available — 1 mark for writing a single equation linking $\overline{M}$, $\sum M^2$ and standard deviation, 1 mark for correct answer]

b) $(3 \times 2.36) + 17.61 = 24.69$ ***[1 mark]***

$26 > 24.69$, so 26 °C would be an outlier ***[1 mark]***

5 a) There is negative correlation between rainfall and hours of sunshine ***[1 mark]***.

b) The gradient shows that for every 1 mm increase in rainfall, you would expect the hours of sunshine to decrease by 0.24291 hours ***[1 mark]***. The intercept shows that when there is no rainfall you would expect to have 6.801 hours of sunshine ***[1 mark]***.

c) Amit's prediction is unreliable as he has extrapolated beyond the range of the sample data, and he doesn't know whether his linear model is valid for data outside this range.

[1 mark for a sensible comment]

6 a)

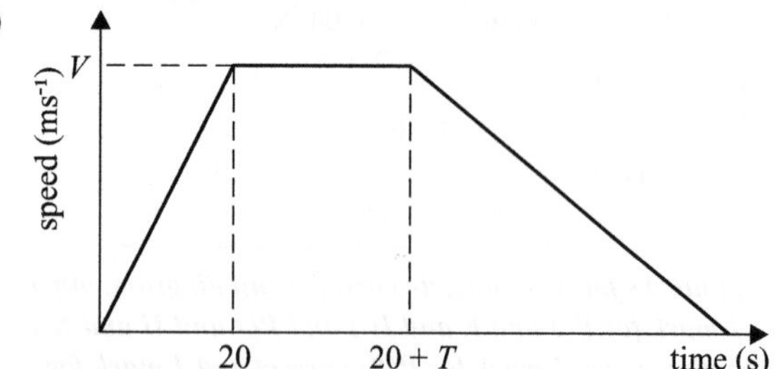

[2 marks available — 1 mark for correct shape, 1 mark for correct labels]

b) Distance travelled = area under the speed-time graph.

For the first 10 s, this is a triangle with a base of 10 and a height of $\frac{V}{2}$.

Area $= \frac{1}{2} \times 10 \times \frac{V}{2} = 100 \Rightarrow V = 40$ ***[1 mark]***

c) Let x be the time taken to decelerate in the last section of the graph. Here, the car decelerates at 0.25 ms^{-2} — this is the gradient of the line, so:

$\frac{40}{x} = 0.25 \Rightarrow x = 160$ s

Area under whole speed-time graph = 6400 m.

$(\frac{1}{2} \times 20 \times 40) + 40T + (\frac{1}{2} \times 160 \times 40) = 6400$

$400 + 40T + 3200 = 6400$

$T = 70$

[4 marks available — 1 mark for writing an equation $\frac{40}{x} = 0.25$, 1 mark for time taken for last section, 1 mark for correct working for area under graph, 1 mark for correct final answer]

Remember to convert distance travelled from km to m, so that it matches the other units in the question.

7 a) Use $F = ma$ to form equations of motion for both P and Q:

P: $T - 30 = 5a$ ① ***[1 mark]***

Q: $5g - T = 5a$ ② ***[1 mark]***

① + ② gives:

$5g - 30 = 10a$ ***[1 mark]***

$\Rightarrow a = \frac{(5 \times 9.8) - 30}{10} = 1.9$ ms^{-2} ***[1 mark]***

Substitute a back into ①:

$T - 30 = 5 \times 1.9 \Rightarrow T = 39.5$ N ***[1 mark]***

b) First, find the speed of Q at the point when the string snaps.

Taking $t = 0$ to be when the system is released:

$u = 0$ ms^{-1}, $a = 1.9$ ms^{-2}, $s = 0.95$ m

So $v^2 = u^2 + 2as \Rightarrow v^2 = 0^2 + (2 \times 1.9 \times 0.95) = 3.61$

Therefore $v = 1.9$ ms^{-1} ***[1 mark]***.

This is the initial speed of free fall, so from the point when the string snaps until Q hits the floor:

$s = (3 - 0.95) = 2.05$ m ***[1 mark]***, $u = 1.9$ ms^{-1}, $a = 9.8$ ms^{-2}

$v^2 = u^2 + 2as$

$= 1.9^2 + (2 \times 9.8 \times 2.05)$ ***[1 mark]***

$= 43.79 \Rightarrow v = 6.617....$ 6.62 ms^{-1} (to 3 s.f.) ***[1 mark]***

8 a) Differentiate the displacement function with respect to time to find a function for velocity: ***[1 mark]***

$v = \frac{ds}{dt} = 18t - 6t^2$ ***[1 mark]***

When the particle reaches its maximum displacement, $v = 0$:

$18t - 6t^2 = 0$ ***[1 mark]*** $\Rightarrow 6t(3 - t) = 0$

$v = 0$ when $t = 0$ s and $t = 3$ s ***[1 mark]***

When $t = 0$, $s = 11$ m

When $t = 3$, $s = 9(3^2) - 2(3^3) + 11 = 38$ m ***[1 mark]***

So the maximum displacement from O is 38 m.

b) Differentiate the velocity function with respect to time to find a function for acceleration:

$a = \frac{dv}{dt} = 18 - 12t$ ***[1 mark]***

Using $F = ma$:

$F = 3(18 - 12t) = (54 - 36t)$ N ***[1 mark]***

9 From passing the sign to entering the tunnel:

$s = ut + \frac{1}{2}at^2 \Rightarrow 110 = 8u + \frac{1}{2}(a \times 8^2)$ ***[1 mark]***

$\Rightarrow 110 = 8u + 32a$ ① ***[1 mark]***

From passing the sign to leaving the tunnel:

$s = ut + \frac{1}{2}at^2 \Rightarrow 870 = 32u + \frac{1}{2}(a \times 32^2)$ ***[1 mark]***

$\Rightarrow 870 = 32u + 512a$ ② ***[1 mark]***

② − 4 × ① gives: ***[1 mark]***

$430 = 384a \Rightarrow a = 1.119... = 1.12$ ms^{-2} (3 s.f.) ***[1 mark]***

Substitute back into ① to find u:

$110 = 8u + 32a$

$u = \frac{110 - 32(1.119...)}{8} = 9.270... = 9.27$ ms^{-1} ***[1 mark]***

Statistical Tables

The binomial cumulative distribution function

The values below show $P(X \leq x)$, where $X \sim B(n, p)$.

	$p =$	0.05	0.10	0.15	0.20	0.25	0.30	0.35	0.40	0.45	0.50
$n = 5$	$x =$ 0	0.7738	0.5905	0.4437	0.3277	0.2373	0.1681	0.1160	0.0778	0.0503	0.0313
	1	0.9774	0.9185	0.8352	0.7373	0.6328	0.5282	0.4284	0.3370	0.2562	0.1875
	2	0.9988	0.9914	0.9734	0.9421	0.8965	0.8369	0.7648	0.6826	0.5931	0.5000
	3	1.0000	0.9995	0.9978	0.9933	0.9844	0.9692	0.9460	0.9130	0.8688	0.8125
	4	1.0000	1.0000	0.9999	0.9997	0.9990	0.9976	0.9947	0.9898	0.9815	0.9688
$n = 6$	$x =$ 0	0.7351	0.5314	0.3771	0.2621	0.1780	0.1176	0.0754	0.0467	0.0277	0.0156
	1	0.9672	0.8857	0.7765	0.6554	0.5339	0.4202	0.3191	0.2333	0.1636	0.1094
	2	0.9978	0.9842	0.9527	0.9011	0.8306	0.7443	0.6471	0.5443	0.4415	0.3438
	3	0.9999	0.9987	0.9941	0.9830	0.9624	0.9295	0.8826	0.8208	0.7447	0.6563
	4	1.0000	0.9999	0.9996	0.9984	0.9954	0.9891	0.9777	0.9590	0.9308	0.8906
	5	1.0000	1.0000	1.0000	0.9999	0.9998	0.9993	0.9982	0.9959	0.9917	0.9844
$n = 7$	$x =$ 0	0.6983	0.4783	0.3206	0.2097	0.1335	0.0824	0.0490	0.0280	0.0152	0.0078
	1	0.9556	0.8503	0.7166	0.5767	0.4449	0.3294	0.2338	0.1586	0.1024	0.0625
	2	0.9962	0.9743	0.9262	0.8520	0.7564	0.6471	0.5323	0.4199	0.3164	0.2266
	3	0.9998	0.9973	0.9879	0.9667	0.9294	0.8740	0.8002	0.7102	0.6083	0.5000
	4	1.0000	0.9998	0.9988	0.9953	0.9871	0.9712	0.9444	0.9037	0.8471	0.7734
	5	1.0000	1.0000	0.9999	0.9996	0.9987	0.9962	0.9910	0.9812	0.9643	0.9375
	6	1.0000	1.0000	1.0000	1.0000	0.9999	0.9998	0.9994	0.9984	0.9963	0.9922
$n = 8$	$x =$ 0	0.6634	0.4305	0.2725	0.1678	0.1001	0.0576	0.0319	0.0168	0.0084	0.0039
	1	0.9428	0.8131	0.6572	0.5033	0.3671	0.2553	0.1691	0.1064	0.0632	0.0352
	2	0.9942	0.9619	0.8948	0.7969	0.6785	0.5518	0.4278	0.3154	0.2201	0.1445
	3	0.9996	0.9950	0.9786	0.9437	0.8862	0.8059	0.7064	0.5941	0.4770	0.3633
	4	1.0000	0.9996	0.9971	0.9896	0.9727	0.9420	0.8939	0.8263	0.7396	0.6367
	5	1.0000	1.0000	0.9998	0.9988	0.9958	0.9887	0.9747	0.9502	0.9115	0.8555
	6	1.0000	1.0000	1.0000	0.9999	0.9996	0.9987	0.9964	0.9915	0.9819	0.9648
	7	1.0000	1.0000	1.0000	1.0000	1.0000	0.9999	0.9998	0.9993	0.9983	0.9961
$n = 9$	$x =$ 0	0.6302	0.3874	0.2316	0.1342	0.0751	0.0404	0.0207	0.0101	0.0046	0.0020
	1	0.9288	0.7748	0.5995	0.4362	0.3003	0.1960	0.1211	0.0705	0.0385	0.0195
	2	0.9916	0.9470	0.8591	0.7382	0.6007	0.4628	0.3373	0.2318	0.1495	0.0898
	3	0.9994	0.9917	0.9661	0.9144	0.8343	0.7297	0.6089	0.4826	0.3614	0.2539
	4	1.0000	0.9991	0.9944	0.9804	0.9511	0.9012	0.8283	0.7334	0.6214	0.5000
	5	1.0000	0.9999	0.9994	0.9969	0.9900	0.9747	0.9464	0.9006	0.8342	0.7461
	6	1.0000	1.0000	1.0000	0.9997	0.9987	0.9957	0.9888	0.9750	0.9502	0.9102
	7	1.0000	1.0000	1.0000	1.0000	0.9999	0.9996	0.9986	0.9962	0.9909	0.9805
	8	1.0000	1.0000	1.0000	1.0000	1.0000	1.0000	0.9999	0.9997	0.9992	0.9980
$n = 10$	$x =$ 0	0.5987	0.3487	0.1969	0.1074	0.0563	0.0282	0.0135	0.0060	0.0025	0.0010
	1	0.9139	0.7361	0.5443	0.3758	0.2440	0.1493	0.0860	0.0464	0.0233	0.0107
	2	0.9885	0.9298	0.8202	0.6778	0.5256	0.3828	0.2616	0.1673	0.0996	0.0547
	3	0.9990	0.9872	0.9500	0.8791	0.7759	0.6496	0.5138	0.3823	0.2660	0.1719
	4	0.9999	0.9984	0.9901	0.9672	0.9219	0.8497	0.7515	0.6331	0.5044	0.3770
	5	1.0000	0.9999	0.9986	0.9936	0.9803	0.9527	0.9051	0.8338	0.7384	0.6230
	6	1.0000	1.0000	0.9999	0.9991	0.9965	0.9894	0.9740	0.9452	0.8980	0.8281
	7	1.0000	1.0000	1.0000	0.9999	0.9996	0.9984	0.9952	0.9877	0.9726	0.9453
	8	1.0000	1.0000	1.0000	1.0000	1.0000	0.9999	0.9995	0.9983	0.9955	0.9893
	9	1.0000	1.0000	1.0000	1.0000	1.0000	1.0000	1.0000	0.9999	0.9997	0.9990

The binomial cumulative distribution function (continued)

	$p =$	0.05	0.10	0.15	0.20	0.25	0.30	0.35	0.40	0.45	0.50
$n = 12$	$x =$ 0	0.5404	0.2824	0.1422	0.0687	0.0317	0.0138	0.0057	0.0022	0.0008	0.0002
	1	0.8816	0.6590	0.4435	0.2749	0.1584	0.0850	0.0424	0.0196	0.0083	0.0032
	2	0.9804	0.8891	0.7358	0.5583	0.3907	0.2528	0.1513	0.0834	0.0421	0.0193
	3	0.9978	0.9744	0.9078	0.7946	0.6488	0.4925	0.3467	0.2253	0.1345	0.0730
	4	0.9998	0.9957	0.9761	0.9274	0.8424	0.7237	0.5833	0.4382	0.3044	0.1938
	5	1.0000	0.9995	0.9954	0.9806	0.9456	0.8822	0.7873	0.6652	0.5269	0.3872
	6	1.0000	0.9999	0.9993	0.9961	0.9857	0.9614	0.9154	0.8418	0.7393	0.6128
	7	1.0000	1.0000	0.9999	0.9994	0.9972	0.9905	0.9745	0.9427	0.8883	0.8062
	8	1.0000	1.0000	1.0000	0.9999	0.9996	0.9983	0.9944	0.9847	0.9644	0.9270
	9	1.0000	1.0000	1.0000	1.0000	1.0000	0.9998	0.9992	0.9972	0.9921	0.9807
	10	1.0000	1.0000	1.0000	1.0000	1.0000	1.0000	0.9999	0.9997	0.9989	0.9968
	11	1.0000	1.0000	1.0000	1.0000	1.0000	1.0000	1.0000	1.0000	0.9999	0.9998
$n = 15$	$x =$ 0	0.4633	0.2059	0.0874	0.0352	0.0134	0.0047	0.0016	0.0005	0.0001	0.0000
	1	0.8290	0.5490	0.3186	0.1671	0.0802	0.0353	0.0142	0.0052	0.0017	0.0005
	2	0.9638	0.8159	0.6042	0.3980	0.2361	0.1268	0.0617	0.0271	0.0107	0.0037
	3	0.9945	0.9444	0.8227	0.6482	0.4613	0.2969	0.1727	0.0905	0.0424	0.0176
	4	0.9994	0.9873	0.9383	0.8358	0.6865	0.5155	0.3519	0.2173	0.1204	0.0592
	5	0.9999	0.9978	0.9832	0.9389	0.8516	0.7216	0.5643	0.4032	0.2608	0.1509
	6	1.0000	0.9997	0.9964	0.9819	0.9434	0.8689	0.7548	0.6098	0.4522	0.3036
	7	1.0000	1.0000	0.9994	0.9958	0.9827	0.9500	0.8868	0.7869	0.6535	0.5000
	8	1.0000	1.0000	0.9999	0.9992	0.9958	0.9848	0.9578	0.9050	0.8182	0.6964
	9	1.0000	1.0000	1.0000	0.9999	0.9992	0.9963	0.9876	0.9662	0.9231	0.8491
	10	1.0000	1.0000	1.0000	1.0000	0.9999	0.9993	0.9972	0.9907	0.9745	0.9408
	11	1.0000	1.0000	1.0000	1.0000	1.0000	0.9999	0.9995	0.9981	0.9937	0.9824
	12	1.0000	1.0000	1.0000	1.0000	1.0000	1.0000	0.9999	0.9997	0.9989	0.9963
	13	1.0000	1.0000	1.0000	1.0000	1.0000	1.0000	1.0000	1.0000	0.9999	0.9995
	14	1.0000	1.0000	1.0000	1.0000	1.0000	1.0000	1.0000	1.0000	1.0000	1.0000
$n = 20$	$x =$ 0	0.3585	0.1216	0.0388	0.0115	0.0032	0.0008	0.0002	0.0000	0.0000	0.0000
	1	0.7358	0.3917	0.1756	0.0692	0.0243	0.0076	0.0021	0.0005	0.0001	0.0000
	2	0.9245	0.6769	0.4049	0.2061	0.0913	0.0355	0.0121	0.0036	0.0009	0.0002
	3	0.9841	0.8670	0.6477	0.4114	0.2252	0.1071	0.0444	0.0160	0.0049	0.0013
	4	0.9974	0.9568	0.8298	0.6296	0.4148	0.2375	0.1182	0.0510	0.0189	0.0059
	5	0.9997	0.9887	0.9327	0.8042	0.6172	0.4164	0.2454	0.1256	0.0553	0.0207
	6	1.0000	0.9976	0.9781	0.9133	0.7858	0.6080	0.4166	0.2500	0.1299	0.0577
	7	1.0000	0.9996	0.9941	0.9679	0.8982	0.7723	0.6010	0.4159	0.2520	0.1316
	8	1.0000	0.9999	0.9987	0.9900	0.9591	0.8867	0.7624	0.5956	0.4143	0.2517
	9	1.0000	1.0000	0.9998	0.9974	0.9861	0.9520	0.8782	0.7553	0.5914	0.4119
	10	1.0000	1.0000	1.0000	0.9994	0.9961	0.9829	0.9468	0.8725	0.7507	0.5881
	11	1.0000	1.0000	1.0000	0.9999	0.9991	0.9949	0.9804	0.9435	0.8692	0.7483
	12	1.0000	1.0000	1.0000	1.0000	0.9998	0.9987	0.9940	0.9790	0.9420	0.8684
	13	1.0000	1.0000	1.0000	1.0000	1.0000	0.9997	0.9985	0.9935	0.9786	0.9423
	14	1.0000	1.0000	1.0000	1.0000	1.0000	1.0000	0.9997	0.9984	0.9936	0.9793
	15	1.0000	1.0000	1.0000	1.0000	1.0000	1.0000	1.0000	0.9997	0.9985	0.9941
	16	1.0000	1.0000	1.0000	1.0000	1.0000	1.0000	1.0000	1.0000	0.9997	0.9987
	17	1.0000	1.0000	1.0000	1.0000	1.0000	1.0000	1.0000	1.0000	1.0000	0.9998
	18	1.0000	1.0000	1.0000	1.0000	1.0000	1.0000	1.0000	1.0000	1.0000	1.0000

The binomial cumulative distribution function (continued)

$p =$		0.05	0.10	0.15	0.20	0.25	0.30	0.35	0.40	0.45	0.50
$n = 25$ $x =$	0	0.2774	0.0718	0.0172	0.0038	0.0008	0.0001	0.0000	0.0000	0.0000	0.0000
	1	0.6424	0.2712	0.0931	0.0274	0.0070	0.0016	0.0003	0.0001	0.0000	0.0000
	2	0.8729	0.5371	0.2537	0.0982	0.0321	0.0090	0.0021	0.0004	0.0001	0.0000
	3	0.9659	0.7636	0.4711	0.2340	0.0962	0.0332	0.0097	0.0024	0.0005	0.0001
	4	0.9928	0.9020	0.6821	0.4207	0.2137	0.0905	0.0320	0.0095	0.0023	0.0005
	5	0.9988	0.9666	0.8385	0.6167	0.3783	0.1935	0.0826	0.0294	0.0086	0.0020
	6	0.9998	0.9905	0.9305	0.7800	0.5611	0.3407	0.1734	0.0736	0.0258	0.0073
	7	1.0000	0.9977	0.9745	0.8909	0.7265	0.5118	0.3061	0.1536	0.0639	0.0216
	8	1.0000	0.9995	0.9920	0.9532	0.8506	0.6769	0.4668	0.2735	0.1340	0.0539
	9	1.0000	0.9999	0.9979	0.9827	0.9287	0.8106	0.6303	0.4246	0.2424	0.1148
	10	1.0000	1.0000	0.9995	0.9944	0.9703	0.9022	0.7712	0.5858	0.3843	0.2122
	11	1.0000	1.0000	0.9999	0.9985	0.9893	0.9558	0.8746	0.7323	0.5426	0.3450
	12	1.0000	1.0000	1.0000	0.9996	0.9966	0.9825	0.9396	0.8462	0.6937	0.5000
	13	1.0000	1.0000	1.0000	0.9999	0.9991	0.9940	0.9745	0.9222	0.8173	0.6550
	14	1.0000	1.0000	1.0000	1.0000	0.9998	0.9982	0.9907	0.9656	0.9040	0.7878
	15	1.0000	1.0000	1.0000	1.0000	1.0000	0.9995	0.9971	0.9868	0.9560	0.8852
	16	1.0000	1.0000	1.0000	1.0000	1.0000	0.9999	0.9992	0.9957	0.9826	0.9461
	17	1.0000	1.0000	1.0000	1.0000	1.0000	1.0000	0.9998	0.9988	0.9942	0.9784
	18	1.0000	1.0000	1.0000	1.0000	1.0000	1.0000	1.0000	0.9997	0.9984	0.9927
	19	1.0000	1.0000	1.0000	1.0000	1.0000	1.0000	1.0000	0.9999	0.9996	0.9980
	20	1.0000	1.0000	1.0000	1.0000	1.0000	1.0000	1.0000	1.0000	0.9999	0.9995
	21	1.0000	1.0000	1.0000	1.0000	1.0000	1.0000	1.0000	1.0000	1.0000	0.9999
	22	1.0000	1.0000	1.0000	1.0000	1.0000	1.0000	1.0000	1.0000	1.0000	1.0000
$n = 30$ $x =$	0	0.2146	0.0424	0.0076	0.0012	0.0002	0.0000	0.0000	0.0000	0.0000	0.0000
	1	0.5535	0.1837	0.0480	0.0105	0.0020	0.0003	0.0000	0.0000	0.0000	0.0000
	2	0.8122	0.4114	0.1514	0.0442	0.0106	0.0021	0.0003	0.0000	0.0000	0.0000
	3	0.9392	0.6474	0.3217	0.1227	0.0374	0.0093	0.0019	0.0003	0.0000	0.0000
	4	0.9844	0.8245	0.5245	0.2552	0.0979	0.0302	0.0075	0.0015	0.0002	0.0000
	5	0.9967	0.9268	0.7106	0.4275	0.2026	0.0766	0.0233	0.0057	0.0011	0.0002
	6	0.9994	0.9742	0.8474	0.6070	0.3481	0.1595	0.0586	0.0172	0.0040	0.0007
	7	0.9999	0.9922	0.9302	0.7608	0.5143	0.2814	0.1238	0.0435	0.0121	0.0026
	8	1.0000	0.9980	0.9722	0.8713	0.6736	0.4315	0.2247	0.0940	0.0312	0.0081
	9	1.0000	0.9995	0.9903	0.9389	0.8034	0.5888	0.3575	0.1763	0.0694	0.0214
	10	1.0000	0.9999	0.9971	0.9744	0.8943	0.7304	0.5078	0.2915	0.1350	0.0494
	11	1.0000	1.0000	0.9992	0.9905	0.9493	0.8407	0.6548	0.4311	0.2327	0.1002
	12	1.0000	1.0000	0.9998	0.9969	0.9784	0.9155	0.7802	0.5785	0.3592	0.1808
	13	1.0000	1.0000	1.0000	0.9991	0.9918	0.9599	0.8737	0.7145	0.5025	0.2923
	14	1.0000	1.0000	1.0000	0.9998	0.9973	0.9831	0.9348	0.8246	0.6448	0.4278
	15	1.0000	1.0000	1.0000	0.9999	0.9992	0.9936	0.9699	0.9029	0.7691	0.5722
	16	1.0000	1.0000	1.0000	1.0000	0.9998	0.9979	0.9876	0.9519	0.8644	0.7077
	17	1.0000	1.0000	1.0000	1.0000	0.9999	0.9994	0.9955	0.9788	0.9286	0.8192
	18	1.0000	1.0000	1.0000	1.0000	1.0000	0.9998	0.9986	0.9917	0.9666	0.8998
	19	1.0000	1.0000	1.0000	1.0000	1.0000	1.0000	0.9996	0.9971	0.9862	0.9506
	20	1.0000	1.0000	1.0000	1.0000	1.0000	1.0000	0.9999	0.9991	0.9950	0.9786
	21	1.0000	1.0000	1.0000	1.0000	1.0000	1.0000	1.0000	0.9998	0.9984	0.9919
	22	1.0000	1.0000	1.0000	1.0000	1.0000	1.0000	1.0000	1.0000	0.9996	0.9974
	23	1.0000	1.0000	1.0000	1.0000	1.0000	1.0000	1.0000	1.0000	0.9999	0.9993
	24	1.0000	1.0000	1.0000	1.0000	1.0000	1.0000	1.0000	1.0000	1.0000	0.9998
	25	1.0000	1.0000	1.0000	1.0000	1.0000	1.0000	1.0000	1.0000	1.0000	1.0000

The binomial cumulative distribution function (continued)

	p =	0.05	0.10	0.15	0.20	0.25	0.30	0.35	0.40	0.45	0.50
n = 40	x = 0	0.1285	0.0148	0.0015	0.0001	0.0000	0.0000	0.0000	0.0000	0.0000	0.0000
	1	0.3991	0.0805	0.0121	0.0015	0.0001	0.0000	0.0000	0.0000	0.0000	0.0000
	2	0.6767	0.2228	0.0486	0.0079	0.0010	0.0001	0.0000	0.0000	0.0000	0.0000
	3	0.8619	0.4231	0.1302	0.0285	0.0047	0.0006	0.0001	0.0000	0.0000	0.0000
	4	0.9520	0.6290	0.2633	0.0759	0.0160	0.0026	0.0003	0.0000	0.0000	0.0000
	5	0.9861	0.7937	0.4325	0.1613	0.0433	0.0086	0.0013	0.0001	0.0000	0.0000
	6	0.9966	0.9005	0.6067	0.2859	0.0962	0.0238	0.0044	0.0006	0.0001	0.0000
	7	0.9993	0.9581	0.7559	0.4371	0.1820	0.0553	0.0124	0.0021	0.0002	0.0000
	8	0.9999	0.9845	0.8646	0.5931	0.2998	0.1110	0.0303	0.0061	0.0009	0.0001
	9	1.0000	0.9949	0.9328	0.7318	0.4395	0.1959	0.0644	0.0156	0.0027	0.0003
	10	1.0000	0.9985	0.9701	0.8392	0.5839	0.3087	0.1215	0.0352	0.0074	0.0011
	11	1.0000	0.9996	0.9880	0.9125	0.7151	0.4406	0.2053	0.0709	0.0179	0.0032
	12	1.0000	0.9999	0.9957	0.9568	0.8209	0.5772	0.3143	0.1285	0.0386	0.0083
	13	1.0000	1.0000	0.9986	0.9806	0.8968	0.7032	0.4408	0.2112	0.0751	0.0192
	14	1.0000	1.0000	0.9996	0.9921	0.9456	0.8074	0.5721	0.3174	0.1326	0.0403
	15	1.0000	1.0000	0.9999	0.9971	0.9738	0.8849	0.6946	0.4402	0.2142	0.0769
	16	1.0000	1.0000	1.0000	0.9990	0.9884	0.9367	0.7978	0.5681	0.3185	0.1341
	17	1.0000	1.0000	1.0000	0.9997	0.9953	0.9680	0.8761	0.6885	0.4391	0.2148
	18	1.0000	1.0000	1.0000	0.9999	0.9983	0.9852	0.9301	0.7911	0.5651	0.3179
	19	1.0000	1.0000	1.0000	1.0000	0.9994	0.9937	0.9637	0.8702	0.6844	0.4373
	20	1.0000	1.0000	1.0000	1.0000	0.9998	0.9976	0.9827	0.9256	0.7870	0.5627
	21	1.0000	1.0000	1.0000	1.0000	1.0000	0.9991	0.9925	0.9608	0.8669	0.6821
	22	1.0000	1.0000	1.0000	1.0000	1.0000	0.9997	0.9970	0.9811	0.9233	0.7852
	23	1.0000	1.0000	1.0000	1.0000	1.0000	0.9999	0.9989	0.9917	0.9595	0.8659
	24	1.0000	1.0000	1.0000	1.0000	1.0000	1.0000	0.9996	0.9966	0.9804	0.9231
	25	1.0000	1.0000	1.0000	1.0000	1.0000	1.0000	0.9999	0.9988	0.9914	0.9597
	26	1.0000	1.0000	1.0000	1.0000	1.0000	1.0000	1.0000	0.9996	0.9966	0.9808
	27	1.0000	1.0000	1.0000	1.0000	1.0000	1.0000	1.0000	0.9999	0.9988	0.9917
	28	1.0000	1.0000	1.0000	1.0000	1.0000	1.0000	1.0000	1.0000	0.9996	0.9968
	29	1.0000	1.0000	1.0000	1.0000	1.0000	1.0000	1.0000	1.0000	0.9999	0.9989
	30	1.0000	1.0000	1.0000	1.0000	1.0000	1.0000	1.0000	1.0000	1.0000	0.9997
	31	1.0000	1.0000	1.0000	1.0000	1.0000	1.0000	1.0000	1.0000	1.0000	0.9999
	32	1.0000	1.0000	1.0000	1.0000	1.0000	1.0000	1.0000	1.0000	1.0000	1.0000

The binomial cumulative distribution function (continued)

	$p =$	0.05	0.10	0.15	0.20	0.25	0.30	0.35	0.40	0.45	0.50
$n = 50$	$x =$ 0	0.0769	0.0052	0.0003	0.0000	0.0000	0.0000	0.0000	0.0000	0.0000	0.0000
	1	0.2794	0.0338	0.0029	0.0002	0.0000	0.0000	0.0000	0.0000	0.0000	0.0000
	2	0.5405	0.1117	0.0142	0.0013	0.0001	0.0000	0.0000	0.0000	0.0000	0.0000
	3	0.7604	0.2503	0.0460	0.0057	0.0005	0.0000	0.0000	0.0000	0.0000	0.0000
	4	0.8964	0.4312	0.1121	0.0185	0.0021	0.0002	0.0000	0.0000	0.0000	0.0000
	5	0.9622	0.6161	0.2194	0.0480	0.0070	0.0007	0.0001	0.0000	0.0000	0.0000
	6	0.9882	0.7702	0.3613	0.1034	0.0194	0.0025	0.0002	0.0000	0.0000	0.0000
	7	0.9968	0.8779	0.5188	0.1904	0.0453	0.0073	0.0008	0.0001	0.0000	0.0000
	8	0.9992	0.9421	0.6681	0.3073	0.0916	0.0183	0.0025	0.0002	0.0000	0.0000
	9	0.9998	0.9755	0.7911	0.4437	0.1637	0.0402	0.0067	0.0008	0.0001	0.0000
	10	1.0000	0.9906	0.8801	0.5836	0.2622	0.0789	0.0160	0.0022	0.0002	0.0000
	11	1.0000	0.9968	0.9372	0.7107	0.3816	0.1390	0.0342	0.0057	0.0006	0.0000
	12	1.0000	0.9990	0.9699	0.8139	0.5110	0.2229	0.0661	0.0133	0.0018	0.0002
	13	1.0000	0.9997	0.9868	0.8894	0.6370	0.3279	0.1163	0.0280	0.0045	0.0005
	14	1.0000	0.9999	0.9947	0.9393	0.7481	0.4468	0.1878	0.0540	0.0104	0.0013
	15	1.0000	1.0000	0.9981	0.9692	0.8369	0.5692	0.2801	0.0955	0.0220	0.0033
	16	1.0000	1.0000	0.9993	0.9856	0.9017	0.6839	0.3889	0.1561	0.0427	0.0077
	17	1.0000	1.0000	0.9998	0.9937	0.9449	0.7822	0.5060	0.2369	0.0765	0.0164
	18	1.0000	1.0000	0.9999	0.9975	0.9713	0.8594	0.6216	0.3356	0.1273	0.0325
	19	1.0000	1.0000	1.0000	0.9991	0.9861	0.9152	0.7264	0.4465	0.1974	0.0595
	20	1.0000	1.0000	1.0000	0.9997	0.9937	0.9522	0.8139	0.5610	0.2862	0.1013
	21	1.0000	1.0000	1.0000	0.9999	0.9974	0.9749	0.8813	0.6701	0.3900	0.1611
	22	1.0000	1.0000	1.0000	1.0000	0.9990	0.9877	0.9290	0.7660	0.5019	0.2399
	23	1.0000	1.0000	1.0000	1.0000	0.9996	0.9944	0.9604	0.8438	0.6134	0.3359
	24	1.0000	1.0000	1.0000	1.0000	0.9999	0.9976	0.9793	0.9022	0.7160	0.4439
	25	1.0000	1.0000	1.0000	1.0000	1.0000	0.9991	0.9900	0.9427	0.8034	0.5561
	26	1.0000	1.0000	1.0000	1.0000	1.0000	0.9997	0.9955	0.9686	0.8721	0.6641
	27	1.0000	1.0000	1.0000	1.0000	1.0000	0.9999	0.9981	0.9840	0.9220	0.7601
	28	1.0000	1.0000	1.0000	1.0000	1.0000	1.0000	0.9993	0.9924	0.9556	0.8389
	29	1.0000	1.0000	1.0000	1.0000	1.0000	1.0000	0.9997	0.9966	0.9765	0.8987
	30	1.0000	1.0000	1.0000	1.0000	1.0000	1.0000	0.9999	0.9986	0.9884	0.9405
	31	1.0000	1.0000	1.0000	1.0000	1.0000	1.0000	1.0000	0.9995	0.9947	0.9675
	32	1.0000	1.0000	1.0000	1.0000	1.0000	1.0000	1.0000	0.9998	0.9978	0.9836
	33	1.0000	1.0000	1.0000	1.0000	1.0000	1.0000	1.0000	0.9999	0.9991	0.9923
	34	1.0000	1.0000	1.0000	1.0000	1.0000	1.0000	1.0000	1.0000	0.9997	0.9967
	35	1.0000	1.0000	1.0000	1.0000	1.0000	1.0000	1.0000	1.0000	0.9999	0.9987
	36	1.0000	1.0000	1.0000	1.0000	1.0000	1.0000	1.0000	1.0000	1.0000	0.9995
	37	1.0000	1.0000	1.0000	1.0000	1.0000	1.0000	1.0000	1.0000	1.0000	0.9998
	38	1.0000	1.0000	1.0000	1.0000	1.0000	1.0000	1.0000	1.0000	1.0000	1.0000

Formula Sheet

These are the formulas you'll be given in the exam, but make sure you know exactly **when you need them** and **how to use them**.

Binomial Series

$$(a+b)^n = a^n + \binom{n}{1}a^{n-1}b + \binom{n}{2}a^{n-2}b^2 + \dots + \binom{n}{r}a^{n-r}b^r + \dots + b^n \quad (n \in \mathbb{N})$$

$$\text{where } \binom{n}{r} = {}^nC_r = \frac{n!}{r!(n-r)!}$$

Exponentials and Logarithms

$$\log_a x = \frac{\log_b x}{\log_b a}$$

$$e^{x \ln a} = a^x$$

Mensuration

Surface area of sphere $= 4\pi r^2$

Area of curved surface of cone $= \pi r \times$ slant height

Differentiation from First Principles

$$f'(x) = \lim_{h \to 0} \frac{f(x+h) - f(x)}{h}$$

Probability

$$P(A') = 1 - P(A)$$

Standard Deviation

Standard deviation $= \sqrt{\text{variance}}$

Interquartile range $= \text{IQR} = Q_3 - Q_1$

For a set of n values $x_1, x_2, \dots x_i, \dots x_n$

$$S_{xx} = \Sigma(x_i - \bar{x})^2 = \Sigma x_i^2 - \frac{(\Sigma x_i)^2}{n}$$

$$\text{Standard deviation} = \sqrt{\frac{S_{xx}}{n}} = \sqrt{\frac{\Sigma x^2}{n} - \bar{x}^2}$$

Kinematics

For motion in a straight line with constant acceleration:

$$v = u + at$$

$$s = ut + \frac{1}{2}at^2$$

$$s = \left(\frac{u+v}{2}\right)t$$

$$s = vt - \frac{1}{2}at^2$$

$$v^2 = u^2 + 2as$$